The College Experience

Second Edition

The College Experience

Amy Baldwin
University of Central Arkansas

Brian Tietje
California Polytechnic State University

Paul G. Stoltz
Peak Learning

PEARSON

Boston   Columbus   Hoboken   Indianapolis   New York   San Francisco
Amsterdam   Cape Town   Dubai   London   Madrid   Milan   Munich   Paris   Montréal   Toronto
Delhi   Mexico City   São Paulo   Sydney   Hong Kong   Seoul   Singapore   Taipei   Tokyo

VP Student Success & Career Development: Jodi McPherson
Program Manager: Anne Shure
Senior Development Editor: Elana Dolberg
Executive Marketing Manager: Amy Judd
Senior Media Producer: Tracy Cunningham
Senior Development Editor: Charlotte Morrissey
Associate Content Specialist: Celeste Kmiotek
Project Manager: Rebecca Gilpin
Project Coordination and Text Design: MPS North America LLC

Electronic Page Makeup: Laserwords Private Ltd
Associate Director of Design: Andrea Nix
Program Design Lead: Beth Paquin
Cover Design: MPS North America LLC
Cover Image: Duncan1890/Getty Images
Interior Design Images: Lusikkolbaskin/Fotolia, Rawpixel/Fotolia
Senior Manufacturing Buyer: Roy L. Pickering, Jr.
Printer/Binder: Courier/Kendallville
Cover Printer: Courier/Kendallville

Credits and acknowledgments borrowed from other sources and reproduced, with permission, in this textbook appear on the appropriate page within text.

Library of Congress Cataloging-in-Publication Data
Baldwin, Amy, date
    The college experience / Amy Baldwin, University of Central Arkansas, Brian Tietje,
California Polytechnic State University, Paul G. Stoltz, Peak Learning.—Second edition.
    pages cm
Includes bibliographical references and index.
ISBN 978-0-321-98003-8
1. College student orientation—United States. 2. College students—Conduct of life.
I. Tietje, Brian C. II. Stoltz, Paul G. III. Title.
LB2343.32.B238 2016
378.1'98—dc23

2014040904

10 9 8 7 6 5 4 3 2 1—CRK—17 16 15 14

www.pearsonhighered.com

Student Edition ISBN 10:   0-321-98003-4
Student Edition ISBN 13: 978-0-321-98003-8
A la Carte ISBN 10:   0-13-4-03883-5
A la Carte ISBN 13:   978-0-13-403883-4

PEARSON

About the Authors

AMY BALDWIN, MA, is a pioneering educator and educational entrepreneur. She wrote the first, groundbreaking student success textbook for community colleges and for first-generation students. In response to nationwide demand, in 2011 she founded Educational Frontiers Group (EFG), which provides educational services such as consulting, professional development, and educational novelties. As a result of her work with national initiatives such as Complete College America, Achieving the Dream, and the Developmental Education Initiative, she has become one of the most sought-after keynote speakers and workshop facilitators on student success and engagement topics. After 18 years as a community college professor at Pulaski Technical College, where she was awarded the 2006 Susan Faulkner Award for Exceptional Teaching for the Two-Year College English Association Southwest Chapter, she now serves as director of University College at the University of Central Arkansas. She has gained considerable acclaim for her efforts toward helping students get in, get through, get out, and get paid.

BRIAN TIETJE, PhD, is a thought leader in higher education and a passionate advocate for student success, particularly for students who face challenging circumstances and who aren't familiar with the unwritten rules of college and career success. Brian took his life experiences and determination from rural Ohio cross-country as he traversed educational and corporate ladders to reach an executive leadership position in higher education. He presently serves as vice provost of International, Graduate, and Extended Education at Cal Poly State University, and serves on the board of directors of several private and not-for-profit organizations. He is continually pursuing opportunities for educational innovation to meet the needs of students and employers. Prior to his administrative leadership career, Brian was awarded the Orfalea College of Business Distinguished Teacher Award in 2000 and 2001 at Cal Poly, and the Most Outstanding Marketing Faculty award in 2002, 2003, and 2004, also at Cal Poly.

PAUL G. STOLTZ, PhD, is a *New York Times* number 1 bestselling author and considered the world's foremost authority on the science and method of measuring and strengthening GRIT™, also known as "GRIT 2.0." His methods and teachings are used at Harvard, MIT, Cornell, Stanford, Carnegie Mellon, and by top organizations in 63 countries. Paul has been selected as one of the Top Ten Most Influential Global Thinkers by *HR Magazine,* one of the Top 100 Thinkers of Our Time by *Executive Excellence,* and the Millennial Thought Leader in Singapore. He's the originator of the globally acclaimed AQ® (Adversity Quotient®) method, adopted worldwide, and has written four bestselling books on the subject—published by Wiley, Harper-Collins, Simon & Schuster, and Penguin—in 17 languages. Paul has been featured in much of the world's top media, including *Fortune, Forbes, Success, Business Week, Financial Times, Wall Street Journal, Asia 21,* Fox, ABC Nightly News, NBC, CBS, *The Today Show,* and multiple appearances on *The Oprah Show.* He is the founding director of the GRIT Institute and the Global Resilience Institute, conducting research in 29 countries, as well as founder and CEO of PEAK Learning, Inc., the global research and consulting firm he formed in 1987. Applying his vast experience and research in higher education specifically to students in their first year of college is a long-term goal of his. Developing effective strategies toward college completion—and sustainable employment—has never been timelier.

Brief Contents

Contents

10 Studying and Taking Tests   177

Acknowledgments

Amy Baldwin

To my family, Kyle, Emily, and Will: Thank you for your continued support and patience.

To my Pearson family, Jodi McPherson, Katie Mahan, Elana Dolberg, Amy Judd, and all those who have provided feedback and creative ideas: Thank you for your hard work and your friendship.

Brian Tietje

I thank God for Debbie, my awesome wife who encourages and inspires me; Amy and Paul, the best (and grittiest) coauthors on the planet; and Jodi, Elana, Shannon, and the Pearson team who work so hard to support our success.

Paul G. Stoltz

I thank Ronda, my inspiration and the living exemplar of good, smart, and massive GRIT, my generous coauthors Amy and Brian for welcoming my child (GRIT) into their home (Student Success), Shannon for stepping up and climbing strong, Jodi and the Pearson team for having the vision to equip students with the GRIT it takes to get in, get through, get out, and get paid, the enlightened professors who commit to GRIT, and all the gritty students out there who find a way to dig deep and do whatever it takes to make a positive impact on the world, in spite of whatever gets in their way!

Thanks also from all of us to the reviewers of this edition:

Gabriel Adona, *San Diego Mesa College*
Pamela Bilton Beard, *Houston Community College Southwest*
Mei Mei Burr, *Northern Kentucky University*
Donna Colondres, *Chaffey College*
Lory Conrad, *University of Arkansas–Fort Smith*
Christine Crowe, *Suffolk Community College*
Raven Davenport, *Houston Community College*
Luke E. Faust, *Indiana University of Pennsylvania*
Shirley Flor, *San Diego Mesa College*
Alonzo Flowers, *Blinn College*
Kim Forcier, *University of Texas–San Antonio*
Barry Foster, *Brazosport Community College*
Patricia S. Foster, *Stephen F. Austin State University*
Altheria Gaston Monique Gilchrist, *Community College of Philadelphia*
Mary Gumlia, *Solano Community College*
Linda M. Hensen-Jackson, *Arkansas Tech University*
Lauren Hensley, *The Ohio State University*
Robert Irizarry, *Brazosport College*
Kimberly Koledoye, *Houston Community College Northwest*
Rula Mourad Koudsia, *Ivy Tech Community College Northeast*
Alice Lanning, *University of Oklahoma*
Catherine Lee, *Cape Fear Community College*
Rhonda Lee Meadows, *West Virginia University*
Shannon E. McCasland, *Aims Community College*
Cynthia Pascal, *The Art Institute of Washington*
Melissa Rathburn, *University of South Florida*
Jacqueline Robinson, *Milwaukee Area Technical College*

Amy Skeens, *West Virginia University*
Leigh Smith, *Lamar Institute of Technology*
Ellen Stohl, *California State University–Northridge*
Margaret A. Soucy, *Western New Mexico University*
Victoria Washington, *Houston Community College*
Cornelia Wills, *Middle Tennessee State University*
Jennifer Woltjen, *Broome Community College*

Preface

Your Challenge, Our Promise

Beat the Odds. Graduate Strong!

While many of your students have worked very hard to be in your class this semester and are eager to start their college career, most college students stumble, fall short, or even quit as they strive to *get in, get through, get out, and get paid.* The statistics and trends can seem pretty dismal. That's the bad news.

The Good News

The good news is this book will equip your students to beat the odds. It will give them exactly what they need to not just survive, but to also come out strong.

How? To help them build the necessary skills to complete college successfully, this book provides powerful, proven content and tools through information about what it takes to meet the academic, social, personal, and professional expectations of college.

This book also has a cutting-edge advantage over other student success books: it includes content and applications for GRIT, the capacity to dig deep and do whatever it takes. Research has proven that GRIT is the single most powerful predictor of success. By including GRIT coupled with direct information about the way college works, we'll show what it *really* takes to succeed. That's our promise.

- **GETTING IN**   Whether or not your students are truly college ready, they will need help understanding the unwritten rules of transitioning from high school or work to college. *This book provides the basic, no-fluff information that helps students learn how college works.*

- **GETTING THROUGH**   Your students need more than just help getting settled into college; they also need to know how to keep going when they hit roadblocks along the way. *This book gives students the tools to overcome the obstacles with resilience and tenacity.*

- **GETTING OUT**   Graduating from college with a degree in hand is every student's dream. However, not all students know what it takes to finish college. *This book delivers both content and strategies for reaching long-term goals by showing students the steps to college completion and equipping them with the GRIT it will take to walk across the graduation stage.*

- **GETTING PAID**   Your students want to move from college to a career with as few challenges as possible, but they often do not connect the work they are doing in college to the world of work. *This book lays the groundwork for building on professional skills that will lead to career success.*

New to This Edition

This edition is tailored to the four-year college experience and framed in a practical, situational way that helps students navigate *what* to do, *when* do it, and *where* to go for support.

Develop GRIT

How do students from any background beat the odds, regardless of their advantages or disadvantages in life? Research has proven that GRIT is the single most powerful predictor of student success, both in and beyond school. Now available for the first time to the academic market, this book provides the scientifically grounded, simple, practical, proven tips and tools students need to grow greater GRIT.

- **GRIT Tips** are quick, practical tips to effectively apply all four dimensions of **GRIT** (**G**rowth, **R**esilience, **I**nstinct, and **T**enacity) to each of the lessons.
- **GRIT Gainers** are tough, edgy, inspirational applications related to each section.
- **How Gritty Are You?** is a "get real" moment for students to assess and amplify their motivation and mindset to put the chapter's lessons to work.
- **Putting It in Practice: The GRIT Advantage** equips and compels students to put the chapter's tools into practice.

Getting In

College acceptance rates have dropped, making it harder for students to get in. In 2014, Stanford University had an acceptance rate of 5.7%! And getting into college is just the first step. This book provides students who beat these odds with a firm foundation of GRIT-based, scientifically grounded tools and skills necessary to be successful.

Getting Through

Only 55 percent of students in two-year public schools returned in the second year. Students in four-year public schools performed a bit better (64.9%), but over a third of freshmen did not return as sophomores. This book provides students with strategies to develop a gritty mindset and skillset to get through college.

- **The Unwritten Rules** let students know what college is really like, as the feature shares the secrets to college success by telling them what usually takes years to figure out on their own.
- **It's in the Syllabus** reminds students to review one of the most important documents in college—the "contract" between their instructors and themselves—by asking them a few questions about the document. Knowing how to use the syllabus will help students get through college.
- **Integrity Matters** provides students the opportunity to think critically about strengthening their integrity with real-life college situations, as acting with integrity is a big part of getting through.
- **Opening stories** run throughout the book and present four characters on their journey as first-time college students. The stories provide opportunities for your students to relate to their situations and end-of-story questions that help students think about the challenges they face and what choices they can make.
- **Your Terms for Success** provides students with an easy "cheat sheet" of common terms that they will be using in college, so they can speak the language.

Getting Out

Only 39 percent of students complete a bachelor's degree in four years; after six years, the graduation rate is 58.7 percent. This book provides the first-ever blend of the gritty skillset and mindset needed to graduate.

Getting Paid

Forty-six schools on the 2013 Payscale College ROI report had a negative 20–year net ROI, meaning the costs of attending these schools outweigh the financial benefit. This book equips students with the practical skillset and GRIT-based mindset that global research reveals is what employers crave most.

- **From College to Career** provides updated information about how to translate college skills to career success.

- **In-chapter and end-of-chapter exercises,** as noted in the previous section, also reinforce getting out and getting paid.

- **A career planning chapter** offers students the opportunity to apply all that has been learned in order to prepare for the next steps toward life and career planning and set goals for achieving them.

MyStudentSuccessLab™

This title is also available with MyStudentSuccessLab—an online homework, tutorial, and assessment program designed to work with this text to engage students and improve results. Within its structured environment, students practice what they learn, test their understanding, and pursue a plan that helps them better absorb course material and understand difficult concepts.

Personalize Learning with MyStudentSuccessLab

This learning outcomes-based technology promotes student engagement through the following:

- **Full course pre- and post-diagnostic** tests based on Bloom's taxonomy are linked to key learning objectives in each topic.

- Each individual topic in the Learning Path offers a **pre- and post-test** dedicated to that topic, an **overview** of objectives to build vocabulary and repetition, access to **video interviews** to learn about key issues "by students, for students," **practice exercises** to improve class prep and learning, and **graded activities** to build critical thinking skills and develop problem solving abilities.

- **Student resources** include Finish Strong 247 YouTube videos, calculators, and professionalism/research and writing/student success tools.

- **Student inventories** increase self-awareness and include Golden Personality (similar to Myers-Briggs and gives insights on personal style) and Conley Readiness Index (CRI) (measures readiness and likelihood for success and gives insight into student aspirations).

- A **title-specific version** is available as an option for those who teach closely to their text. This course would include the national eText, chapter-specific quizzing, and Learning Path modules that align with the chapter naming conventions of the book. Also included are the Experience Series audience-specific booklets *Adult Learners, International Learners, Men of Color,* and *Student Athletes.*

Version Overview

You and Your Students Have Unique Needs

Experience books have changed to fulfill your unique needs. The *Experience* books recognize how student and instructor needs have evolved, and have made the change from editions that catered to all institutions to specific programs. In learning environments, it is important to get relevant information at the time you need it. Now you can select course materials from *Experience* that reinforce your institution's culture (four-year, two-year, or one credit hour and/or blended and online) and speak directly to your specific needs.

The Choice Is Yours

Experience combines student success skills with the world's leading method for growing greater GRIT (Growth, Resilience, Instinct, and Tenacity). With a focus on student experience specific to institution type, the *Experience* series for college students incorporates the GRIT framework, supplying learners with powerful success strategies and tools for college completion and career success—*get in, get through, get out,* and *get paid.* The authors recognize that understanding what it takes to succeed in college is one thing, but having the personal GRIT to make it happen is what makes the difference. Framed in a practical, situational manner, the book helps students navigate *what* to do, *when* to do it, and *where* to go for support. It provides scientifically grounded yet practical tips and tools students need to grow greater GRIT, which research shows is the most powerful predictor of success in school and beyond. Students "get in and get through" using a firm foundation of distinctive features to stay in and get through college with academic, social, and transitional skills. In order to "get out and get paid," students are equipped with a blend of professional and GRIT-based mindsets required to successfully graduate and enter a career that fulfills their educational and personal goals.

Choose the version of *Experience* that aligns best with your institution and student population, all while getting the hallmark features and content you've come to expect.

- *The College Experience,* second edition. Written for students attending four-year programs, it addresses today's university and college students.
- *The Community College Experience,* fourth edition. Written for students attending two-year programs, it addresses students in community, technical, and career colleges.
- *The College Experience Compact,* second edition. Written for one credit hour student success courses and/or those with blended and online students, it addresses the needs and challenges of students as digital learners. It aligns with learning outcomes from both the MyStudentSuccessLab (www.mystudentsuccesslab.com) and Student Success CourseConnect online course (www.pearsonlearningsolutions.com/courseconnect). This book is designed for use as a standalone text or a print companion with one of these technologies for blended, online, or one credit hour student success courses.

Instructor Resources

Online Instructor's Manual

(www.pearsonhighered.com/irc)

This manual provides a framework of ideas and suggestions for activities, journal writing, thought-provoking situations, and online implementation, including MyStudentSuccessLab recommendations.

Online PowerPoint Presentation

(www.pearsonhighered.com/irc)

This comprehensive set of PowerPoint slides can be used by instructors for class presentations and also by students for lecture preview or review. The PowerPoint presentation includes summary slides with overview information for each chapter to help students understand and review concepts within each chapter.

MyStudentSuccessLab

(www.mystudentsuccesslab.com)

This title is also available with MyStudentSuccessLab—an online homework, tutorial, and assessment program designed to work with this text to engage students and improve results. Within its structured environment, students practice what they learn, test their understanding, and pursue a plan that helps them better absorb course material and understand difficult concepts. Beyond the full course pre- and post-diagnostic assessments and pre- and post-tests within each module, additional learning outcomes-based tests can be created or selected using a secure testing engine and may be printed or delivered online. If you are interested in adopting this title with MyStudentSuccessLab, ask your Pearson representative for the correct package ISBN and course to download.

Course Redesign

(**www.pearsoncourseredesign.com**)

Collect, measure, and interpret data to support efficacy. Our resources can help you rethink how you deliver instruction, measure the results of your course redesign, and get support for data collection and interpretation.

Implementation and Training

(**www.mystudentsuccesscommunity.com**)

Access MyStudentSuccessLab training resources such as the Best Practices implementation guide, How Do I videos, self-paced training modules, 1:1 Expert on Demand sessions with a faculty advisor, and videos, posts, and communication from student success peers.

CourseConnect

(**www.pearsonlearningsolutions.com/courseconnect**)

This title is also available with CourseConnect—designed by subject-matter experts and credentialed instructional designers, it offers customizable online courses with a consistent learning path, available in a variety of learning management systems as self-paced study.

CourseSmart Textbooks Online

(**www.coursesmart.com**)

As an alternative to purchasing the print textbook, students can subscribe to the same content online and save up to 50 percent off the suggested list price of the print text. With a CourseSmart eTextbook, students can search the text, make notes online, print out reading assignments that incorporate lecture notes, and bookmark important passages for review.

Custom Services

(**www.pearsonlearningsolutions.com**)

With this title, we offer flexible and creative choices for course materials that will maximize learning and student engagement. Options include custom library, publications, technology solutions, and online education.

Professional Development for Instructors

(**www.pearsonhighered.com/studentsuccess**)

Augment your teaching with engaging resources. Visit our online catalog for our Ownership series, Engaging Activities series, and Audience booklets.

Resources for Your Students

(**www.pearsonhighered.com/studentsuccess**)

Help students save and succeed throughout their college experience. Visit our online catalog for options such as Books à la Carte, CourseSmart eTextbooks, Pearson Students program, IDentity Series, Success Tips, and more.

Pearson Course Redesign
Collect, measure, and interpret data to support efficacy.

Rethink the way you deliver instruction.

Pearson has successfully partnered with colleges and universities engaged in course redesign for over 10 years through workshops, Faculty Advisor programs, and online conferences. Here's how to get started!

- Visit our course redesign site at www.pearsoncourseredesign.com for information on getting started, a list of Pearson-sponsored course redesign events, and recordings of past course redesign events.

- Request to connect with a Faculty Advisor, a fellow instructor who is an expert in course redesign, by visiting www.mystudentsuccesslab.com/community.

- Join our Course Redesign Community at www.community.pearson.com/courseredesign and connect with colleagues around the country who are participating in course redesign projects.

Don't forget to measure the results of your course redesign!

Examples of data you may want to collect include:

- Improvement of homework grades, test averages, and pass rates over past semesters

- Correlation between time spent in an online product and final average in the course

- Success rate in the next level of the course

- Retention rate (i.e., percentage of students who drop, fail, or withdraw)

Need support for data collection and interpretation?

Ask your local Pearson representative how to connect with a member of Pearson's Efficacy Team.

MyStudentSuccessLab™

MyLab from Pearson has been designed and refined with a single purpose in mind—to help educators break through to improving results for their students.

MyStudentSuccessLab™ (MSSL) is a learning outcomes-based technology that advances students' knowledge and builds critical skills, offering ongoing personal and professional development through peer-led video interviews, interactive practice exercises, and activities that focus on academic, life, and professional preparation.

The **Conley Readiness Index (CRI), developed by Dr. David Conley, is now embedded in MyStudentSuccessLab.** This research-based, self-diagnostic online tool measures college and career readiness; it is personalized, research-based, and provides actionable data. Dr. David Conley is a nationally recognized leader in research, policy, and solution development with a sincere passion for improving college and career readiness.

Developed exclusively for Pearson by Dr. Conley, the Conley Readiness Index assesses mastery in each of the "Four Keys" that are critical to college and career readiness:

KEY COGNITIVE STRATEGIES	KEY CONTENT KNOWLEDGE	KEY LEARNING SKILLS & TECHNIQUES	KEY TRANSITION KNOWLEDGE & SKILLS
Think	**Know**	**Act**	**Go**
Problem Formulation Hypothesize Strategize	**Structure of Knowledge** Key Terms and Terminology Factual Information Linking Ideas Organizing Concepts	**Ownership of Learning** Goal Setting Persistence Self-awareness Motivation Help-seeking Progress Monitoring Self-efficacy	**Contextual** Aspirations Norms/Culture
Research Identify Collect			**Procedural** Institution Choice Admission Process
Interpretation Analyze Evaluate	**Attitudes Toward Learning Content** Challenge Level Value Attribution Effort	**Learning Techniques** Time Management Test Taking Skills Note Taking Skills Memorization/recall Strategic Reading Collaborative Learning Technology	**Financial** Tuition Financial Aid
Communication Organize Construct			**Cultural** Postsecondary Norms
Precision & Accuracy Monitor Confirm	**Technical Knowledge & Skills** Specific College and Career Readiness Standards		**Personal** Self-advocacy and Institutional Context

Topics include:

Student Success Learning Path

- Conley Readiness Index
- College Transition
- Communication
- Creating an Academic Plan
- Critical Thinking
- Financial Literacy
- Goal Setting
- Information Literacy
- Learning Preferences
- Listening and Note Taking
- Majors and Careers Exploration
- Memory and Studying
- Online Learning
- Problem Solving
- Reading and Annotating
- Stress Management
- Test Taking
- Time Management

Career Success Learning Path

- Career Portfolio
- Interviewing
- Job Search
- Self-Management Skills at Work
- Teamwork
- Workplace Communication
- Workplace Etiquette

Assessment

Beyond the Pre- and Post-Full Course Diagnostic Assessments and Pre- and Post-Tests within each module, additional learning-outcome-based tests can be created using a secure testing engine, and may be printed or delivered online. These tests can be customized by editing individual questions or entire tests.

Reporting

Measurement matters—and is ongoing in nature. MyStudentSuccessLab lets you determine what data you need, set up your course accordingly, and collect data via reports. The high quality and volume of test questions allows for data comparison and measurement.

Content and Functionality Training

The Instructor Implementation Guide provides grading rubrics, suggestions for video use, and more to save time on course prep. Our Best Practices Guide and "How do I…" YouTube videos indicate how to use MyStudentSuccessLab, from getting started to utilizing the Gradebook.

Peer Support

The Student Success Community site is a place for you to connect with other educators to exchange ideas and advice on courses, content, and MyStudentSuccessLab. The site is filled with timely articles, discussions, video posts, and more. Join, share, and be inspired!
www.mystudentsuccesscommunity.com

The Faculty Advisor Network is Pearson's peer-to-peer mentoring program in which experienced MyStudentSuccessLab users share best practices and expertise. Our Faculty Advisors are experienced in one-on-one phone and email coaching, presentations, and live training sessions.

Integration and Compliance

You can integrate our digital solutions with your learning management system in a variety of ways. For more information, or if documentation is needed for ADA compliance, contact your local Pearson representative.

MyStudentSuccessLab users have access to:

- Full course Pre- and Post-Diagnostic Assessments linked to learning outcomes

- Pre- and Post-tests dedicated to individual topics

- Overviews that summarize objectives and skills

- Videos on key issues "by students, for students"

- Practice exercises that instill student confidence

- Graded activities to build critical-thinking and problem-solving skills

- Journal writing assignments with online rubrics for consistent, simpler grading

- Resources like Finish Strong 24/7 YouTube videos, calculators, professionalism/research & writing/student success tools

- Student inventories including **Conley Readiness Index** and **Golden Personality**

Students utilizing MyStudentSuccessLab may purchase Pearson texts in a number of cost-saving formats—including eTexts, loose-leaf Books à la Carte editions, and more.

CourseConnect™

Trust that your online course is the best in its class.

Designed by subject matter experts and credentialed instructional designers, CourseConnect offers award-winning customizable online courses that help students build skills for ongoing personal and professional development.

CourseConnect uses topic-based, interactive modules that follow a consistent learning path—from introduction, to presentation, to activity, to review. Its built-in tools—including user-specific pacing charts, personalized study guides, and interactive exercises—provide a student-centric learning experience that minimizes distractions and helps students stay on track and complete the course successfully. Features such as relevant video, audio, and activities, personalized (or editable) syllabi, discussion forum topics and questions, assignments, and quizzes are all easily accessible. CourseConnect is available in a variety of learning management systems and accommodates various term lengths as well as self-paced study. And, our compact textbook editions align to CourseConnect course outcomes.

Choose from the following three course outlines ("Lesson Plans")

Student Success

- Goal Setting, Values, and Motivation
- Time Management
- Financial Literacy
- Creative Thinking, Critical Thinking, and Problem Solving
- Learning Preferences
- Listening and Note-Taking in Class
- Reading and Annotating
- Studying, Memory, and Test-Taking
- Communicating and Teamwork
- Information Literacy
- Staying Balanced: Stress Management
- Career Exploration

Career Success

- Planning Your Career Search
- Knowing Yourself: Explore the Right Career Path
- Knowing the Market: Find Your Career Match
- Preparing Yourself: Gain Skills and Experience Now
- Networking
- Targeting Your Search: Locate Positions, Ready Yourself
- Building a Portfolio: Your Resume and Beyond
- Preparing for Your Interview
- Giving a Great Interview
- Negotiating Job Offers, Ensuring Future Success

Professional Success

- Introducing Professionalism
- Workplace Goal Setting
- Workplace Ethics and Your Career
- Workplace Time Management
- Interpersonal Skills at Work
- Workplace Conflict Management
- Workplace Communications: Email and Presentations
- Effective Workplace Meetings
- Workplace Teams
- Customer Focus and You
- Understanding Human Resources
- Managing Career Growth and Change

Custom Services
Personalize instruction to best facilitate learning.

As the industry leader in custom publishing, we are committed to meeting your instructional needs by offering flexible and creative choices for course materials that will maximize learning and student engagement.

Pearson Custom Library

Using our online book-building system, create a custom book by selecting content from our course-specific collections that consist of chapters from Pearson Student Success and Career Development titles and carefully selected, copyright-cleared, third-party content and pedagogy.
www.pearsoncustomlibrary.com

Custom Publications

In partnership with your Pearson representative, modify, adapt, and combine existing Pearson books by choosing content from across the curriculum and organizing it around your learning outcomes. As an alternative, you can work with your Editor to develop your original material and create a textbook that meets your course goals.

Custom Technology Solutions

Work with Pearson's trained professionals, in a truly consultative process, to create engaging learning solutions. From interactive learning tools, to eTexts, to custom websites and portals, we'll help you simplify your life as an instructor.

Online Education

Pearson offers online course content for online classes and hybrid courses. This online content can also be used to enhance traditional classroom courses. Our award-winning CourseConnect includes a fully developed syllabus, media-rich lecture presentations, audio lectures, a wide variety of assessments, discussion board questions, and a strong instructor resource package.

For more information on custom Student Success services, please visit www.pearsonlearningsolutions.com.

The College Experience

1 College Culture and the Campus

Chapter goals to help you *get in, get through, get out, and get paid:*

The purpose of this book is to help you get in, get through, get out, and get paid. If you're reading this book, it's likely that you already made it into college. Congratulations! Now the focus is on equipping you with both the world-class skillset (tools) and mindset (GRIT) to perform well in your classes, complete all of the requirements for your degree, and prepare you to get a great job when you get out. To accomplish these important achievements, you need to understand what college is like, how it's different from high school or work, and how to get access to the resources you'll need to be successful. That's the purpose of this first chapter.

To meet those goals, *this chapter will help you:*

- Transition successfully into college
- Meet the expectations of college
- Adjust to the rhythm of the college experience
- Find and use the resources on campus that are available to you
- Grow and show the **GRIT** it takes to dig deep and achieve your goals, no matter what

MyStudentSuccessLab™

Log in to MyStudentSuccessLab.com to deepen your **GRIT** mindset and build the skills you'll need to get through the college experience.

Four Student Stories: Orientation

"Destination: Degree," the travel-themed orientation, is winding down after an afternoon of skits, presentations, and door prizes.

"If everyone will score their inventories, we will explain how learning style preference affects your study habits," says Jason, an orientation leader.

"Hey, I am 'kinesthetic.' That kind of makes sense. I teach kickboxing and learned how to do it by working out almost every day," Evan says.

"I thought I would be more of a social learner, but my learning style preference is 'individual,'" says Michael as he rubs his head. "I spent so much time leading troops when I was in the military."

"I am definitely 'auditory,'" Laura says to the group. "I got through all my classes in high school by listening to the lectures. I rarely took notes because I liked to listen."

"Yeah, I can see that. You talked during every presentation!" Evan jokes.

"Will you be able to do that in college, just listen?" Juanita, the youngest of the group, asks. "I mean, I have heard that the professors expect so much more of you when it comes to being in class."

"I am sure you will," says Michael. "My girlfriend graduated last year with a degree in nursing. All she did was read for class and then study her notes every night."

"I know Laura is the talkative one, but give me a call if you ever need anything. Good luck to everyone!" Jason says.

Now, what do you think?

- How would you use information about yourself to connect to the expectations of college?

  a. Not at all. I don't think I will need to do anything to meet college expectations.

  b. Learn more about myself and how I can use that knowledge to help me meet college expectations.

  c. Avoid challenges to understanding myself better and my environment better.

- Do you see college as an opportunity to learn more about yourself and those around you?

  a. Most definitely. Knowing more about myself will help me learn and work with others more effectively.

  b. Not really. I have a good understanding of who I am and don't need to change.

  c. Only in certain circumstances when I feel most comfortable learning new things about myself.

- When you are unsure of the expectations of college, do you:

  a. Figure it out on your own

  b. Complain to your peers about not understanding what you need to do to meet expectations

  c. Make a plan to learn more about college expectations from your classmates and professors and put those ideas into practice

Your Terms for success

when you see . . .	it means . . .
Academic integrity	Doing honest work on all assignments and tests
Core curriculum	Also called general education requirements or basic courses; the common courses that almost all students who earn a bachelor's degree complete
Corequisite	A course that can be taken at the same time as another course
Course content	The material that will be covered in a course
Course objectives	The goals of a course
Credit hour	The unit of measurement that colleges use that usually equals the amount of time you are in class each week during a 16-week semester
Degree plan	A list of classes that you must complete successfully in order to be awarded a degree

Disability accommodation policy	A policy that states how accommodations for documented disabilities will be handled
FERPA	Family Educational Rights and Privacy Act; federal law that regulates the communication and dissemination of your educational records
GPA	Grade point average; each grade that is earned is awarded grade points that are multiplied by the number of credit hours taken
Grading criteria	The standards by which an assignment is graded
Prerequisite	A course that must be taken *before* one can take a course
Quality points	The points determined by a grade point multiplied by the credit hours for a course; e.g., an A (4 grade points) in a writing class (3 credit hours) will equal 12 quality points; used to calculate grade point average
Syllabus	The contract between an instructor and a student; provides information about the course content, course objectives, grading criteria, and course schedule

As You Get into College, Be Prepared for Change

This is an exciting time for you as you transition into college life. The definition of *transition* means a change or a modification, and you will find that going to college will create a change in you—and not just in your schedule and your workload. You will find that your concept of yourself will change, your relationships will change, and your outlook on your future will change. All of these changes will require an investment of your time and reflection to make it happen. At the end of your college experience, you will find yourself *transformed* into a new person. You will most likely be more thoughtful and more confident about your abilities; most certainly, you will be more aware of the skillset and mindset (GRIT) it takes to earn a degree. However, this change or transformation won't be easy. The following section on transitioning from where you are now to where you want to be will give you a better understanding of what you need to do to make the change happen.

Transitioning from High School or Work Offers Distinct Challenges

For some students, the move from high school to college seems fairly simple—both require reading, writing, testing, and attending class. Students who are taking the step from work to school may also see some

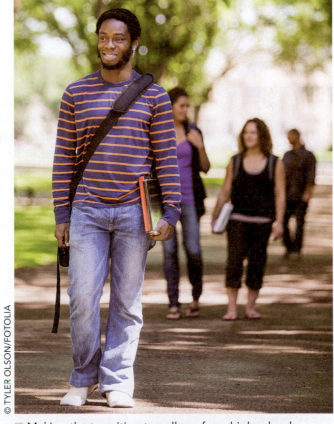

© TYLER OLSON/FOTOLIA

◼ Making the transition to college from high school or work will mean learning what is expected of you academically and personally.

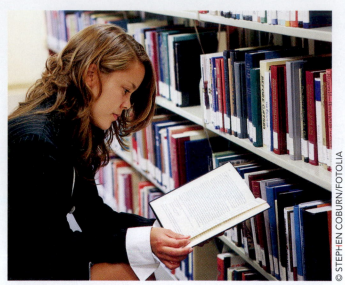

© STEPHEN COBURN/FOTOLIA

■ Getting familiar with library services and other services on campus and online will be essential to your transitioning smoothly.

similarities between their jobs and their classroom work—both require working hard, keeping yourself motivated, and following the rules. If the realties of high school or work and college are that similar, then why do so many college students have difficulty making a successful transition?

The answer to that question can be given by the instructors who see smart, competent students have trouble adjusting to the climate and culture of college, because either they do not understand what is expected of them, or they lack the personal GRIT to persevere through all the uncertainty, frustrations, and challenges that are a rich part of the experience. In other words, in order to be successful, students must know what is expected of them beyond the questions on the next test.

Students need to know how college works and how to navigate through not only their courses, but also the common challenges that they will face as they work toward a degree.

The Biggest Change Involves Personal Responsibility

GRIT
Tenacity

Research clearly shows that students who develop the greatest GRIT get the best results. Period.

Exhibit 1.1 illustrates some of the differences and similarities among high school, a full-time job, and college. As you take a look at the column labeled "college" in Exhibit 1.1, you'll notice a pattern emerge—compared to their high school classes or full-time jobs, college students experience a dramatic increase in the amount of personal responsibility they must handle. In high school, teachers, counselors, and coaches provide significant oversight and direction to students, and carefully manage everything from school lunches to study hall. In the workplace, employers oversee their employees using timesheets, employee policy manuals, and supervisors. High school teachers and supervisors provide clear guidance, both about expectations and how to achieve them. In college, however, the student is responsible for understanding the expectations for academic and career success and developing a strategy for meeting those expectations. In other words, you have to figure it out for yourself. You have to find a way to persevere, especially when it gets frustrating and difficult.

There have probably been some times during your high school or work experience when you wished that you had more freedom to make your own decisions and pursue your own interests. As you step into college, these wishes indeed come true. The range of opportunities and alternatives that lie before you is so broad and diverse that you'll find yourself making important decisions every day.

Which general education (GE) courses will you take next term? Do you want to take classes primarily in the morning or later in the day? Which dorm or apartment do you want to live in and with whom? Do you want to join a club or Greek organization? Should you participate in a study abroad program? What kind of internship should you be looking for and how? How often should you go home and visit your family? Do you maintain your friendships with your high school friends, or move on to new relationships? Do you attend all of your classes? And even if you do, to what extent do you do whatever it takes to learn what you need to learn and to achieve your goals?

The list of questions, decisions, and responsibilities that you face affords you tremendous freedom to chart your own course in college and your career. This broad range of personal responsibility

GRIT
Tenacity

As you grow and apply your GRIT, you'll find you get energized by challenges. You'll expand your capacity, taking on more, even tougher courses and professors, with greater success. And most importantly, it will fuel you to get through, get out, and get paid.

EXHIBIT 1.1   Differences Among High School, Full-Time Work, and College

High School	Full-Time Work	College
Attendance is mandatory in order to meet requirements	Attendance is mandatory in order to stay employed	Attendance may not be mandatory
At least six continuous hours spent in class each day	At least eight continuous hours spent at work each day	Different amounts of time spent in class and between classes each day
Very little choice in what classes you take and when you take them	May have little choice in work assignments and when the work is to be completed	More flexibility in when you work on assignments and how soon you complete them before the due date
Moderate to no outside work necessary to be successful	Moderate to no overtime work necessary to complete job duties	Substantial amount of outside work to complete assignments and to be successful
Teachers check homework and keep you up to date on progress; they will inform you if you are not completing assignments and progressing well	Supervisors check completion and quality of work at regular intervals; they will inform you if you are not meeting the standards for the position	Professors may not check all homework or provide feedback on progress at regular intervals; they may not inform you if you are not meeting the standards of the course
Teachers go over material and expect you to remember facts and information	Employers provide basic information and expect you to use it to complete the job effectively	Professors provide concepts and theories and expect you to evaluate the ideas, synthesize the ideas with other concepts you have learned, and develop new theories
Frequent tests over small amounts of material allow for grades to be raised if needed	Supervisors create employee improvement plans to allow you to improve your ratings if needed	Professors provide the standards and grading criteria but often allow only a few chances (through infrequent testing/assignments) to meet them
You may be able to skate by	Your boss determines how hard you work	It takes GRIT to succeed; you determine how hard you work, what approach to take, and how much you are willing to own your success

is exciting, but it can also become overwhelming at times, and you can find yourself suffering significant consequences for poor decisions along the way. That's why GRIT is so critical.

It's important, then, to develop your signature approach for stepping into and getting the most out of this amazing experience that offers so much personal responsibility and autonomy.

Make a Plan for Exercising Your New Freedom

Before you start making a lot of important decisions that affect your academics, social life, and physical and psychological health, take some time to consider how you want to approach these decisions so that you exercise good judgment. Consider whom you will consult when you encounter important decisions and personal freedoms. Who are your "go to" people that help you develop a more resilient approach? Identify individuals in your life who can help you think through important decisions and consider all the important factors. Specific family, friends, classmates, advisors, professors, and mentors may come to mind. Seek their counsel and input as you explore your alternatives in college.

G R I T
Resilience

A big part of being a gritty, successful student is becoming more resilient. Resilience is about more than bouncing back when you fall. It's also about having a safety or support network so you don't fall as far, and you can rebound and learn faster.

GRIT GAINER™

GET GOING WITH GRIT Remember: GRIT is your capacity to dig deep and do whatever it takes—even sacrifice, struggle, and suffer—to achieve your goals. Try these GRIT Gainers to enjoy the energizing upsides and avoid the dangerous downsides of personal freedom and responsibility.

1. Upperclassmen sometimes make fun of first-year students for their innocence, ignorance, and foolish mistakes. Accelerate your wisdom by picking two or three more experienced students you respect and asking them, "When you look back on your first year, what are the two or three specific things you wished you had done differently in order to be more successful?"

2. Whenever you get stuck, or when you think something is impossible, ask yourself, "What are the facets of the situation I can potentially influence to get what I want or need?"

Instinct

Values are meaningless without GRIT. Who you are and what you say and do when something goes wrong, when you're tired and fed up, or when everything conspires against you reveals your true values. The stronger your GRIT, the more likely you are to show real moral fortitude, staying true to what matters most, no matter what. People respect that. And it will help you succeed.

Another consideration is what personal values or principles you want to uphold in your life. It's important to keep your values in your sights as you experience a range of new opportunities and diversions that might either reinforce your values or undermine them.

It therefore makes sense to give careful consideration to how your decisions will affect others. Although we refer to this topic as "personal" responsibility, it's important to recognize that every decision you make will affect not only your life, but others' as well. For example, a decision to miss a meeting for a group project in a class not only affects your performance in the class, but that of your team members also. Similarly, if you exercise your personal freedom to stay up late at night watching TV or playing videogames, your decision will have an impact on your roommates.

Having greater personal freedom is an exciting component of the college experience, and it's an important part of your transformation. The advice we've offered is intended to help you navigate this wider road with success, GRIT, and good judgment.

Higher Education Brings High Expectations

A marathon is a 26.2 mile run, and regardless of whether a participant runs full speed or walks, it's an event that is challenging for everyone. Similarly, college is a demanding experience. There is no way to avoid that reality. If it were easy, more people would complete their degrees. If it were easy, it would also be less meaningful and powerful to achieve. Regardless of the national or international reputation of your university, your college experience will challenge you mentally, physically, and emotionally. It will take a lot of GRIT not only to persevere, but ideally to flourish and grow in the process. We don't tell you this to intimidate or discourage you, but to help you get into the right mindset for success. New students can fall prey to rumors and suggestions that college is easy, or that one college is easier than another. Don't fall for these myths! If you start college with the expectation that it will be easy, you'll run the risk of stumbling during your very first semester in college, and you'll have to work even harder to recover. Doing well at anything requires serious effort. It's tough.

A typical bachelor's degree requires 120 semester units or 180 quarter units, and most students take four, five, or even six years to finish their degree. Along the way, if you're a full-time student, you'll be expected to attend four to five classes every semester, study several hours outside of class, meet with team members, participate in club activities and other extracurricular events, and perhaps even work part-time or full-time to pay for school.

Even though your professors know that you face all of these responsibilities, each professor will expect you to give your very best effort and quality of work to her class.

Because of their experience in teaching hundreds if not thousands of students over time, professors know that students can succeed when they are challenged. Most won't teach you GRIT, but they will require you to have and show it. Here, we offer some tips for getting yourself in shape, so to speak, for a successful and challenging college experience. We build our recommendations around the four Cs:

G R I T
Growth

1. Computers and supplies
2. Classroom preparation, attendance, and behavior
3. Constructive criticism
4. Controversial content

> Professors don't appreciate excuses for why things don't or can't get done. They simply grade (and respect) you for what you do get done and how well you do it. That's why GRIT earns you results and respect.

Computers and Supplies

In high school, books and course materials are provided for each student, but in college, you will be responsible for obtaining and purchasing your own materials—and you will need to do that before or at the very beginning of the semester. Here's a quick list of "the right stuff" that you will likely need:

- Access to a computer and a working knowledge of how to use one. Most colleges provide computer labs, email accounts, and printers for student use, but their hours may be limited; they may be crowded at busy times during the semester; and you may have to pay for the pages that you print. Thus, having the necessary computer skills as well as regular access to a computer will be integral to your success, and if you need some help honing those skills, your college may offer computer classes.

- Textbooks and course materials. Usually an exact list of course materials is included in your syllabus. If not, the bookstore may have this information. If you find yourself unable to acquire or buy your materials, then you will need to talk to your professor immediately to ask about alternative arrangements. For example, some professors put a copy of the textbook on reserve in the library, which means that students can borrow the book for limited periods of time.

- Access to online course materials. Most colleges have a website or "portal" that has special links to specific courses where professors will post the syllabus, assignments, class notes, and, in some cases, quizzes and tests. To gain access to these materials, you'll need to be officially enrolled in the class and you'll need to have access to your college's web portal, which requires a user name and password. Make sure you have all of this covered before the first day of class.

- Writing materials, including notebooks (one for each class), printer paper, pens, highlighters, and #2 pencils.

- Depending on the type of math, engineering, or science classes, you will probably need a scientific calculator. Check with your professor first for any requirements or recommendations before purchasing one.

- A good, sturdy backpack that allows you to carry all your books and notebooks. Because you will not have a locker or place to store your things between classes, you will have to find a bag that holds up to the task of carrying heavy materials over a period of weeks.

- A portable storage device that will hold your computer files and allow you to access them at any computer. Thumb drives, also known as flash drives and pin drives, are increasingly popular because they hold a large number of files and are easy to carry. Use a permanent marker or tape to put your name on the drive, save a Word file on the drive labeled "If found, please contact," and include your contact information. University computer labs have hundreds of these thumb drives that were misplaced by students in just one semester.

Classroom Preparation, Attendance, and Behavior

In addition to your supplies, knowing and meeting your professor's expectations in the classroom will make a great foundation for success. One essential expectation that professors have is preparation—yours. You should be prepared *before* you get to class by reading the assigned pages or completing the homework. Professors who assign reading or homework expect students to prepare—they may even administer quizzes—and to ask questions about anything they did not understand. Professors assume that if you don't ask questions or participate in a discussion, you understand the assignment. They may also hold you accountable for the assigned reading on exams even if it was not discussed in class.

Another expectation is that out-of-class assignments must be typed; in fact, unless otherwise stated, assume that all outside assignments should be typed, because they are easier to read and they look more professional. If you don't know how to create written documents on a computer, now is the time to learn; relying on others to create these documents will put you at a disadvantage. You may not be able to control when the person can complete the work, which can make you miss important due dates.

G R I T
Growth

> Gritty students take the most advantage of the resources available and are least likely to let any lack of resources prevent them from getting what they need. They show up for their professors' office hours when they need to, so they can better accomplish their goals.

Professors also expect that college students are able to access technology regularly and use it competently. What this means is that your professor will assume and expect that you have consistent access to a computer and the Internet. She will also believe that you have an email account and can send emails— even messages with attachments—successfully. If these are skills and equipment that you do not have, you will need to find out where you can access a computer on or off campus and make sure that you have the ability to use it properly.

Finally, instructors expect you to use their office hours—the time when they are formally available to meet with students—to meet with them. This is a time not only to address any questions or concerns you may have about your progress, but it is also a wonderful time to get to know your professors better. Professors typically post their office hours in their syllabi, on their course websites, and on the doors of their offices.

Regular attendance in your classes is crucial so that you can obtain information and guidance about assignments, tests, and grading. Especially in courses that build on concepts (such as math, foreign languages, and writing), regular attendance is essential to help you overcome problems with challenging assignments and prepare for tests. If you are receiving financial aid through grants or loans, your attendance may be important to your continuing to receive funds in the future.

If you miss a class or intend to miss a class, you should contact your professor in writing. You may need a doctor's excuse if you missed an exam or assignment, and if your absence wasn't due to a medical situation, you should be prepared to justify your absence. Most professors, though, may not care why you were absent or may not distinguish between excused or unexcused absences. Instead, they use your attendance as an indication of your effort and contribution to the class. Many professors base a portion of their grades on attendance and/ or class participation. Because you can't participate in a class discussion while absent, your attendance will likely have a direct impact on your grades.

Attending class is just part of the effort you will put forth; you will also need to produce quality work. Writing a paper and turning it in is only part of the requirement. You also have to adhere to the standards of the course. If your professor asks for a 10-page paper that argues a contemporary topic and uses five sources, you must follow those guidelines. In some instances, you may receive no credit for completing an assignment if you have not followed these requirements.

The more time you work to complete an assignment *usually* translates to better quality, but this is not always the case. For example, someone who types 40 words a minute will need less time to produce the same typographical-error-free assignments as someone who "hunts and pecks" at the keyboard. The quality of your work is what you will be graded on, not the number of hours you spend doing it.

No doubt you already juggle numerous responsibilities, and going to class and studying are just more tasks that you must complete each week. Handling your responsibilities skillfully will take the right mindset, respect for yourself, and some basic maturity. Laura knows how important being responsible for herself and her son is. She has had many years of relying on herself and a few family members to meet her responsibilities. Obviously, as a student she has the responsibility to take notes, study for tests, and attend classes regularly. But she also has the responsibility to ask questions when she doesn't understand or to resolve any conflict that may occur.

G R I T
Tenacity

Do whatever it takes to get what you need from a class. With tough subjects, set aside some prime time—when your mind is sharpest—to review, prepare, and stay on top. Strive to *exceed* professors' expectations, and build in a buffer, in case anything goes wrong. Like Laura, the tougher it gets, the deeper you dig to do well.

With responsibility also comes maturity, which is the foundation for many of the other components of college culture. Without a mature and gritty mindset, the other parts are unattainable. There are, however, less obvious actions that can help you present yourself as a dedicated, mature student. The first one is paying attention during lectures, presentations, talks by guest speakers, and videos. Although this sounds obvious, it is sometimes forgotten after the first few weeks of the semester. Work on looking at the front of the room and avoiding distractions. A common barrier to paying attention, besides staring out the window, is doing homework in class. Instructors frown on students who use class time to study for other classes or complete assignments that were due at the beginning of class. Students are often amazed at how visible everything is from the front of class. Just remember that the instructor sees that you are not paying attention and will make note of it.

Small actions, but equally important ones, that convey maturity and readiness to meet college expectations include staying for the duration of the class, limiting off-topic conversations with classmates, refraining from eating or participating in distracting activities, and getting ready to exit class only after the instructor has dismissed everyone.

One small activity that causes big problems in class is the use of phones or other personal electronics. Professors generally view it as rude and disruptive, unless they are having you intentionally use a device as a learning tool. In some classes, such as a chemistry lab, the distraction can be dangerous. Some colleges have strict policies forbidding the use of personal electronics in class. There may be exceptions, however. For example, if you work in a field that requires your immediate attention in the event of an emergency or if you have a gravely ill family member, ask if you may leave these electronic devices turned on. If your college does not have a policy, turn off your phone in class anyway. Students who answer social calls in class appear immature and unconcerned about their education.

the unwritten rules
of College Culture and the Campus

- **The unwritten rules are just that—unwritten.** Learning the unwritten rules will take time and trial and error, but everyone feels as if they are in a different country when they first enroll at college. This feeling will pass as you begin to learn more about how the college works.

- **Upperclassmen, also known as students who are further ahead of you in their degree completion, can help you learn the rules more quickly.** Find someone who is a second-year or third-year student who can show you the ropes. Maybe you need to know where the best place to park is or how to sign up for a campus organization; a student who has been at your college for over a year can speed up your mastery of the unwritten rules. A big part of GRIT is learning from others and adjusting your approach along the way.

- **The campus has people who can help you.** No matter what you need, there is most likely an office or person that handles it. Get to know your campus early and well by finding out what each building houses and what the office or position can do for you if you need it.

Constructive Criticism

Another important way to demonstrate maturity in college is to understand and appreciate, even seek and welcome, constructive criticism from your professor. Your professors will provide feedback on your assignments, exams, projects, and presentations both in writing and verbally, and sometimes the feedback will be challenging. Because professors are busy, because they work with a lot of students each semester, and because they have high expectations for student work, they may deliver feedback in a way that can be tough to hear. For example, your professor might return your term paper covered in red ink with comments and corrections throughout the document.

Growth

Here's where you can show some real GRIT. If you get this kind of feedback, don't take it personally, and don't jump to the conclusion that your work was poor. Clarify to make sure you understand. Take it in the spirit of improving yourself and consider it a compliment. Use it to fuel your determination to earn more positive feedback next time.

Getting a lot of feedback and response from your professor is actually a really positive opportunity. No matter how much you may dislike how the feedback is delivered, your professor's ultimate intention is to help you learn and improve your performance. Read the professor's feedback carefully and identify the lessons you can learn from the feedback to improve the quality of future assignments. Gritty learners use feedback like a GPS, helping them reroute to get to their goal even better and faster.

The more GRIT you grow, the quicker, better, and more positively you will respond to any feedback. But if the feedback triggers an emotional response, give yourself a day or two before you respond. Even better, share the professor's feedback with a trusted classmate or friend and invite their advice on how you can best learn from it. Some of you may have experienced athletic coaches or high school teachers who were tough on their students, but in a well-intentioned manner that brought out the best in student performance. Professors who provide challenging feedback are similarly effective at facilitating high performance among students, especially for students who are open to constructive criticism and who view it as an opportunity to learn and grow.

GRIT
Tenacity

Years later, you may look back on your toughest professors as your favorite, because they helped you grow the most. They made you show some GRIT.

Controversial Content

For the most part, college will be a straightforward experience—you will learn the expectations and when you meet them, you will be successful. There are, though, other aspects of college culture that may be uncomfortable or even shocking to you. All colleges value diversity, whether it is in the student body population or in the backgrounds of its faculty. Most definitely, you will find diversity in ideas and theories among the subjects that are offered, which may challenge your beliefs and values. Still other subjects may contain material that you find disrespectful, offensive, distasteful, or disturbing. Besides the reading and discussion of controversial issues, your college may produce student and faculty work that contains language, images, or situations that you find offensive.

What should you do if you encounter college "culture shock"? First, remember that the purpose of college is to provide you with a wider worldview and understanding of diversity—even if that diversity involves different ideas and theories. Second, remember that you have the right to opinions and feelings about what you encounter in college. There is no reason you should hide your feelings or attitudes about what you are learning and encountering. With this said, the third point to remember is that with your right to an opinion, you also have an obligation as a college student to examine your previously held beliefs and evaluate how they are being challenged in your courses or as you participate in college activities. You also have the obligation to appreciate that there is more than one way to view an "offensive" idea or image. Exhibit 1.2 provides a list of possible subjects that could be controversial to you or other students.

You will learn about diversity and relationships in depth in another chapter, but it is worth mentioning here that dealing with diversity, conflict, and controversy takes a certain level of maturity. Effectively meeting any challenge to your belief system or values will demand that you act with integrity and openness. Because the purpose of getting an education is to stretch your mind and expand your ideas, you will need maturity to help you put all that new information into perspective.

It's in the
syllabus

What are your instructors' expectations? Look at your syllabus for each class you are taking and determine what each one expects of you.

- Are you supposed to do the majority of your work outside of class?
- Are you expected to be responsible for completing a group project?
- What kinds of supplies are you required to have for each class?
- Will you need computer access to complete assignments?
- How will you purchase or access the required supplies?

The College Experience Has a Rhythm

Now you know what to expect and what is expected of you in college, but understanding a few other customary practices will help you go from being a "tourist" to a "native." One of the characteristics of a university environment that you'll start to notice over time is that there's a rhythm that drives the pace and intensity of the college experience. In the same

---

EXHIBIT 1.2   A Sample of Possible Controversial Subjects

The existence of God, higher being	The theory of extraterrestrial life
Conservatism and liberalism	Evolution
Nudity in art, photography	The beginning of life
Sexuality, including homosexuality and adultery	Scientific investigation and experimentation (stem cells, cloning)
The creation of the universe	Socioeconomic theory

GRIT GAINER™

GRITTY MINDSET   Right from the start, you have to decide if you are going to be the kind of student who owns and takes full responsibility for your achievement and success. Are you going to claim it or blame it when you fall short or things go wrong? Are you going to be one of those students who does the bare minimum? Or are you going to strive to do and become more? Try these GRIT Gainers to become unstoppable.

1. Any time you face a challenge, get stuck, feel frustrated, or are disappointed, ask yourself, "Ultimately, what do I really want to get out of this class (or degree)?" The clearer you are on your goals and the more compelling your goals are, the grittier you become.

2. Whenever you feel like giving up or compromising your standards for success, ask yourself, "If my life depended on my getting a good grade in this class (or achieving this goal), what would I do (that I haven't yet done) to make sure that happened?"

way that a 24-hour period in your life tends to have variations in what you're doing and how intense your schedule is, the college experience has predictable variations that you can expect and anticipate.

Schedules

First, it is helpful to note that universities organize their annual calendar around semesters, terms, or quarters, which can be as short as four weeks, usually during the summer, or as long as 16 weeks. Many universities have at least four semesters: fall, spring, first summer term, and second summer term, with the summer terms being shorter than the fall and spring terms. Other colleges organize the academic calendar around 10- or 11-week quarters. If you are unsure how many weeks the semester is, count the number of weeks from the first day of class until the last day of finals. You can find the information in the college catalog or in the course outline of your syllabus.

No matter how many weeks you spend taking a course, classes are scheduled at different days during the week. This arrangement may differ significantly from your high school schedule. In college, you may take classes once a week, as is the case in evening or night classes, or you may take them on Mondays, Wednesdays, and Fridays or just Tuesdays and Thursdays. Usually, colleges do not offer classes on Friday nights, so if you take classes in the evening, you will take them either once a week or twice a week, Mondays through Thursdays.

Exceptions to this schedule occur during shortened terms such as summer semesters or intersession terms in which you may go every day during the week. Also, you may have a lab or special class that meets only once a week, but is tied to another class such as biology or chemistry. The best advice for new students is to read the schedule of classes carefully before registering, and as always, ask an advisor, counselor, professor, or fellow student if you have trouble reading your schedule.

Colleges award credit hours based on how many hours a week you are in class during a regular semester (summer or intersession terms will double or quadruple the number of hours a week as compared to a regular semester). Thus, a three-credit-hour class will require that you spend about three hours in class per week—some classes may last only 50 minutes three times a week. Exceptions do exist: Labs are often worth one credit hour, but they may meet for more than one hour one day a week.

Exhibit 1.3 shows a typical schedule of a full-time student. Notice the "TR" under the "Days" column; "T" stands for Tuesday and "R" stands for Thursday. Thus, the biology class

EXHIBIT 1.3 Sixteen-Week Class Schedule

FALL 2016 (16-WEEK) SCHEDULE				
COURSE ID	COURSE NAME	DAYS	TIME	CREDIT HOURS
Engl 030	Composition 1	M W F	8:00–8:50 A.M.	3.0
Biol 110	Biology	T R	8:00–9:15 A.M.	3.0
Biol 112	Biology Lab	R	9:25–11:25 A.M.	1.0
Math 034	College Algebra	M W F	10:00–10:50 A.M.	3.0
Coll 101	Freshman Seminar	T R	12:15–1:30 P.M.	3.0
TOTAL HOURS				13.0

meets both Tuesday and Thursday while the lab meets on Thursday only. Labs and other special classes may meet for more than one hour a week, but they are usually worth only one credit hour. Although the classes in this schedule meet two and a half hours each week, they are given three credit hours. Three hours is often an approximation of the time spent in class.

If the schedule in Exhibit 1.3 reflects a 16-week semester, this student will spend over 40 hours in class for the semester. During summer or intersession terms, you will spend about the same number of hours in class, but you will attend class more often and for a longer period of time.

Because Exhibit 1.4 is a schedule for a four-week term, the classes meet for more than three hours a week. In this case, students meet for 10 hours a week for four weeks, which will equal 40 hours or the equivalent of the total number of hours a three-credit-hour class will meet during a 16-week term.

As you build your schedule each semester, here are a few tips to consider:

- To get through, identify the courses you need to make progress toward your degree. Meet with your advisor well in advance of when you need to formally enroll in the next semester, and make sure you know what general education (GE) courses you should take next and what required and elective courses you should be taking for your major. Don't build your schedule around classes that are interesting or fit the time of day when you want to attend class—focus on the courses you need to move closer toward graduation.

EXHIBIT 1.4 Four-Week Class Schedule

SUMMER 2016 (4-WEEK) CLASS SCHEDULE				
COURSE ID	COURSE NAME	DAYS	TIME	CREDIT HOURS
MATH 101	College Algebra	M T W R F	8:00–10:00 A.M.	3.0
Engl 101	Composition I	M T W R F	10:10–12:10 P.M.	3.0
TOTAL HOURS				6.0

Growth

Think beyond. Imagine the career you'd like to pursue once you complete your degree. If you were to dig deep and do whatever it takes *now* to enhance your chances of making it happen, what courses (or other learning) beyond your requirements might you go after to help fulfill your ambitions?

Instinct

Being denied admission to a specific class doesn't always mean you can't get it. Exercise some GRIT, approach the professor, express your enthusiasm for the subject, and see if there is a way to make it happen.

Tenacity

Employers value GRIT. When asked, 98 percent would rather hire a graduate who did reasonably well taking tough courses while working his way through school and shouldering a lot of responsibilities over the graduate with an easy life and perfect grades in easy courses. Don't get seduced by easy, when at times the tougher path may pay off in the long run.

- Have a contingency plan or alternative courses in mind. Depending on the balance between student demand and the supply of courses at your university, you may encounter situations in which the classes you want to take are either not being offered next term (not every class listed in the university catalog is offered every term) or are already full by the time you register for classes. For that reason, identify courses that could be appropriate second options for you. For example, some GE requirements provide several options. Your top choice might be a popular culture class that you know you would really enjoy, but it's a good idea to identify another suitable GE course that you could take if that class is full or not scheduled.

- Don't make your schedule a popularity contest. If you rely on fellow classmates to tell you when you should take class and which professor you should choose, you'll find yourself competing against everyone else for the same classes. This doesn't always work in your favor. Sometimes an "unpopular" 7 A.M. class may be your best option because it fits your schedule well, and you may discover that you think most clearly in the morning. You might also discover that a professor is "unpopular" simply because he challenges his students to work hard, and you actually learn a lot in his course. Select courses for the right reasons, not the popular reasons.

- Build in time for individual study and to meet with study groups. As you build your schedule, insert blocks of time when you can go to the library or other study space to review lecture notes, read the textbook, and complete homework and assignments. Also, set time aside for study group meetings and team projects.

There are other factors you'll want to consider when you build your schedule—such as your part- or full-time job, eating, exercising, sleeping, and social activities—so take time to build a complete schedule before you have to officially enroll in the next term. The schedule you build will determine the rhythm of each term, and you want that rhythm to fit you well.

Grades

What is a discussion about college expectations without mentioning grades? For sure, grades are an important part of your education, but they aren't the only measure of your learning and success. Grades are important because they reflect your level of achievement on an assignment or in a course, they are often used for obtaining and maintaining scholarships and financial aid, and they are a relevant piece of news to family, friends, and employers who may be supporting you financially and emotionally. Many people view grades as a reflection of a level of success. For instance, most of the people you ask would view a student who has straight A's as someone who is smart and successful. Earning good grades can motivate you to do your best and give you more confidence as you earn them.

Although good grades feel great when you earn them, grades are not always an indication of your success or lack of success in mastering a subject. Grades are important because they are a way to describe the work you have done in a class, and you'll have to earn a certain level of grades in your classes to officially pass and move on. However, grades alone are not the magic carpet to success in college; they are only part of the story of your achievements. Your goal should be to strike a balance between caring about your grades and caring about improving your skills and increasing your knowledge.

EXHIBIT 1.5 Grading Criteria for an A Paper

An excellent introduction with engaging hooks, setup, plan for essay; and/or main idea

An original significant thesis that offers insightful interpretation or thought

An inventive and logical organizational plan

Smooth and varied transitional expressions, phrases, and sentences that provide unity and coherence

Strong conclusion that ends the essay effectively

Expressive, clear style with sophisticated sentence structure and word choice

No more than three major grammatical errors

As stated earlier, college professors grade a student on his or her ability to meet the standards of the course or of a particular assignment. Effort is definitely a necessary part of earning good grades—and you will earn the respect of your professor and fellow students by demonstrating an intense effort to master the concepts of a class—but it is only one part of achieving success in a course. College professors expect that you also meet the standards, sometimes called grading criteria, of the course. Exhibit 1.5 shows a potential set of criteria for a college-level paper. In this case, the criteria are for an A paper.

Knowing how your college assesses student performance is a start to improving your overall outlook on grading. The following is a typical grading scale in college:

90–100 A   80–89 B   70–79 C   60–69 D   0–59 F

Some colleges may use a + or – next to a letter grade, such as A– or C+. Usually, colleges that allow for +'s and –'s will also alter the grading scale to designate the different grades. Here is an example of a grading scale that includes +'s and –'s:

94–100 A   90–93 A–   89–87 B+   86–84 B   80–83 B–

Each semester, the Registrar's Office, which maintains your official academic records, will calculate your grade point average (GPA) and post it to your transcript, or your list of classes and grades. Because the calculation of your GPA requires a little mathematical skill, it is important to know how the registrar figures it. Hours are the number of hours you are in class each week. As discussed previously, classes are usually three credit hours. Science or specialized classes that have labs usually carry four-credit hours. Depending on the course and the program, credit hours can be as many as six or as few as one. To know how many hours a course carries, check the description in the college catalog, because some classes meet for more hours a week than they are worth in terms of credit.

Letter grades carry a point value called *quality points*. Exhibit 1.6 shows how many quality points each letter grade is worth.

Courses that are designated developmental or remedial usually do not figure into your grade point average, so they do not carry any quality points. If you audit a course or receive AP or CLEP credit for a course, you will not receive quality points either. In other words, although you receive credit on your transcript for taking the course or taking an equivalent of the course, the course will not factor into your grade point average. Before you figure your GPA, you will need to figure your grade points for each class (see Exhibit 1.6). You arrive at

EXHIBIT 1.6 Grades and Quality Points

Letter Grade	Quality Points
A	4
B	3
C	2
D	1
F	0

EXHIBIT 1.7   GPA Calculation Table

Hours	Grade (Quality Points)	Grade Points (Hours × Quality Points)
3	A (4)	$3 \times 4 = 12$
3	B (3)	$3 \times 3 = 9$
3	C (2)	$3 \times 2 = 6$
3	C (2)	$3 \times 2 = 6$
3	C (2)	$3 \times 2 = 6$
15 Hours		39 Grade Points

your grade points by multiplying the quality points for the grade you received by the number of hours the class is worth. For instance, if you took a four-hour class and you made a B, then you will multiply 4 (hours) by 3 (quality points for a B).

Evan is taking 15 hours (5 three-hour courses) this semester; if he receives an A, B, and three C's, then his grade would be calculated as shown in Exhibit 1.7.

Finally, divide the total grade points by the total hours (39/15). Evan's GPA would be 2.6.

Building your schedule every term and tracking your grades will establish a regular rhythm for your college experience. Other activities may be part of this rhythm as well, such as club or Greek life responsibilities, intramural sports, academic competitions, career fairs and workshops, and on-campus events like concerts and sporting events. Over time, you'll adapt to the ebbs and flows of these activities and the intensity of your work to meet all of the expectations and responsibilities that you face. As you learn to anticipate these variations in intensity and pace, you'll be able to prepare for them and succeed.

integrity matters

Your college transcript, which includes your grade point average, can reveal more than just the grades you earned in courses. For example, some colleges make notations on students' transcripts if they have failed a class because of plagiarism or cheating. These marks can be evidence that a student did not follow academic integrity policies.

In some cases, these marks can be deleted from transcripts if the student successfully completes an academic integrity workshop.

YOUR TURN

In 250 words, discuss the specifics of your college's academic integrity policy. Describe how your university records failing grades that are due to academic integrity violations. Also include in your discussion whether or not there there any programs at your college to help students understand and follow the academic integrity policy.

GRIT GAINER™

> **THE GRITTY GAMEPLAN**   Fewer and fewer employers are fooled by graduates with great grades in easy courses. More value the hardship, struggle, adversity you face to achieve your goals. Build a Gritty GamePlan using these simple tips:
>
> 1. Is your schedule challenging enough? Does it stretch you to learn, grow, adapt, and perform? What adjustments can you make so it does?
>
> 2. Add something new to your schedule every term, or at least every year. Take on new challenges and new pursuits that expand your capacity and capabilities. College is the perfect time to do it.

There Are Helpful Resources on Your Campus to Help You Succeed

Now that you have a better understanding of college culture and what is expected of you, it is time to examine how your college looks. Getting to know the layout of the campus and the people who work there is important to understanding the culture and getting the help you need to support your success. A big part of being a gritty learner is proactively and creatively tapping the resources around you to fill in any gaps and to get what you need to accelerate and fortify your success both inside and outside the classroom.

For example, knowing where to go when you need to use a computer will make your ability to complete an assignment a little easier. Finding your professor's office may save you time and stress when you need to talk to him about an upcoming test. Going out of your way to take advantage of these resources can make a huge difference. The more you are on campus, the better able you will be to find people and places that will help you no matter what you need, but it will help if you take some time to study your campus so you know where to look.

Explore Your Campus

Find a map of your campus and study it for a few minutes. How many buildings does it have? How much parking space? How much "green" space or landscaping? Are there any unique features to your campus that make it an inviting and exciting place? Familiarizing yourself with your campus is probably the first activity you did when you enrolled in classes. If you have not taken a tour or simply walked around the campus, do so within the first few weeks of the semester. Locate the library, the student center, student parking, the bookstore, the business office, and the registrar's office—just to name a few destinations.

The more you know about your campus's layout, the easier it will be to find what you are looking for when you need it most. Using your map of the campus or your memory, check off in Exhibit 1.8 the types of buildings or departments within buildings that you know are present at your college.

If your university has more than one campus, familiarize yourself with the layout of other college property. You may have to travel to a satellite campus to take a test or to pick up materials for a class. If you have the time and the other campus is not too far away, ask for a tour. At the very least, familiarize yourself with any of the items you marked "not sure" in Exhibit 1.8.

EXHIBIT 1.8   **Campus Layout Checklist**

Building or Area	At My College	Not Sure
Student center or union		✗
Library	✗	
Bookstore	✗	
Administration building		✗
Theater or auditorium	✗	
Snack bars, food courts, and other dining facilities	✗	
Athletic training facilities (indoor or outdoor)	✗	
Science labs	✗	
Computer labs	✗	
Individual colleges and departments (such as business, psychology, engineering, and graphic communication)	✗	
Student parking	✗	
Benches and tables for meeting outside	✗	
Quiet study space inside	✗	
Disability Resource Center		✗
Health Center		✗
Cashier's Office		✗
Housing Office		✗
Registrar's Office		✗

Locate Information about Campus Resources

Knowing where to go to find services and people is only part of learning about your college. Another important aspect is finding and using the information that the college produces for students. College publications are a great place to find information about courses, programs, scholarships, activities, and policy changes. It is important that you regularly read these publications in order to stay up to date with what is going on.

College Catalog

The college catalog is an essential document during your academic career. All the information that you need to apply for financial aid, choose courses, and complete a degree is contained in the catalog. The academic calendar is usually placed at the beginning of the catalog. There you will find the dates for registering, dropping courses, and taking final exams.

It is important to read and keep your college catalog because if the college changes any requirements of your degree program, you will be able to follow the guidelines that were published the year you began the program. For instance, if you are working on a psychology degree and you have taken three semesters of courses so far, you will not necessarily have to adhere to new requirements that are made at a later date.

Student Handbook

The student handbook, which provides you with specific information about student conduct, academic standards, and services, is another valuable publication. Usually, the handbook contains descriptions of career services, the bookstore, computer labs, and financial aid offices. Academic information such as terms for probation and suspension for misconduct and qualifications for making the dean's list can also be found in the student handbook. Most schools view the student handbook as a legal document that outlines what students can do in certain situations, so be sure to read it closely and keep a copy at home or in your bookbag.

College Newspaper

College newspapers differ from the college catalog and student handbook in that students are usually the ones who are responsible for the content. Within a college newspaper, you will find articles about upcoming events, reports on changes on the college campus, editorials on important student issues, profiles of programs, and advertisements for used books, musical performances, and anything else that students want to announce. The college newspaper is also a forum to explore controversial topics and to discuss sensitive issues.

Newspapers always need students to interview, write, edit, and publish. If you are interested in working for the newspaper, contact the editor or visit a journalism or composition professor.

■ Students who have "the right stuff"—such as access to a computer, textbooks, and other materials and equipment that are required for classes—are much more likely to be successful.

© PEARSON EDUCATION

Bulletin Boards

Even with the increased use of the Internet, the bulletin board is still an important way to get a message to students. Found all over campus, bulletin boards usually advertise used books, needs for roommates and part-time jobs, and upcoming campus events. Bulletin boards within academic buildings often announce study abroad opportunities, summer workshops, special events, and other types of notable activities.

It's in the Syllabus

Anything that professors hand out in class is a communication tool. The syllabus is one of the most important documents that you will receive in class, so be sure to read it carefully. In the syllabus you will usually find the following information:

- Instructor's name, office location, phone number, hours open to students, and email address
- Prerequisites for the course
- Course description from the catalog
- Textbook information
- Course objectives, or what you will accomplish by the time you finish the class
- Course content, or what topics will be covered throughout the semester
- Assignments and due dates
- Grading criteria
- Attendance and late-work policies
- Academic integrity statement (which also appears in the student handbook)

- Disability accommodations policy
- General policies for classroom conduct

The syllabus is considered a contract between the student and the instructor. This means that not only will the syllabus contain what is expected of you during class, but it will also contain what you can expect from the professor. Both of you—the student and the professor—will be bound by what is stated in the document. Reading the syllabus closely and following it regularly will keep you on top of the policies, expectations, and assignments.

Other essential information that is handed out in class includes directions to assignments, photocopied readings, study questions, and notes. Regard anything that is given to you by the instructor as important, even if you are told "This won't be on the test."

You should also consider the grades and written comments you receive as communication from your instructors. Be sure to read any comments or suggestions that are written on papers and exams, ask questions if you don't understand them or they are illegible, and save all feedback until the semester is over.

Online Resources

The college's website is where you can find the most current information about classes, academic programs, and contact information for professors. It is easier to update information on a website because it doesn't involve printing and distribution, so it is more likely to provide the most accurate information. College websites usually list phone numbers and email addresses of professors and deans, which makes contacting them easier.

In addition to general information about degrees and departments, your college's website may give you access to professors' syllabi and assignments. This provides a good opportunity to investigate what courses you want to take based on the course objectives and activities and information about the professor.

Campus Organizations

Campus organizations or student groups are another part of college life you will want to learn more about. Depending on how large your college is and how involved the students are, you may find a variety of student organizations and clubs in which to participate. Even if your time is limited, consider getting involved in some way, because these activities can enhance your college experience, and employers value extracurricular leadership experience when they recruit potential employees. Campus organizations include, but are not limited to, student clubs, fraternities and sororities, student government, student leadership programs, and clubs focused on certain interests (e.g., gay, lesbian, bisexual and transgendered issues; political action; community service; academic honors and distinctions; religious or spiritual development; and career exploration). Getting involved will help you transition to the college and provide immediate connections with students, faculty, and staff. You can learn about these opportunities on the university website, through on-campus club fairs and information sessions, and by asking upperclassmen about their own experiences.

A university is an exciting place with a wide variety of activities and experiences that can enrich your life and help you succeed. Because there are many options for how you can get involved, you'll need to gather information about them and carefully choose the best opportunities in which you'll invest time and effort. It's a common mistake among students to get excited about all these opportunities and then overcommit. This leads to avoidable disappointment and failure. As you begin your college career, carefully select only one or two extracurricular activities until you can gain experience with your academic responsibilities and determine how much capacity you have for commitments outside the classroom.

Growth

Surround yourself with and join the organizations full of students who get stuff done, make it happen, and set a high standard for themselves. GRIT is contagious.

GRIT GAINER™

GO GET WHAT YOU NEED Any professor can spot which students sit back versus those who step up. A big part of adopting a gritty mindset is actively seeking out, going after, and getting the information, wisdom, and resources you need to succeed. Try these simple GRIT Tips to come out ahead:

1. Ask your professors, "Excuse me, professor, but I'm curious, beyond the syllabus, what two or three pieces of advice would you offer me to at least increase my chances of success in your class?" Most will be impressed. Write/record what they say.

2. When you face a struggle or obstacle, don't let it beat you down. Seek out and ask a few of the wisest people you can find where they would go to get resources or what they would do to deal with a situation like yours. Most will be happy to help.

3 things future professionals need to know about college culture

your ability to adapt to change is a lifelong skill

Transitioning from high school or work to college requires you to change. Change isn't always easy, and it may not be fun, but it's a necessary and important part of life as you move through life in pursuit of your goals and your values. As you successfully transition to college, you're gaining experience in how to adapt to and ideally harness change. That ability will help you adapt to and get the most out of the next big transition from college to career.

the college experience is a safe and supportive time for you to prepare for your career

Before a skydiver jumps out of an airplane, he puts on his goggles and gloves, double-checks all of his equipment, and prepares himself for the conditions he'll face when he jumps out. The airplane serves as a safe place for the skydiver where he can get the final advice from the instructor before making the leap. In some ways, college is like this. Your professors, advisors, and mentors are all there to help you prepare for the conditions you face after you graduate. They may even try to simulate those conditions for you to help you get ready. Eventually, however, you'll have to make that jump, and it's a thrilling and challenging experience.

the habits you establish in college can propel you into your career

The tools and methods you use to manage your time, money, assignments, projects, and other responsibilities while in college will lead to habits over time. You'll have a tendency to carry habits from college into your career. For example, if you habitually arrive to your classes late or with only a minute to spare, you'll have a tendency of doing the same when you attend meetings at work. Is that going to give you the best chance for success in your career? If not, you need to change your habits now so that you have successful habits when you graduate.

THE G R I T ADVANTAGE

Here's a simple, quick challenge for you to put this chapter into immediate action. Check the boxes (below) next to the actions you'd like to take. They are based on the four dimensions of GRIT. Pick the ones that would at least increase your chances of successfully and enjoyably getting through, getting out, and getting paid.

Growth

☐ Ask my professor when I'm stuck or confused

☐ Ask more senior students I respect for their advice

☐ Immediately get familiar with the campus resources, where they are, and what they offer me

☐ Look for fresh angles, approaches, and ideas for how I can succeed in class and at college

Resilience

☐ Focus on what I can influence and what can be done, rather than on what cannot

☐ Take ownership for my success, choices, learning, and behavior

☐ Get what I need in spite of whatever frustrations, limitations, or injustices I may face

☐ Work to minimize the downside of any setback

☐ Learn from every adversity, so I get stronger, smarter, and better

Instinct

☐ Step back and ask, "What do I really want to get out of this course (or degree)?"

☐ Ask, "How can I adjust my approach or strategy to at least increase the chances I get what I need and want?"

☐ Figure out ways to work smarter, rather than just harder, so I can make more efficient and effective use of both my energy and time

Tenacity

☐ Refuse to give up on my main goals

☐ Surround myself with more go-getters than quitters

☐ Don't take "no" for an answer on the stuff that matters

☐ Reroute or take a different approach if what I'm doing now, even with my best effort, is not getting me anywhere

HOW **GRITTY** ARE YOU?

Score yourself on each of these items. Be brutally honest.

Now that you've completed this chapter, how committed are you to:

1. Doing whatever it takes to get what you need from your professors and your courses?

    Zero Commitment 0 ——————————————————————————— 10 **Fully Committed**

2. Getting to know and make good use of campus resources?

    Zero Commitment 0 ——————————————————————————— 10 **Fully Committed**

3. Sticking to my values, especially in the moments of truth?

    Zero Commitment 0 ——————————————————————————— 10 **Fully Committed**

4. Setting and living up to high expectations for myself?

    Zero Commitment 0 ——————————————————————————— 10 **Fully Committed**

2 Goal Setting, Motivation, and Learning Styles

Chapter goals to help you *get in, get through, get out, and get paid:*

In order to get in, get through, get out, and get paid, you need to know yourself well and establish goals that motivate you and keep you on track. This chapter puts the focus on you and helps you identify the reasons why you are pursuing a college degree and how it will lead you to achieving your personal goals and dreams.

To meet those goals, *this chapter will help you:*

- Discover your story
- Develop a personal strategy for achieving your goals and fulfilling your dreams
- Develop your support system
- Determine your learning style preference
- Dig deep, with **GRIT**, and do whatever it takes to fulfill your goals

MyStudentSuccessLab™

Log in to MyStudentSuccessLab.com to deepen your **GRIT** mindset and build the skills you'll need to get through the college experience.

Juanita's Story

© ANDRESR/SHUTTERSTOCK

Juanita calls her mother for the second time in two hours. She just created her schedule, visited with her advisor, and now is looking for where her classes will be. Juanita's mom answers immediately. "Do you think I can do this?"

"Juanita," her mother says, "you always overthink these things. I know you like to be prepared, but things will be different. It's not high school."

The classes seem different from the dual enrollment classes Juanita took in high school.

"Yeah, but I didn't have to make a life decision in high school. It made me nervous when my advisor asked me to choose a degree plan," she replies.

"You did choose electrical engineering, just like we talked about, right?" her mother asks.

"Well, I wanted to talk to you about that. I think I want to go into nursing," Juanita says.

"But you don't like working with people who are sick, Juanita. Besides, engineering is more prestigious," her mother replies. Because of the classes she has taken in her high school's dual enrollment program, Juanita could graduate earlier than her classmates who started this fall, but she knows it will still take a lot of money to do it.

"I will be proud of you whatever you decide, but make a choice and stick with it," her mother says.

Juanita knows her mother is right. She has a goal of getting a degree, but she is not sure how to make the right decisions today.

Now, what do you think?

- How will you handle the added responsibility of making important decisions about your future in college?
  - **a.** Not worry too much; everything will work out
  - **b.** Aim high, even if it requires more work and takes longer
  - **c.** Learn as much as I can about my options by talking to people on campus and attending events geared toward my future
  - **d.** Avoid any major decisions for as long as possible

- What would you do if your plans for the future conflicted with your family's plans for you?
  - **a.** Explain clearly why my plans are better than my family's plans for me
  - **b.** Give serious consideration to my family's ideas about what I should do
  - **c.** Try to get really clear on and stay true to what matters most, no matter what
  - **d.** Do what my family wants me to do; they have supported me and know what is best

Your Terms for success

when you see . . .	it means . . .
Background	The experiences you have had that make up who you are
Learning style preference	The learning style that you prefer or the one in which you learn best
Long-term goal	A goal that will take a month, a semester, a year, or several years to complete
Mission statement	A statement in which you describe how your values and goals will create your life's mission
Motivation	What keeps you moving toward your goal
Multiple Intelligences	Learning style preferences, or "intelligences," that include bodily/kinesthetic, intrapersonal, interpersonal, musical, spatial-visual, logical-mathematical, linguistic, and naturalistic
Priority	Something that is important at that moment
Short-term goal	A goal that takes an hour, a day, or a week to complete
Value	What you believe in

Begin with Your Story

The question "Who are you?" sounds easy to answer. You may start by listing a variety of characteristics. For example, you are a male, age 25, married, father of a son, an electrician, and a Native American. Or you are a single female, age 19, part-time sales assistant, full-time student, and mountain climber. But what are you beyond those labels? Where have you been? What are you doing now? Where are you going and where do you want to be? Now the questions get a little more difficult and take more time and thought to answer. The point is that you need to have some idea of who you are, or at least an idea of where you want to be, when you begin college.

Maybe you can say that you don't know who you are yet, but you hope that enrolling in classes and pursuing a degree will help you come to a better understanding of who you are. Don't worry if you cannot immediately articulate the essence of you. This question—"Who are you?"—and the possible answers have been intriguing human beings for thousands of years. The ultimate goal is to know yourself and your environment well enough to reach your goals.

Of course, who you are will change, maybe dramatically, as you take classes, encounter new subjects, and research interesting topics. But taking the time now to think and reflect about yourself will help you map your course throughout your university experience and beyond—from returning to work, to raising a family, to having a fulfilling career. This chapter assists you in understanding who you are by helping you identify what you know and how you learn. This chapter also aids in your decisions about who and what you want to be while helping you make the transition into college.

Your Background Is the First Chapter of Your Story

To discover your story—and write your future—you will need to consider from where you have come. Your background, which includes your family, your culture, and your experiences, will serve as a foundation for creating a life. Think about what experiences you have had and how they have shaped who you are. Consider how your family has influenced you as well—what beliefs have they instilled in you? What is their attitude toward your college aspirations? Who you are and how you have developed will be part of your value system as well as part of the foundation for setting goals for future achievements.

Think about the role adversity—difficulties, challenges, hardships, obstacles, limitations—has played in your life so far. Has it been an easy or difficult road? How much GRIT has it taken just to get to where you are today? How deep have you had to dig? How much have you had to struggle, sacrifice, even suffer in order to enroll in college and pursue your dreams?

If you have had great support and good educational experiences, the prospect of completing your degree may seem relatively easy and attainable. You may not know how much GRIT you hav, or how you will handle things if it gets more challenging.

However, if you have had an adversity-rich history with plenty of tough challenges, you may have exceptional GRIT. Or you may need more support and resources, and to grow more GRIT, to equip you for success. No matter what your background, attacking your college experience with a decent dose of GRIT will give you the chance to write a life story that includes a college degree.

Your Values Drive Your Goals

Part of your life story will include your value system. Values can be inherited from your parents, or they can come from what your culture, religion, or ethnicity regards as important. Values can also be formed from both positive and negative experiences. For example, you may value honesty, which means that you try to be truthful and straightforward in most situations

EXHIBIT 2.1   Table of Values

Advancement	Excitement	Learning	Security
Authority	Family	Money	Social status
Beauty	Fast pace	People	Solitude
Challenge	Financial stability	Physical challenge	Spirituality
Creativity	Friendship	Power	Structure
Community	Helping others	Pressure	Teamwork
Competence	Independence	Recognition	Tranquility
Decision making	Influence	Relationships	Travel
Education	Knowledge	Safety	Variety

and that you expect others to be honest with you. If you value hard work, then you strive to do your best in your life. If a friend has treated you with compassion, you may value sensitivity to others. On the other hand, if you have been discriminated against in the past, you may now value open-mindedness in others. Exhibit 2.1 provides a list of values that may drive your goals. Mark the ones that drive you.

The importance of knowing and understanding your values is that this knowledge can help you set realistic goals. If you value a satisfying career, for instance, you will set goals that support that value. Therefore, you will probably investigate careers and fields that are challenging and interesting. If you value a stable financial future, you will set goals that enable you to earn enough money to provide for your needs and wants. If you value your family, you will make spending time with them a priority. Your values should be a true reflection of who *you* are and what *you* believe.

Think about Juanita's conversation with her mother. Her mother wants Juanita to consider electrical engineering, perhaps because she values financial stability and success or career prestige. What if one reason Juanita hesitates at choosing a major and career path is that she values a career that helps the human condition? What if she also wants to learn more about how we recover from illness? If she decides to adopt her mother's values and ignore her own, what kind of future can you envision for her? Although her mother's intentions may be good, Juanita will have to compromise herself in order to meet her parents' goals for her, and she will probably suffer some regret in the future.

Does this example mean that you should ignore others who have helped you figure out what you want to be? Certainly not. But you should pay attention to what you want when you do get help with your educational and career goals. Be open to others' suggestions, but make sure that your final decisions are consistent with your own values. Those who truly want you to succeed will be proud of you when they know you have achieved your heart's desire, not theirs.

Your Dreams Are Worth Pursuing

As you consider your goals, you will also want to think about your dreams. Dreams are the big ideas and bold achievements that you sometimes imagine and for which you secretly hope. What do you

G R I T
Resilience

Whatever values you claim can be pretty meaningless until tested by adversity. It is in these moments of truth that you and the people in your life get to see who you really are and what you truly stand for. Be ready to sacrifice for what you believe in. This makes your values real.

■ If you value an education and it is part of your overall goal to graduate with a degree, then studying will be one way to achieve your goal and support your values.

© LAURENCE GOUGH/FOTOLIA

integrity matters

Staying true to your values is part of integrity. If you try to please others or adopt their values when you do not completely agree with them, you will lack integrity. For example, you may have been raised with the value of staying true to your ethnic or cultural heritage, even at the expense of meeting someone new or experiencing a new culture. Now that you are in college, you may find that you are exposed to a variety of ethnicities and cultures and that you enjoy and appreciate learning more about others.

YOUR TURN

In 250 words, discuss a time in which you took on someone else's values. Discuss your motivations for doing so, as well as the outcome. Finally, explain what you learned in the process.

want to do or achieve that you have not written down because you feel it is too far-fetched? There are many stories of people who ignored their dreams and took jobs that provided them with financial security and prestige, only to discover that their lives were not fulfilled because they regretted giving up on their dreams. There are also many exciting stories about people who never forgot their dreams and who eventually achieved them through hard work and determination.

Why don't more people follow their dreams? First, they may not know what their dreams are. Sometimes day-to-day life takes up so much of our time, attention, and energy that we don't take time to reflect on our lives and consider our dreams. Second, we may be scared. Pursuing your dreams is a risky proposition, and there's always the chance that circumstances or events could bring disappointment and failure in this pursuit. Third, some people need to make the "safe" choice first before they feel confident that they can pursue their dreams. Personal responsibilities and family obligations may dictate that you choose a path that provides a predictable source of income and security for now, with the hope that you will have a chance to pursue your dream sometime in the future.

Although you may not be able to fulfill your dreams in the immediate future, don't lose sight of them. Your life experiences and personal background, your values, and your dreams all shape who you are and who you can become.

Your Personal Strategy Can Bring Your Dreams to Life

The fact that you are reading this book is evidence that you are someone who not only has a purpose, but also is willing to take action to fulfill that purpose. These two elements—defining your purpose and taking action—are important components of something we'll call your

GRIT GAINER™

IMAGINE YOUR MOUNTAIN   You want who you are and what you do to make some sort of difference. Your highest aspiration defines your mountain. You want to move forward and up in life, to ascend. Staying true to your values, dreams, and purpose is difficult. The weather on the mountain can be harsh. Some people quit. Most go partway and camp; they stop short and play it safe. Be a *climber*. It takes some serious GRIT. But the views are unmatched.

Tenacity

Climbers reroute. Why do most people camp rather than climb? Why do people give up on fulfilling their dreams and having a life rich in purpose? It's tough. The weather on the mountain can be intense, and along your ascent, you are sure to face some obstacles, hardships, and setbacks. Campers get stuck. Climbers have the GRIT to reroute, even if you have to temporarily lose altitude, in order to move forward and up.

personal strategy. Your personal strategy is what you can plan and implement to fulfill the dreams that you've imagined and achieve the goals that you have set for your life.

The first step in developing a personal strategy is to define your mission statement. Your personal mission statement describes your purpose in life. It defines your mountain. We'll cover that first in the next section. Once you've defined your mission statement, you can develop specific goals, which, if achieved, bring your mission statement to life.

Goals lay out the trail map for you to know how well you're staying on path to live out your mission statement. With a mission statement and goals in place, with your mountain and trail map laid out, your next step is to develop a strategy—a course of decisions and actions that you can implement to achieve your goals and fulfill your mission statement.

Your strategy starts with some big-picture action items and decisions and narrows to more tactical elements such as day-to-day activities and short-term decisions. These building blocks—mission statement, goals, and strategy—will help you life a purposeful life that you can examine each hour, day, month, and year and say to yourself, "I'm on my way to living my dreams."

Your Mission Statement Defines Your Purpose

Mission statements are statements of purpose. Most companies develop a mission statement for themselves because it defines their purpose and answers the crucial questions: "Why do I exist?" and "What is my purpose?" Your personal mission statement, therefore, should explain your purpose in life from a very broad perspective. Your personal values are the foundation of your mission statement. Once you've identified your values and what is most important to you, your next step is to describe your mission statement to establish your purpose.

As you meet your goals and learn new things, your mission will likely change and your mission statement will need to be revised. The following is an example of a mission statement that you can use as a model for defining your own mountain.

> **Sample Personal Mission Statement**
> My mission is to have a fulfilling personal and professional life that allows me to meet new people, take on new challenges, and have flexibility in my schedule. As a mother and wife, I want to have a close relationship with my family, and as a teacher, I want to help prepare students to have successful lives and careers.

Your Goals Set the Bar for Achievement

To build on your mission statement—and to fulfill that mission in the process—you will need to set goals that elevate you, goals you want to strive for and achieve. A goal is something that you work toward—it may be to learn how to cook macaroni and cheese, to quit a bad habit, or to write a novel.

Whatever your goals, they should describe outcomes that may stretch you, but you believe are both achievable and will help you advance toward longer-term goals in the future. They should also describe the desired outcome in a way that can be defined and observed. For example, setting a goal to "become a better person" might be a noble vision or mission, but it's not an effective goal because it doesn't specify an actual outcome. Consider, instead, a goal like "accumulate $1,000 in my emergency savings account by next February." This goal defines the outcome and provides a clear method for measuring its attainment.

We've adopted the "get in, get through, get out, get paid" theme for this book and our work in higher education. We think it effectively describes, in practical terms, why students pursue a college education and what's necessary for them to achieve personal and professional success.

If you're reading this book, chances are that you're already in college, so you achieved the "get in" goal. To "get through," you need to set goals to identify the classes you need to complete your degree, enroll in them, and successfully pass them. To "get out," you need to set a goal to meet all of the requirements of your chosen degree within a specific time period, typically two years for an associate's degree or four years for a bachelor's degree. You'll also need to establish goals to have the financial resources you need to complete all of these requirements. To "get paid," you need to set goals for getting an internship or job while in college and engaging in a successful career search before graduation so that you can secure a good job offer and have a great career waiting for you after commencement.

Exhibit 2.2 provides some sample goals that reflect the "get in, get through, get out, get paid" approach. Certainly, you may have other goals during the next few years relating to other important dimensions of your life like your health and relationships, so you can add those goals to these academically focused examples.

Here are a few other tips for writing effective goals:

- **Write your goals down.** No matter what you want to achieve, be sure that you write down all your goals and review them every few months to assess your progress. The process of writing down your goals tells your mind to start paying attention to your ambitions and makes you aware of opportunities to achieve them. Stating them and saying them out loud to others also makes your goals more real.

- **Break larger goals into smaller goals that will lead to fulfillment.** A 10-year goal of running a successful landscape design firm can be broken into smaller goals with shorter time periods that contributed to the larger goal.

- **Regularly review your goals and make changes as necessary.** A big part of GRIT is adjusting your path as things change but remaining relentless in achieving your goals. The weather on the mountain constantly changes. You may set goals now that change over time as you discover new things about yourself or learn about new career and personal opportunities. Climbers are agile. They reassess and reroute.

- **Reach out to others who care about you to help you achieve your goals.** Once you have written down your goals, communicate them to your coworkers, family, and friends. Enlist them to help you meet your goals, especially if you need to schedule time to study and complete assignments. For example, tell them that you must have the evenings free of distractions, or make arrangements with them to have a weekend or

EXHIBIT 2.2   SMART Goal and Action Plan

LONG-TERM SMART GOAL: Graduate with a bachelor's degree in biology by May 2018	
Action Steps	
Register by April 2015 for summer 2015 classes to get ahead on my degree plan	Meet with my advisor June 2015 to plan my schedule for fall 2015 and spring 2016
Register for required courses for fall 2016 by April 2016	Register by April 2016 for summer 2016 classes to get ahead on my degree plan or to retake any classes I need to retake
Meet with an advisor May 2017 to ensure I am on track to graduate in May 2018	Apply for graduation by February 2018

weekday to yourself to study. Don't assume that because they know you are in school they will also know you need extra time and personal space to get your work finished. Managing your time will be much easier if your priorities and goals are concrete, realistic, and communicated to those around you.

Growth

Whom in your life can you count on to show no mercy, hold you to your commitments, and help you stay gritty and focused, especially when faced with an avalanche of adversity? Explain your goals. Enlist that person to be the one who urges you on, forward, and up, like a personal climbing coach. No excuses.

- **Identify habits or challenges that could interfere with your goals.** As you work toward your goals, make an effort to eliminate anything that keeps you from focusing on them. If you think you don't have time to accomplish two short-term goals during the week, don't give up. Challenge yourself. Examine where you have been spending your time and eliminate the activities that do not contribute to your goals. Making a goal of staying healthy (e.g., eating right, exercising, de-stressing your life) is not only helpful, but achieving the goal will help you achieve your other goals. If you are unsure whether your activities contribute to your goals, take a few minutes to list what you have done this week and determine how each activity has supported or not supported one of your goals. Exhibit 2.3 gives some examples.

Your Strategy Is Your Action Plan

With a mission statement that reflects your values and long- and short-term goals that set the bar for your achievement, you can now move into the most exciting part of your personal strategy—strategic implementation. You can begin your climb. The word *implementation* means to put something into action and to commit to certain decisions. It means taking real steps along your trail map. The word *strategic* means that your decisions and actions are consistent with a course of action, which you've defined in terms of your mission statement and goals. If you enjoy board games like Monopoly, for example, your decisions to purchase certain properties will be guided by a particular goal, like owning all the utilities or the most expensive hotels. When you have a clear mission statement and goals, you will have clear guidance for your decisions and actions on a day-to-day, week-to-week, term-to-term, and year-to-year basis.

If you've written your goals effectively, the action plan that you need to implement to achieve those goals should be relatively clear. For example, if one of your goals is to achieve your bachelor's degree in landscape design in four years, your action plan will consist of taking (and passing) the courses you need to fulfill those degree requirements. If another goal is to lose 10 pounds in the next four months, your action plan will include proper nutrition and exercise and a plan to set time aside each day to prepare healthy meals and work out. Sometimes it

---

EXHIBIT 2.3   Activities That Contribute to and Distract from Your Goals

Activities That Contribute to Your Goals	Activities That May Distract You from Your Goals
Practicing car maintenance allows you to get to school and work safely.	Socializing excessively depletes the time and energy you have to focus on your goals.
Exercising allows you to remain healthy and reduce stress.	Mindlessly watching TV may not contribute to learning.
Eating well and getting enough sleep keeps you healthy and reduces stress regularly.	Using drugs and alcohol keeps you from focusing on goals and is dangerous.
Reading the newspaper keeps you informed, helps improve reading skills, and contributes to learning.	Sleeping and eating irregularly creates stress, which inhibits the ability to reach goals.

won't be entirely clear where your goals end and your strategies begin, but that distinction isn't as important as defining what you want to accomplish and making decisions and performing activities that move you forward toward those accomplishments.

Some people are really good at setting goals, but they struggle with the actual behaviors and decisions that are necessary to reach those goals. Other individuals are really good at taking action and making decisions, but their actions and decisions aren't consistent with a cohesive strategy. The balance between goals and actions will shift over time, but just keep your eyes on both, and you'll find yourself making progress over time.

Gritty students constantly reassess by asking, "Am I pursuing the right things in the best ways?" As we point out in other chapters, you can develop the climber's rhythm. Assess, adjust, and ascend. Assess, adjust, and ascend.

Perhaps the most important benefit of having a strategy and specific action steps is that you can pursue really big goals, reach higher elevations—and the dreams they fulfill—by breaking them down into achievable steps. Becoming a highly successful business owner is a wonderful goal and an exciting aspiration. If you're in the first semester of a bachelor's degree, however, that goal may seem so far away. Setting mid-range and shorter-term goals that lead up to your 10-year goal can help, but the most important activity that can build your confidence and hope is to start making decisions and performing activities that move you toward that 10-year goal.

Growing your own garden to develop your knowledge and understanding of plants is an example. Volunteering for community service will give you relevant experience and confidence that you'll need someday to become a major contributor to your community's well-being. During each day of your life, you'll encounter decisions and responsibilities that may seem relatively unimportant by themselves, but they add up every day to put you on a path toward achieving major goals in your life and fulfilling your dreams.

Another benefit of having a strategy is that you'll be able to identify the alternatives and activities around you that are *not* good options for your life. Your college experience will be full of many opportunities, and almost all of them have some kind of desirable qualities or apparent benefits. Having the personal GRIT to say "no" is as important as having the courage to say "yes." For example, in addition to pursuing a major, some students choose to also earn a minor or even a double major while they are in college. Student clubs, Greek organizations, study-abroad programs, weekend road trips, and spring break vacations are all examples of activities that may sound appealing and offer great opportunities for new experiences. However, not all of these opportunities are going to help you achieve your goals and fulfill your dreams. In fact, your decision to pursue some of these opportunities might actually distract you or hinder you from achieving the more important goals in your life. If you take time to develop a personal mission statement, establish long- and short-term goals, and develop an action plan for achieving those goals, you'll find yourself making far better decisions over time and feeling a sense of purpose and accomplishment each day.

■ Celebrate when you complete your goals.

© PAUL MATTHEW PHOTOGRAPHY/SHUTTERSTOCK

Priorities Determine Your Next Steps

A discussion of values and goals cannot be complete without also talking about priorities. Simply stated, a priority is something that is important at the moment. Today your top priority could be studying for an exam, but later in the day, it could be taking care of a sick child, which means that studying will have to come second, if at all. Priorities, by their very nature, can change weekly, daily, or even hourly.

Your actions also reflect your priorities. If you say that your first priority is to pass your classes this semester but you spend all your spare time playing basketball with friends, then your social life as well as a little exercise is really your top priority. You must make sure you know what your priorities are and take action to satisfy them. You may also need to express to others what your priorities are so that they can help you stick to them.

GRIT GAINER™

GRIT YOUR GOALS GRIT is the most important factor in completing your goals and fulfilling your dreams. Try these two tips to put some GRIT in your goals. Before you decide on or finalize your goals, ask yourself:

1. How can I kick it up a notch and stretch myself by making this goal a little more challenging?

2. If my life depended on me getting this goal accomplished quickly (and well), how much sooner could I get it done?

You'll be amazed at how your capacity to climb continues to grow.

Maintain Your Motivation

One of the hardest parts of setting goals is maintaining the momentum to achieve them. This is where your GRIT and goals work together. There will be times in your academic career when you will feel overwhelmed by the responsibilities you have and unsure of your ability to handle it all. When you feel weighed down by all that you have to accomplish for a particular week or day, try to calm down first. If you can, talk with a friend, an instructor, or a counselor and explain your frustration and stress. Sometimes, if an instructor knows you are feeling overwhelmed by expectations in a course, he or she will assist you by helping you find resources that will keep you on track. A friend may also volunteer to help by studying with you.

To stay motivated and to resist the temptation to give up because of the stress, review your short- and long-term goals. Is there anything that you can change that will make your goals more reasonable or attainable? Or are they challenging enough to bring out your best? Have you allowed enough or too much time to achieve them? Revising your goals or your timeline may be necessary to keep yourself on track.

Finally, think positively about yourself and your progress. Many students before you have successfully juggled a job, classes, and a family. That is not to say that they did not doubt themselves along the way or suffer any setbacks. The difference between these students and those who were not successful is their GRIT. They persevered because they believed in themselves and dug deep to make progress more often than not. Tap your GRIT to bring light and hope in your darkest moments. Tell yourself that you can get through stressful times.

Your Support System Is a Key to Success

Even the most dedicated student cannot do it all alone. Climbers are typically "on rope" with others. In fact, behind every successful college graduate is a good support system, usually comprising family, friends, and community members. It is no secret that succeeding in college will take more than just studying hard—you will need to surround yourself with people who encourage you to do your best. There will be times when you need others for academic, emotional, and even financial support. Recognizing who in your circle of friends, family, and contacts will be the best resources for you is part of the process of creating a support system that will inevitably be part of your college success. Who will not just support but stretch you to do and become more?

Your Family

Whether you live with your parents, you are a parent, or you are somewhere in between, your family is an important part of who you are and what you will become. Your family has influenced your values and beliefs, and your family members may be a part of the reason you have enrolled in college. For many students, their ability to stay in college and be successful depends on the support of their family. If your family will be an important part of your life as you pursue a degree, then you will need to consider how they will support you and what you need to communicate with them about what to expect when you have to spend more time studying and taking classes than strengthening relationships with them. Questions to ask yourself as you begin your first semester in college include:

- Who in my family will support my decision to attend college?
- What kinds of financial support can I expect?
- What kinds of emotional support can I expect?
- Does my family strengthen or weaken my GRIT?
- How may my relationships with my family change?
- What can I do to communicate my needs while I am in college?

Answering these questions early and communicating your responses at the beginning of the semester will make it easier for you to keep the lines of communication open in the long run. If you don't feel comfortable talking face-to-face with your loved ones, you could write a letter. At the very least, getting your thoughts down on paper first can help you polish what you want to say before you say it.

You may find yourself away from family and friends more often than normal as you begin to work toward your degree.

Your Friends

Another important part of your support system is your friends. Although you may not be able to choose your family members, you will have more choice as to which friends will be positive influences on your college experience. If you have friends who have also attended or are attending college, you will have a great opportunity to connect with each other on this common pursuit. Even if you do not attend the same college, you can develop a support system with them since you will all be having similar experiences. You can share advice and study strategies as well as a shoulder to lean on when you feel stressed. Knowing that a friend is having a similar experience as you can often give you the motivation to continue working hard.

Although friends can provide a solid support system, especially those who are in college too, not all friends will be a positive influence as you work toward your degree. Those who are not supportive may be very open about their anger, jealousy, or disappointment that you are pursuing a different path than the one that they have chosen; others will be more subtle. Some friends may fear that you will not have enough time for them or will find new friends to replace them. In some cases, you may discover that your values no longer match your friends' values, which may signal a time to lessen your contact with them.

For sure, you will be busier than when you were not in college, and keeping in touch will be more difficult for you. Letting these friends know that you may not be able to give them as much time as you did in the past can help you distance yourself from them. Of course, there is always the option of being up front and honest about their lack of support. Telling these friends that you need positive relationships while you are in college may be the message they need to hear to change their attitudes toward your exciting endeavor. If they still don't get the message, it may be time to eliminate them from daily contact.

Your Roommates

If you've chosen to live in a dorm or apartment during your college career, you'll discover that your roommates can be either very helpful or, unfortunately, very destructive influences on your life. Roommates who share the same goals and values as you and who are equally

GRIT GAINER™

CHOOSE YOUR ROPE TEAM When climbers get "on rope" with other people, they do two powerful things. First, they help each other climb. Second, when you slip, they immediately slow or stop the fall. You get to decide who is part of your ascent.

1. Who do you want "on rope" with you? Who elevates, challenges, supports, and believes in you?

2. Who can you count on? Who will inspire you to climb further and higher than you might reach by yourself?

committed to being successful in college can provide a strong support system for you. They can offer encouragement when you're feeling discouraged or companionship when you're feeling lonely. You can provide the same support to them. It will be important for you to have study habits and a personal strategy of your own, but at times you'll benefit greatly from sharing the college experience with your roommates, with whom you may share meals, social activities, and household chores.

Your Community

There are other places you can look for support as you make your way through college. Your community may also offer support to college students such as you. Check out your local community center to see if they offer workshops on time management or study skills; the local library may sponsor book clubs or study groups. Area churches, temples, and synagogues may provide financial support for students in need. Most communities support their residents' goals to go to college and earn a degree because as more residents have college degrees, the more the community improves. A gesture as simple as offering a discount at a local store for college students is a sign that the area businesses recognize and value a student's hard work in college. Local community leaders may be willing to provide internships or mentoring sessions for students who could use extra advice and guidance throughout college. See what your community has to offer or start your own community support group.

Knowing Your Learning Style Is a Useful Insight

Take a Learning Style Inventory

Knowing your learning style preferences provides a foundation for understanding yourself in other aspects of your life. Information about what you like and dislike, how you relate to others, and how to work productively will help you achieve your goals. The VAK learning styles inventory, which you can take for yourself in the MyStudentSuccessLab (MSSL), will help you identify your particular learning style preferences. Consider the results of the inventory as information about a part of who you are. Your values, dreams, mission statement, goals, and learning style work together to create a more complete picture of who you are and how to get where you want to go.

Although learning preferences are not necessarily directly linked to college majors or careers, you can easily see that your learning style preference will come into play when you choose your major and your career. Kinesthetic learners, for example, may be drawn to majors or careers that allow them to move about or use their bodies to complete tasks. Landscape design, theater, culinary arts, and nursing are just a few college degree programs that would appeal to kinesthetic learners. Review Exhibit 2.4, which lists possible majors and careers for some of the learning style preferences, but note that it is not considered an exhaustive list. Also, some majors and careers may speak to more than one learning style preference—for example, an advertising executive who writes, edits, and directs commercials may rely on almost all the learning style preferences on a daily basis. For sure, she will need to work individually, with peers, and with her boss on different aspects of a project, and she may find that she is needed to complete tasks at different times of the day, even late at night when filming continues long after the typical workday ends.

Different Types of Intelligence

Harvard psychologist Howard Gardner is well known for his theory of multiple intelligences. Gardner has created eight categories of how we can know and learn.

Verbal/linguistic intelligence is evident in people who can use language with ease. People who demonstrate verbal/linguistic intelligence enjoy reading and writing and may be journalists, novelists, playwrights, or comedians. Logical/mathematical intelligence is demonstrated by an ease and enjoyment with numbers and logic problems. People who have a strong leaning toward logical/mathematical intelligence like to solve problems, find patterns, discover relationships between objects, and follow steps. Career choices for logical/mathematical people include science, computer technology, math, and engineering.

Visual/spatial is an intelligence that is characterized by anything visual—paintings, photographs, maps, and architecture. People who have a strong visual/spatial sense are usually good at design, architecture, painting and sculpture, and map making. Body/kinesthetic is an intelligence that focuses on movement. Body/kinesthetic people enjoy using their bodies to express themselves. Obvious career choices for this intelligence include dancing, sports, and dramatic arts. Musical/rhythmic intelligence encompasses the mind's proficiency with the rhythms of music and hearing tones and beats. People who have strong musical/rhythmic intelligence may use musical instruments or the human voice to express themselves. Career choices for this intelligence include all types of musical performers.

How you relate to others and yourself is part of the interpersonal and intrapersonal intelligences. People with strong interpersonal intelligence relate well with others. They read others' feelings well and act with others in mind. Intrapersonal intelligence centers around the ability to understand oneself. People who possess intrapersonal intelligence know how and why they do what they do. Naturalistic, the eighth intelligence, refers to people who enjoy and work well in an outdoor environment. Naturalistic people find peace in nature and enjoy having natural elements around them.

■ Kinesthetic learning involves using your hands or body to master a concept.

© LAYLAND MASUDA/SHUTTERSTOCK

Different Theories Provide Unique Insights

There are numerous ways to see yourself and understand your behavior in certain situations, and many education specialists and psychologists have provided theories on how we take in and process information. They have developed different inventories and personality profiles to enhance your understanding of yourself. As you will discover in another chapter, the learning process is somewhat complex and involves more than just our preferences in how we create knowledge; there are many factors that influence our ability to take in and process information.

Theories about the two hemispheres of our brain, known as the left brain and the right brain, have given us insight into how people think, learn, and see the world. People who have strong left-brain tendencies are more likely to be logical, to see the parts rather than the whole, and to prefer to do activities step by step. They are also more analytical, realistic, and verbal than their right-brained companions. The right-brained individual shows a preference to see the whole picture rather than the details, to work out of sequence, and to bring ideas together.

The Myers-Briggs Type Indicator® (MBTI®), on the other hand, is a personality assessment that provides you with information about how you prefer to think and act. For example, one dimension of the personality test asks you how outgoing or extroverted you are in certain situations or how reserved or introverted you are in social settings. These questions indicate whether you are Extroverted (E) or Introverted (I). Both left-brain/right-brain inventories, or samples of the complete inventories, as well as the MBTI® can be found in books or online sources.

There are many ways of viewing yourself and creating a plan of action for your work in college, but no single inventory, assessment, or work plan will reflect the exceptional person you are or your unique circumstances. In other words, no matter what inventory you take or what you learn about how you prefer to learn, the results are not the final verdict on your abilities and potential.

The goal, then, of this learning plan is to provide you with an adaptable, flexible model for putting your learning style preference into action. It also gives you a roadmap for accomplishing the many goals that you will set for yourself. Additionally, it can serve as a place to start when faced with situations that require you to work outside your learning preference comfort zone. For example, what will you do, as a morning learner, when faced with completing an important project late at night? Or how will you, as an individual learner, fare when required to collaborate with classmates on an assignment?

One way to move outside your learning preference comfort zones is to read this about the characters whose stories begin each chapter and reflect on how you would act in the same situation and consider how you will meet similar challenges. For example, you have already met Juanita and learned about her relationship with her family. In the previous chapter, you read about all four characters and their experience with orientation.

Although the characters are fictional, representative of the many different college students, their stories ring true because they are based on real-life situations that you may face as well. Reflecting on who you are and how you will get where you want to go will help you create your own story of success.

It's in the syllabus

Your professors' syllabi contain clues about how the content will address learning style preferences. For example, a syllabus for biology may include a description of a kinesthetic class project that will involve creating a 3-D model of DNA replication.

- What learning styles will be addressed through the assignments in your classes this semester?
- Which assignments do you think will be the most challenging for you to complete?
- Which are the most intriguing? Why?

Learning Styles Relate to Career Choices

Discovering your learning style preference and your personality type will definitely help you set realistic short-term and long-term goals. For example, confirming that you have a learning preference and you work well with deadlines and staying organized may help you realize that your long-term goal of being a writer will work well with who you are and how you learn and work. However, identifying your style and type should not limit your choices or keep you from working on areas of your learning style and personality that may be weaker or get less attention. If you are a strong visual learner, but you are taking a class that relies on listening effectively and critically, you should use that opportunity to become a better listener and improve your aural learning style preference by following listening tips like the ones found in another chapter. Likewise, if you work better alone and have a strong kinesthetic learning style preference, choosing a career as a computer technician may play to your strengths, but you may also find yourself working with others collaboratively and communicating frequently in writing and verbally. See Exhibit 2.4 for examples of careers and majors as they connect to learning style preferences.

Whatever your learning style strength and personality preferences are, consider how other styles and types will factor in to your short-term and long-term educational goals. Then, look for opportunities to strengthen those less-developed sides of your learning and personality so that you are more comfortable in a variety of situations and so that you are a well-rounded person.

EXHIBIT 2.4   Learning Style Preferences, Majors, and Careers

Learning Style Preference	College Majors	Careers
VISUAL	Art, graphic design, architecture, video production	Art teacher, artist, graphic designer, architect, interior designer, video producer
AURAL	Music, communications, counseling	Musician, music educator, marketing director, public relations director, counselor
KINESTHETIC	Sciences, sociology, computer technology, culinary arts, theater	Nurse, doctor, theropist, networking specialist, computer technician, thespian, director

the unwritten rules
of Motivation, Goals, and Mission Statements

- **Internal motivation is the key to success.** If most of your reasons for attending college are based on what others have told you, you will need to dig deeper to discover the reasons why *you* want to succeed. This is where your GRIT and goals work together. Find your internal motivation for college success, even if it takes a while to discover it.

- **Goals are dreams with a deadline.** Setting goals to achieve your dream is the only way to make it happen. A student who says she wants to be a doctor will also need to describe when and how that will happen to ensure she has the best trail map to get to her destination.

- **Those who have mission statements will get where they want to go.** Your college has one, and most every business you patronize has one as well. Mission statements keep companies and institutions on track to meeting their goals. Having a personal mission statement will help you determine what paths to take and decisions to make in the future.

GRIT GAINER™

GO BEYOND THE LABEL   Knowing your natural learning style, intelligences, and personality tendencies will help you in countless ways. The danger is that all of these come with potentially limiting labels. Don't camp in your category. Climb beyond:

1. Intentionally put yourself in situations that force you to be uncomfortable and require you to tap and grow some of your less developed capacities.

2. Rather than avoiding, embrace the tough stuff. When adversity strikes—whether it's conflict, frustration, confusion, fatigue, delays, or something else—enter the storm. Try to use its force to propel you onward.

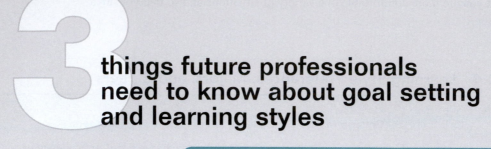

3 things future professionals need to know about goal setting and learning styles

setting goals
will be part of your
performance review

Goal setting is not just a crucial part of getting to graduation; it will also be a required part of any job you have once you graduate. Many employers ask that you set goals for the year and then revisit them at certain periods during your employment. They will want you to set gritty goals that stretch and challenge you. This means that you will be held accountable for achieving them—or not. No longer is setting goals and tracking your progress a private matter. Your future employment—raises and just being able to continue in the position—will depend on them.

juggling multiple priorities
with professionalism
and grace are expected

You may think that college is hectic—just wait until your job requires that you manage your professional priorities with ease and keep your personal priorities, well, personal. Be an agile, gritty climber. Being able to make changes in your schedule quickly and to respond effectively to last-minute needs or crises will be critical to your future. And you will be expected to do this all with patience and confidence that you can meet the demands of the job.

learning
is a constant
on the job

Learning on the job will include both discovering how to do your job and staying updated on the trends in your field. How that education is delivered to you will depend on your employer or the provider of continuing education. That means you will have little choice as to how you receive the training, but you can still play on your learning style preferences to master the content. Continue to use the strategies you develop in your classes to make learning on the job a little easier and maybe even enjoyable.

THE GRIT ADVANTAGE

You want to move forward and up in life, and college will help you get there. You can decide now: how far and high do you want to climb? Don't quit. Don't camp. Do what climbers do:

- **Define your mountain.** Don't let your past define your future. How do you want your life? What do you want it to be all about?

- **Establish your trail map.** Lay out your strategy, set specific, measurable mileposts along the way, and stretch yourself to accomplish more, more quickly than you imagined.

- **Build your rope team.** Decide whom you trust, respect, and want to join up with to help you achieve or surpass your goals.

- **Assess yourself.** Find out your learning preference by completing the personal inventory. Then go beyond the labels. Take on the uncomfortable. Stretch your capacities so you can climb strong.

HOW GRITTY ARE YOU?

It's time to climb! After reading this chapter, how committed are you to:

1. Define your mountain by beginning to shape your personal mission statement?

   Zero Commitment **0** —————————————————————————— **10** Fully Committed

2. Reassess and reroute when needed to stay true to your goals?

   Zero Commitment **0** —————————————————————————— **10** Fully Committed

3. Spend more time and energy climbing, rather than camping or quitting?

   Zero Commitment **0** —————————————————————————— **10** Fully Committed

4. Show moral fortitude, but live your values in the moments of truth?

   Zero Commitment **0** —————————————————————————— **10** Fully Committed

5. Take advantage of the support system and resources around you?

   Zero Commitment **0** —————————————————————————— **10** Fully Committed

6. Pick a strong "rope team," people you can join up with to do great things, and who support your goals?

   Zero Commitment **0** —————————————————————————— **10** Fully Committed

7. Understand, use, and expand your intelligences, capabilities, learning preferences, and more?

   Zero Commitment **0** —————————————————————————— **10** Fully Committed

3 Relationships and Diversity

Chapter goals to help you
get in,
get through,
get out,
and get paid:

In order to get in, get through, get out, and get paid, you will need to get along well with others, including students, faculty, and staff who have different backgrounds, experiences, and perspectives than you. You'll need to learn how to thrive in a diverse environment to be successful in college, your career, and your life.

To meet those goals, this chapter will help you:

- Describe the different types of people on your campus and understand the benefits of cultivating relationships in college
- Recognize the importance of diversity and cultural competence
- Explain how stereotyping, prejudice, and discrimination are related
- Describe the process of resolving conflict in relationships
- Appreciate the diversity in how people show and apply their **GRIT**

MyStudentSuccessLab™

Log in to MyStudentSuccessLab.com to deepen your **GRIT** mindset and build the skills you'll need to get through the college experience.

Michael's Story

© MONKEY BUSINESS IMAGES/SHUTTERSTOCK

"Evan, are you going to be around later today? I may need some help," Michael asks.

One reason Michael felt an instant connection with Evan that first day they met was that Evan is a lot like him.

"Sure, man," Evan says. "Maybe you can help me, too. You think you can lend me a hand with some furniture?"

"Are you sure you can use help from an old man like me?" Michael asks. Michael has never thought much about being a nontraditional student until recently, when some students he is working with on a group project said something about his being "too old" to work with.

"You may be old, man, but I'm pretty sure you can bench press more than me," Evan says as he laughs.

"Maybe when I was your age, but not anymore," Michael says. "Seriously, though, I have this group project, and, well, my group keeps meeting without me."

"Ah, c'mon," Evan says. "I would make you the leader of my group."

"I think that is part of the problem, too," Michael says. "I don't know, maybe I come on too strong, offend people."

"So what do you need from me? Need some boxing tips?" Evan asks.

"Do you think I should talk to the professor?" asks Michael.

"Man, what do you have to lose by asking?" Evan replies.

Now, what do you think?

- What would you do if you were left out of a group assignment?

  a. Ignore the snub and complete the project on my own

  b. Get the professor to intervene on my behalf

  c. Reach out to my group and ask what I can do to contribute

- If you wanted to be sure that you don't experience this again, what would you do?

  a. Cultivate relationships on the first day of class

  b. Do nothing—not everyone will be excited to work with me all the time

  c. Alert the professor to past problems with group work and ask for an alternative assignment

Your Terms for success

when you see . . .	It means . . .
Administrator	A person who manages staff at the college
Advisor	A person who works with students to provide guidance and planning for a degree
Ageism	Discrimination against a person in a certain age group
Counselor	A person who advises students on personal, academic, or career matters
Diversity	A state of difference; variety
Due process	Formal procedures designed to protect a person's rights
Faculty	A person or persons who teach
Homophobia	Irrational fear of homosexuals
Instructor	A person who teaches
Mentor	A person who provides advice or guidance
Peer mentor/peer leader	A person of equal status who provides advice or guidance
Racism	Hatred of a race; discrimination against a person of a certain race
Sexism	Hatred of a gender; discrimination against a certain gender
Sexual harassment	Unwanted or offensive sexual advances, usually by a person in a superior position
Tutor	A person who provides academic support

Relationships Are Part of the College Experience

Research has shown that getting to know at least one person on your campus, no matter who it is, will increase the likelihood that you will stay in college and complete your degree. Whether it is the janitor or a career counselor, getting to know someone beyond just a name, title, and face is to your advantage while you are in college.

You have probably noticed already that there are many people who work at a college—and most of them are there to support and guide you through your college experience. Equally important to understanding where buildings and services are located is knowing who does what on your campus. It saves you time when you know, for example, that to get copies of your transcript will involve speaking with someone in the registrar's office or that checking on loan applications will include contact with a financial aid officer. All of these people are charged with the task of helping you succeed each semester you are in college, and it will make your transition from either high school or the world of work much easier if you are familiar with the common jobs on campus.

Get to Know Your Professors

There may be no one more important to your college and possible future career success than a professor. She does not just provide you with access to the content and challenge you to think critically about the subject matter; she also can be a mentor and a resource as you complete your degree and start your career. One way to start out on the right path to a good relationship is to greet your professor with a smile and a "hello" when you see her in and out of class. College professors see their relationships with their students outside of class as part of their advising and mentoring duties. For many instructors, their students are not only people in their classes, but also potential graduates from their programs and lifelong acquaintances. Being friendly in and outside of class is a great way to start on the path to a strong, valuable relationship during your college career (and maybe even after!).

Growth

Because a big part of GRIT is looking at problems with fresh eyes, from fresh angles, and with fresh ideas, getting to know a variety of people helps you consider more perspectives in anything you take on.

Another way to start developing meaningful relationships with your professors is to appreciate the diversity of disciplines, personality types, and teaching styles among them. You will not love every class (although we professors wish you could), every teaching style, and every personality that you will encounter in college. When you take pleasure in the class and the instructor, enjoy every minute of it; when you don't, use the experience to keep focused on what you want: a college degree. Also realize, however, that what you don't like at first may just be a first impression that will not necessarily be your feelings at the end of the course. Sometimes students' initial experiences in a class are uncomfortable, but turn out to be the ones that they reflect on as the most meaningful because they learned something about the course topic as well as themselves.

Because each instructor's expectations in terms of class preparation and policies regarding attendance, late work, and make-up exams will differ, be mindful that rules that apply in one class may be different in another. Relationships built on acknowledgement of others' boundaries (in this case, professors' expectations and policies) as well as respect and integrity are stronger and more authentic. To cultivate a solid relationship with your professor, make the most of her office hours. Office hours are best used for questions about material that was previously covered, assignments and policies that were previously explained, and anything else that does not pertain to the day's lecture or in-class activity. Sometimes students only see office hours as a time to discuss a problem, but office hours should be used for positive visits as well—stopping by to say hello or to follow up on an idea that sparked your interest in class are great ways to strengthen your relationship.

It would be a perfect world if there were no conflicts in your relationship with your professor. However, there may be a time in your college career when you don't feel as though you have a strong, respectful relationship. If you experience conflict with a professor, be sure to discuss the issue as soon as possible—and in private. Use "I" statements, rather than "you" statements, to explain your perspective. For example, saying "I am confused about what our exam will cover" is better than saying "You were confusing when you talked about the exam." Using "I" statements also underscores your control over your actions and reactions during the conflict. Look, too, for common ground that can help you manage the conflict maturely and respectfully.

A good relationship for its own sake is perfectly acceptable, but also remember that professors can provide a link to other opportunities beyond the classroom. You will most likely turn to a professor when you need a recommendation letter for student activities, scholarships, internships, and jobs. Getting to know at least one professor well will give you an advantage when you want to move forward in your college career. Professors in your major are usually tied closely to the business and industry in which they teach. Thus, a good relationship with a professor may lead to a job opportunity in the field.

Although a good relationship with your professor is a key to your enjoying your education experience, remember that your professor is not an equal in the relationship. She still must challenge you to learn and stretch your concept of yourself and others, as well as evaluate you during and at the end of the term. Creating boundaries in relationships is discussed later in the chapter.

In addition to professors, some of the most important relationships that you will forge during college will be with people whose sole job is to help you succeed. Counselors and advisors will be key people in your academic career, so be sure to take the time to get to know these individuals. College administrators also play an important role.

It's in the
syllabus

- What are your professors' office hours?
- Where are their offices located?
- How do they prefer to be contacted when you have a question?
- What are the expectations regarding meeting with your professors? Should you only meet with them when you have a problem?
- What other reasons would you have to meet with them?

Advisors

Your advisor may be the first person you encounter at college. An advisor explains to you what courses you should take, how many hours you should take per semester, and how to plan remaining semesters. You may be lucky enough to have the same advisor throughout your college career. In that case, regular contact with your advisor will help keep the lines of communication open. If you have a different advisor each semester, you may wish to find one person on whom you can rely to act as regular advisor. That person may be a former professor or a counselor who has advised you in the past. The goal is to find someone on campus who has an interest in your education beyond one semester, and who is knowledgeable about your degree requirements to help you stay on track toward graduation.

G R I T
Instinct

Expect that some professors, counselors, or advisors will be more difficult to get to know. Some may seem cold and unwelcoming. Before you give up on connecting with a valuable resource, ask yourself, "How can I approach this differently to at least increase the chances that it goes well?"

Counselors

You should take the opportunity to get to know at least one counselor on your campus. Whether it is a career counselor or a disability counselor, make it a point to schedule an appointment with one while you are in college. Getting to know counselors is a great way to obtain more information about the school and its services. For example, a career counselor may inform you of a career fair or recruiting day. He can also help you prepare a resume and practice interviewing. Counselors who deal with students who have personal issues are another valuable resource for you. Even if you do not need personal counseling, you may benefit from a relationship with one. This type of counselor can give you tips for managing stress and dealing with difficult people, just to name a few experiences you may have in college.

Administrators

During your college experience, you may have an opportunity to meet or work with university administrators—individuals with titles such as "Dean," "Provost," and even "President." Many administrators were or still are professors themselves, so they understand the college experience very well. Although they may not spend time in the classroom any longer, their sole focus is on student success, and they provide the leadership to your institution to make sure that everyone stays focused on that goal. If you have a chance to spend time with an administrator, share your ideas about student success and take time to learn about the work they're doing to support it.

Tutors, Mentors, and Student Leaders

In addition to the key people you will encounter in college, there are a variety of other people who work or volunteer their time to help you achieve your academic, career, and personal goals. Those people can include tutors in a learning assistance lab. Working one on one with them provides you with a unique relationship in that a tutor can really get to know what your learning needs are and how to help you fulfill them. A tutor can be a great resource for understanding the material for a class because he is often a student himself or has recently taken the class.

Resilience

One of the key elements of GRIT is resilience, and one of the key drivers of your resilience is diversity. Intentionally connecting with a diversity of resources and people enhances your chances of being able to work your way through any adversity.

Student or peer mentors are other people you will find on your college campus who can be instrumental in keeping you on track to success. Peer mentors are usually current students who have been successful in their classes and who are willing to provide support to new students who may need extra encouragement to navigate the choppy waters of the first few semesters. Peer mentors may give you advice for studying, for choosing a degree, or for balancing family, work, and college. And just think—if you are also successful, you may be a great peer mentor for a student who was just like you when you started!

One final group of people with whom you may come in contact is student leaders. You may find them in special clubs, associations, or student government. Unlike peer mentors, whose primary role is to work one on one with a student, student leaders work with both students and the college or organization to provide leadership in certain areas. For example, a student government representative may ask college officials to provide more family-friendly activities so that students can attend with their children. If administrators agree, then the student government association may work with students to find out what types of activities are best and may organize an event to get more students involved.

Classmates

Last, but certainly not least, getting to know your classmates can make the difference between struggling all alone and meeting new challenges with a like-minded support group. Who else can relate to the challenge of studying for a chemistry final exam than the students in the class with you? Think about it: Your classmates will be the majority of the people who populate a college campus. You may get to know well only three or four professors throughout your college career, but you have the potential of meeting and working with hundreds of students.

In addition to sharing experiences with your fellow students, you can also rely on them as study partners or emergency note takers if you can't be in class. Another benefit to making friends with classmates is that you can learn about other classes, instructors, and degree programs from them. Their firsthand knowledge could help you choose the best classes and the most promising programs.

Getting to know your classmates can be relatively simple, especially because you will be sitting close to them during each class. Here are a few tips for creating lasting relationships with fellow students:

- Introduce yourself to those sitting around you. It may be easier to arrive early and start conversations with other students.

- Exchange phone numbers or email addresses with classmates who seem reliable and trustworthy. You may need to call someone if you miss class.

- Offer to study with someone. Not only will you help a classmate, you will also help yourself learn the material.

- Keep in contact with friends even after the semester is over. Although you may not share classes anymore, you still may be able to study and offer support to one another.

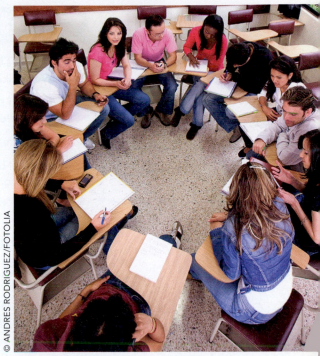

© ANDRES RODRIGUEZ/FOTOLIA

■ Getting along with classmates will be essential to your success both in and out of the classroom.

Family and Friends

Entering college will be a new experience not only for you, but also for your family and friends, especially if they have not gone to college. Communication, then, will be the key to weathering any changes in your relationships. They need to know how you feel about going to college, and they need to be aware that you will be going through changes while you are there. Surely you will be experiencing changes in your outlook on life, your belief in yourself, and your attitude toward the future.

When these changes occur, people around you may react differently. Some will be supportive and excited that you have created personal goals and are achieving them. A few, however, may react negatively. These people may be jealous of your success or your new lease on life because they did not have the same opportunities or because they squandered the opportunities that they did have. Others who react negatively may be insecure about themselves and feel "dumb" around a person in college; these same people often fear that once the college student graduates, he or she will leave them for a "better" spouse or friend. Also, there are parents who do not want to acknowledge that their children are grown adults who are and should be making decisions on their own. Parents are also often worried that their children will be exposed to value systems and beliefs that are very different from what they taught them.

Whatever the reasons that the people around you react to the changes you experience, be comforted by the fact that you will survive, and better yet, you will have more of an understanding of the diversity of opinions that you will encounter. Learning how to deal with different people in college will allow you to apply what you learn to your personal relationships.

GRIT GAINER™

GRITTY STUDENTS GO FOR IT! Use your GRIT to tap the power of diversity by asking these three questions:

1. Who can I have a conversation with today that might help me see things from a different perspective?

2. If I could learn anything from that person, what would I like it to be?

3. How can I best approach him or her to help increase the chances it's a positive conversation?

Value Diversity and Develop Your Cultural Competence

An exciting part of college is that you will meet and work with people from all ages and backgrounds. Universities attract individuals from a wide variety of backgrounds and who have a broad spectrum of opinions and beliefs. Your college experience offers a great opportunity for you to learn how to live, learn, and work with other people who may be very different from you in some ways, but who also share similarities with you as well. The benefits of experiencing diversity in college are many: "Students learn better in . . . [a diverse] environment and are better prepared to become active participants in our pluralistic, democratic society once they leave school. In fact, patterns of racial segregation and separation historically rooted in our national life can be broken by diversity experiences in higher education" (Gurin, 1999).

A simple definition of diversity is "difference" or "variety." Another term heard when diversity is discussed in a college setting is *multiculturalism.* Although the two words have different implications, they often have the same motivation—to expose the community to a variety of ideas, cultures, viewpoints, beliefs, and backgrounds.

When people talk about diversity, they usually mean race, gender, ethnicity, age, and religion. Colleges that want to promote diversity on their campuses often look for opportunities to hire and enroll people who have different backgrounds than the majority of the campus population. They do this with the belief that diversity enriches the educational experience for all, exposing faculty, staff, and students to new ideas and challenging our preconceived notions of the world.

Recognize and Appreciate Gender and Sexual Orientation Diversity

The latest educational statistics show that almost two-thirds of the U.S. college student population is female. In the past few decades, women have enrolled in college in record numbers. It may seem strange to think that several decades ago, there were far fewer women in college, especially in law and medical schools. No doubt, you will encounter gender diversity at your college, and what this means for you is that you will have plenty of opportunities to work with both men and women and explore any preconceptions you may have about the differences between the sexes. You may have to pay more attention to society's assumptions about gender and be more attuned to how language, art, and sciences, among other disciplines, perpetuate gender stereotypes.

Sexual orientation is another type of diversity that you will more than likely encounter in college, if you have not already. Homosexuality and bisexuality are just two categories of sexual orientation diversity. Organizations such as the Human Rights Campaign (www.hrc .org) strive to educate others about discrimination that can—and does—occur because of the stereotypes and prejudice that exist regarding sexual orientation. Why should you know more about sexual orientation as a part of diversity? Sexuality is part of the human experience, and one purpose of higher education is to help you better understand and appreciate your and others' human experience. Recognizing sexual orientation as a category of diversity gives you a more complete picture of humankind.

G R I T
Tenacity

> Ask yourself, "Over the past several months, whom have I tried and failed to really connect with?" Then try two more times, in different ways, to see if you can forge the beginning of a relationship you might enjoy.

Understand and Avoid Sexual Harassment

Colleges and universities as well as the workforce have been working hard to educate students and employees about the definitions and prevention of sexual harassment for decades. Sexual harassment, by legal definition, refers to a superior, or a person in power, harassing a subordinate, or a person with less power than the harasser. College and employee policies often broaden the definition, however, to include any unwanted sexual advances that create an uncomfortable situation or hostile environment. This broader definition means that, in college, a student can sexually harass another student or a student can sexually harass a professor—or any other scenario that involves students, prospective students, and employees and guests of the college. To further round out the definition, women can sexually harass men and people can experience sexual harassment from someone of the same sex.

Despite educational programs for new students and required seminars for employees, colleges—like any place in which people live and work—are not immune to instances of sexual harassment. According to Katz (2005), the American Psychological Association surveyed female graduate students about their experiences in college. The survey results found that 12.7 percent of female students experienced sexual harassment and 21 percent avoided taking certain classes for fear of being sexually harassed. Surveys about sexual harassment in the workplace paint a dimmer picture, with 31 percent of female employees and 7 percent of male employees claiming to be sexually harassed at work.

G R I T
Growth

> Avoiding and helping to prevent sexual harassment requires asking yourself, "What do I need to know to make sure I don't do or say anything inappropriate?" You have to have a gritty growth mindset to effectively navigate diverse relationships.

Educating yourself about the seriousness of sexual harassment, your college's policy on sexual harassment, and the common behaviors that are often considered sexual harassment is a step in the right direction to minimizing incidents. For sure, sexual harassment is no laughing matter, and a review of your college's statement on the matter will reveal what lengths the college will go to discipline those who sexually harass others. Some college policies list the following behaviors as sexual harassment:

- Offensive jokes or comments of a sexual nature
- Requests or demands for sexual favors in return for favorable treatment or rewards (e.g., a good grade)
- Unwanted physical contact or assault

- Showing or distributing sexually explicit materials to others
- Posting sexually explicit images or websites in college-owned online course management systems or emailing those images or websites from college-owned computers

Although it may not be considered sexual harassment if it is not distributed to others, accessing sexually explicit websites with college-owned computer hardware and software may be prohibited conduct that will result in disciplinary action on the part of the college, as well as possible criminal charges.

As with all forms of diversity and possible problems that can arise, be sensitive to others, treat everyone you meet on campus with respect, and be honest with others if you feel uncomfortable in a situation or with certain conversational topics.

Racial, Ethnic, and Cultural Diversity Enables Cultural Competence

The demographic profile of our planet is changing in dramatic ways that affect you wherever you live. The population growth among countries like China and India, the increase in the U.S. Hispanic population, and the growth of the world's Muslim population are just a few examples of demographic trends that will affect not only your college experience, but also your career and personal lives well beyond college. Learning to communicate and work well with individuals who have a different demographic profile than your own is a critical skill for lifelong learning. Exhibit 3.1 provides you with activities that you can do to appreciate diversity.

GRIT
Resilience

Everyone can benefit by diversifying one's relationships and perspectives. Sometimes you have to create a little adversity for yourself by asking, "Who—what person or group—makes me the most uncomfortable? How can I overcome my discomfort to connect and expand my perspective?"

Whereas diversity is a characteristic of the student or geographic population in which you live, *cultural competence* (or cultural competency) is the learned ability to interact effectively with people of a different race, ethnicity, or culture than your own. You could be attending a very diverse campus, but you might not have a well-developed cultural competence. In the same way, you may have cultural competence but attend a campus that is not particularly diverse. Because of the importance of cultural competence for your short- and long-term success, your university will provide courses, activities, and support resources to help you become culturally competent. For example, your campus might host a multicultural event or include a cultural pluralism course in its general education requirements. The university environment also provides the ideal place for you to

---

EXHIBIT 3.1 Tips for Appreciating Racial, Ethnic, and Cultural Diversity

Work to eliminate all racial, ethnic, and cultural stereotypes and slurs, from your thoughts and vocabulary. Stop yourself before you speak and ask, "Is this a stereotype or could it be offensive to some?"

Racial, ethnic, and cultural jokes, images, and cartoons are insensitive at best, harassment at worst. Avoid making fun of others' heritages. Be sensitive to others' backgrounds.

Learn more about your heritage and culture.

Strive to learn more about cultures that are new and different to you.

Participate in college and community cultural celebrations.

Attend seminars, guest lectures, and artistic performances about different cultures and countries.

Do not tolerate others who exhibit racial and cultural insensitivity. If you don't feel comfortable saying something to them, then avoid them and similar situations in the future.

meet people of diverse cultures and backgrounds. Be proactive and seek out these opportunities whenever possible. It may seem intimidating at first, especially if you recognize that you're lacking in certain aspects of cultural competence. But just as the citizens of a foreign country appreciate it when a visitor attempts to speak in their language—even if it's done somewhat poorly—the people of different cultures with whom you engage will welcome and appreciate your efforts to learn more about them and their perspectives.

G R I T
Instinct

People from different backgrounds have learned to handle hardships, stressors, and challenges in different ways. Tap their wisdom by asking for their advice on how to handle yours as they arise.

Generational Diversity

The idea that our parents' generation is vastly different from our own, which will be greatly different from our children's generation, is considered a fact of life. One unifying viewpoint among the generations is that different generations view the world differently.

You will, no doubt, encounter generational diversity at your college and in the world of work—more so than in generations past. A generational cohort is a group of the population that was born within a certain period of time, that marked as important some of the same world events, and that hold certain common values (Zemke et al., 2000). Generational cohorts hold certain values that influence how they work with others and how they achieve personal success.

During your college experience, you will have classmates, professors, employers, employees, or friends from a different generation than your own, and this creates a wonderful opportunity to learn how to work with someone who has a different perspective on life than you do. Your differences with this person may be a source of misunderstanding, miscommunication, and conflict at times, but as you work through these issues you will develop valuable skills and perspectives that will serve you well throughout your lifetime. There are many movies that depict both the challenges and wonderful rewards that occur from generational diversity, including *Finding Forrester* with Sean Connery and *Flipped* with Callan McAuliffe. The key with generational diversity—as with all types of diversity—is to learn more about yourself and others and appreciate the differences. Exhibit 3.2 provides a list of core values for each generation type.

Socioeconomic Diversity Shouldn't Be Overlooked

The forms of diversity we've discussed so far—gender, ethnic, racial, cultural, and generational—tend to be observable characteristics that we recognize about someone when we meet that person. However, there are other forms of diversity that are less visible, but no

EXHIBIT 3.2   Generations, Birth Years, and Core Values

Generation	Birth Years	Core Values
Veterans	1922–1943	Dedication, sacrifice, patience, respect for authority
Baby Boomers	1943–1960	Health and wellness, optimism, personal growth
Generation Xers	1960–1980	Diversity, fun, self-reliance, global thinking
Nexters or Millenials	1980–present	Civic duty, morality, street smarts

less important, such as socioeconomic diversity. Students, faculty, staff, and administrators come from a wide variety of social and economic backgrounds, and this variety provides yet another enrichment opportunity for your college experience.

Because of differences in his socioeconomic background, the student sitting next to you may have a very different set of beliefs, attitudes, abilities, experiences, and motivations than you do. These differences may have little to do with his physical characteristics and far more to do with his childhood experiences in a relatively poor or wealthy family. As you meet people, take time to listen to their life stories. You'll come to appreciate the challenges and obstacles they've overcome, the goals they are trying to achieve, and the beliefs they hold true because of their experiences. To help you explore this dimension of diversity even more, we encourage you to take a look at the book *Bridges Out of Poverty*.

■ Your institution may provide you exposure to a variety of different people.

© MONKEY BUSINESS IMAGES/SHUTTERSTOCK

Look for Other Kinds of Diversity

Dealing successfully with diversity includes more than working well with people from different nations, different religious or political backgrounds, and different disabilities; you will also need to consider the diversity of attitudes and work ethics. For example, not everyone you meet in college or in your career will value the same things you do. What will you do if you work with others whose values conflict with your own? What will you do if the differences between your and others' work ethics cause conflict?

You will get the opportunity to work with others in class when you are assigned a group project or presentation. Even if you all are the same gender, race, religion, and age, you will still find that each of you has different expectations and opinions of the assignment. Being able to work with others, regardless of their learning and work styles, is a skill. The more you are exposed to diversity, the more you will be able to handle and appreciate the differences between you and everyone you meet.

Teaching Styles Will Also Be Diverse

You will encounter many different teaching styles. It has been said that most professors teach the way they learn best, but there are college instructors who use a variety of teaching methods to encourage student learning. You will be more successful if you can identify each teaching style and what you need to do to adapt to it. Gone are the days of saying, "I just can't learn in her class. She doesn't teach the way I need her to." Like the people who must work together in groups and be sensitive to one another's personalities, you, too, will need to recognize what your learning style is and how it will fit into your professor's teaching style. In some cases, your instructor will adapt his course to appeal to different learning styles, but not everyone you encounter in college will vary his teaching style to meet your needs. Your best bet is to be ready to learn no matter what the teaching style. This is, by the way, great preparation for the world of work, in which you will likely encounter supervisors and bosses with different management styles. Rarely will managers adjust to you; they will expect you to adjust to them and their organizational culture.

To help you recognize the different methods of teaching, Exhibit 3.3 contains a description of each and tips for making the most of the different types of classroom instruction.

EXHIBIT 3.3 **Teaching Styles**

Teaching Style	Description	Tips for Success
Lecture	Professor talks for the majority of the class; a brief outline may be inducted; questions are limited or discouraged; usually very structured	Practice good listening skills; record lectures with permission; take good notes during class and review them frequently
Discussion	Professor poses a question and requires students in the class to answer and build on an idea or theme	Practice good listening skills; record theme or question for the discussion; note repeated ideas; record essence of each person's contribution; participate in discussion
Project	Professor bases class learning on projects; provides instruction for assignment; assigns roles; monitors progress	Make connection between project assignments and course objectives: ask for feedback during project to make sure you are progressing; refer to course materials for extra help
Problem solving	Professor poses or writes a problem on the board, then walks through solving the problem	Break process down into steps; identify any step that is unclear; ask for extra practice and feedback if needed

Stereotyping, Prejudice, and Discrimination Are Problems We Face

To understand what a problem hate is in our world, all you have to do is open a newspaper or click on the latest news story online. Hatred for others because of their skin color, their religious beliefs, or their sexual orientation has fueled violence and discrimination all over the world. Whether it is as large as millions of people being slaughtered in a third-world country or as small as a person being beaten up for his beliefs, the remedy to begin to combat hatred is the same: learning to understand others and appreciate diversity. To do that, we must confront the very ideas and processes that lead people to greater acts of hatred.

Stereotypes

A discussion of diversity is not complete without mentioning some common problems. Stereotyping is an oversimplified opinion of someone or something. We often use stereotypes to make quick decisions every day. When choosing a checkout line, we may make a quick decision as to which is the fastest based on the people in line and what they have in their carts. When playing outfield on a softball team, we may stereotype the smaller players as weaker hitters, which will cause us to move closer to the infield. Parents also encourage children, who have difficulty making complex decisions, to stereotype strangers in order to protect them. Although these stereotypes are not necessarily harmful, they can create problems for us. We may get in a line we think will be shorter, but we end up standing in line for a longer time; we may move so close to the infield that the smaller player hits the ball over our heads; we may confuse children about the characteristics of a stranger, making it difficult for them to trust adults.

GRIT GAINER™

FORGE NEW BONDS   Because people are often scared of or hesitant with people who are different from themselves, you have to A) be the one who initiates the effort to connect with people different than you, and B) often try multiple times, in various ways, to make it work.

Stereotypes can serve a purpose in the short run, but as these examples illustrate, stereotypes do not take all the facts into consideration. For the most part, stereotypes keep us from having to think about the complexity of issues, and often, then, we are unable to appreciate the beauty of diversity. In essence, stereotypes are shorthand for evaluating situations and making decisions, but if used inappropriately, they can become prejudice and discrimination.

Prejudice

Prejudice is literally "prejudging" a person or situation without knowing the facts. Prejudice is often based on stereotyping, which is one of the dangers of stereotyping in the first place. Let's take a seemingly harmless example of stereotyping that can result in prejudice: If you assume that all smaller softball players are weak hitters, then you may take that stereotype a bit further by disliking playing with smaller players because they don't make the game very challenging.

Like stereotyping, prejudice is a judgment based on little or no information or misinformation about a person or thing. In other words, it is based on ignorance or lack of correct information. That is why education is so important—you can avoid prejudging people and things by learning about them and making decisions about them based on knowledge rather than ignorance. Although we cannot always avoid stereotyping, we can eliminate prejudice and subsequently eradicate discrimination by making the decision to learn about others.

There are a variety of ways we can categorize and classify ourselves and others. Used as one way of understanding ourselves better, these types of diversity are useful tools. If they are used to stereotype and then make judgments about people based on these stereotypes, then the categories become means to discrimination.

GRIT
Instinct

Remember, there is good GRIT and bad GRIT. Good GRIT means relentlessly pursuing your goals in ways that ultimately benefit instead of hurt or damage others. Expand your awareness about what effect your efforts may have on others.

SEXISM. The increased number of women in college has changed the culture to be more sensitive and inclusive to women, but stereotypes and prejudice about females still exist. However, sexism is not limited to prejudice against women. Men, too, can suffer from sexist attitudes that are based on stereotypes.

HOMOPHOBIA. Sexual orientation prejudice often takes the form of homophobia, or fear of homosexuals. Homophobia is sometimes born out of ignorance of sexual orientation diversity, and sometimes it comes from a person's own background and values.

RACISM. Racist attitudes can be obvious or subtle. People can hold racist views, like all other prejudices, and not realize that they are being intolerant of others. Asking people of other races what kinds of racism they experience is one way to understand what they perceive as prejudice. Monitoring your own words, actions, and attitudes is another way to be more sensitive to other races and cultures. You may think you don't mean any harm by what you say or do, but the recipients of racism don't always agree.

AGEISM. As you read earlier, different generations have different values and viewpoints. An environment in which people from different generations work closely together can be exciting or tense, depending on how much people are willing to recognize, understand, and appreciate their generational differences. Problems arise, though, when people have prejudicial attitudes about a certain age group. We usually think of ageist attitudes as ones that stereotype people older than us, but people can hold prejudicial views against those younger as well.

Discrimination

Discrimination occurs when an action is taken on the basis of the prejudice. If, for instance, you decide that you do not want to play softball with teams with smaller players because you believe they are not as fun as teams with bigger players, then you have discriminated against smaller players and their teams. Because of recent laws and lawsuits, colleges and other

GRIT GAINER™

FORM A DIVERSE GRIT GANG   Check yourself and optimize your GRIT with these three questions:

1. In what ways might my goals or efforts be unintentionally insensitive or hurtful to others?

2. Who don't I reach out to or include but, if I did, might enhance my chances of success in achieving my goals?

3. Who haven't I reached out to, perhaps because it's uncomfortable, who might benefit from my perspective and ideas?

places of business are sensitive to discrimination issues and spend a large amount of time and resources educating employees about it. Sexism, racism, and ageism are types of discrimination that are the most common in the workplace. It will be an important part of your education to understand how and why people discriminate so that you can avoid similar problems that stem from discrimination.

Even though most workplaces strive hard to eliminate sexual, racial, and age discrimination, there are still other types that can appear in everyday situations. For example, a coworker may declare that she won't hire anyone from a certain college because she believes that all its graduates are more interested in partying than working. Your boss may state his disdain for people from a certain part of the country and then refuse to promote an employee who is originally from the same area. Although you may not be able to change everyone's mind, you should be attuned to these more subtle, and sometimes acceptable, forms of discrimination and make an effort to eliminate them.

Conflict in College Will Happen, but You Can Resolve It

While you are in college, you may find yourself in a conflict that must be resolved in order for you to be successful and satisfied. The conflict can arise between you and family member, you and a classmate, or even you and a professor. How you handle the conflict may have long-term consequences that directly tie to your ability to complete a degree. Often a minor conflict such as miscommunication or a misunderstanding can easily be resolved. Other times, the disagreement may be larger than you can handle with a calm conversation.

Boundaries Provide Healthy Limits

Because you will be surrounded by a diverse group of people, it may be difficult for you to create and maintain the traditional boundaries that exist between students and their counselors, professors, administrators, and learning support staff. It almost seems contradictory, but boundaries may be necessary at the same time that you are getting to know others. Why should you refrain from close relationships with professors and advisors when you need them to get to know you if you are to ask for a referral or recommendation?

For one, some colleges discourage intimately personal relationships between professors and students, just as many companies prohibit the same type of overly friendly relationship between supervisors

■ Learning to work well with others and complete tasks as a team, regardless of how different they are from you, is an important skill to develop in college.

© MOODBOARD/FOTOLIA

integrity matters

Integrity is related to trust. If you can trust others, then you will be better able to learn and grow. If you do not have trust, then you may shut yourself off from others and experiences that are new to you. Give people reasons to trust you and then deliver on your promises.

Trust is also reliability, or doing what you say you will do. If your classmate asks you to take notes for him and you fail to do so each time, then you lack reliability.

YOUR TURN

In 250 words, describe a time in which you have demonstrated you are trustworthy. Discuss the effect of the experience and how you felt about it. Then, describe how you plan to achieve greater trust.

and their employees, because such relationships can be problematic. One possible problem is that intimate relationships can result in perceived or actual unfair evaluation or treatment. Because a professor is considered a superior, the college views the professor's role as one of authority and power. Many sexual harassment policies and laws are built on the imbalance of power between a person in authority and a subordinate.

Another possible problem is that other students may see the relationship as favoritism and feel as though they are being treated unfairly. Additionally, there is the possibility of a sexual relationship, which is sometimes strictly prohibited at colleges. If you have not already done so, check your student handbook regarding your college's policy about relationships between students and faculty. Ultimately, you will need to make the decision that is best for you and the situation as to how friendly you should be with faculty or other college officials.

Tenacity

Setting and sticking to boundaries takes tenacity. People will challenge or violate them, even unintentionally. Use your GRIT to set and honor the boundaries that belong in your relationships.

If you get along well with your professor and genuinely enjoy her company, then your best move is to respect the professor–student relationship while you are in class. You can do this by meeting your professor during her office hours on campus and keeping conversations focused on your progress in your classes and your career plans. You can then continue the friendship after you have finished the semester and have no intentions of taking another class with that professor again. Some friendships between professors and students are long lasting, so consider cultivating them once the class is over.

Problems Require Procedures

A time may arise when you have a problem in one of your classes. If it does, you can be assured that the college's employees will work with you to resolve it. There are, however, rules and procedures regarding how to resolve a problem at a college. Knowing and following these procedures will ensure that a problem is handled appropriately and quickly.

The first step to resolving a conflict in class is to define the problem. Is it a communication problem? Is it a problem with the course material? Is it a problem with the course standards? Once you have defined the problem, your next step is to discuss the problem with the person directly. If the problem is with your instructor, make an appointment during her office hours to discuss the issue. If you are emotional—angry, upset, nervous—wait until you have calmed down to discuss the problem. Your goal in meeting with the instructor is to resolve the conflict.

For the process of conflict resolution to work, you will need to complete the first two steps. If you are not satisfied with the result or if you feel the problem has gotten worse, not better, move to the next step: talking to the department chair or dean. You will no doubt be asked if you have met with the instructor. Again, your goal at this step is to resolve the issue. Occasionally, the instructor may be called in to help resolve the issue. Staying calm and focused on resolving the conflict will be to your advantage. In the event that the problem is not solved at this level, your last stop is with the dean of students or vice president for academic affairs. Starting at the top will only delay resolution. See Exhibit 3.4 for common issues that can cause conflict for college students.

Lasting Relationships Need Time and Attention

It can be a challenge to cultivate friendships because of busy schedules and competing priorities. Despite these challenges, what can you do to forge relationships in college?

Leave time in your schedule to talk with friends or meet with professors. If you must leave directly after class to get to work, you will not be as successful in cultivating important relationships. One way to ensure that you connect with your professors is to make an appointment with them during the semester to ask questions or get feedback on your progress. Your ulterior motive is to cultivate a relationship with them. Also, be sure to approach conflict as an opportunity to learn more about yourself and always act with integrity. Lasting relationships are ones that are built on trust and doing what is right.

the unwritten rules
of Relationships and Diversity

- **Students who learn to communicate with diverse audiences are better equipped to succeed in life and their careers.** If you attend a campus that is extremely diverse by any definition, the practice and experience you'll gain from learning to communicate in this environment will set you up well for future success. Conversely, if you're on a campus that tends to lack diversity, look for opportunities to engage with diverse audiences by participating in activities that may be outside your comfort zone. The extra effort will yield rewards later.

- **Working on a project with a team will take more time, but will also yield a better project than an individual effort.** You may encounter some difficult team situations that make you wonder if it would be easier to just do the project on your own. In the long run, a project that's been developed by a team always tends to be a better project than an individual effort. That's why so many companies and professionals use teams to accomplish their objectives.

- **The most common mistake that people make in conflict resolution is bringing other people into the conflict too early.** People have a tendency to want to talk about a problem with everyone but the person with whom they have the problem. This will only complicate the problem and escalate the conflict. Once you have identified the problem (step one), take time to have a one-on-one conversation with the person you're having the conflict with. It may be a tough conversation, but it's worth it.

EXHIBIT 3.4 **Potential Conflict Issues**

Potential Conflict Issues	Tips tor Managing Conflict
Conflicts with Professors	
Grades	Make sure you read the syllabus, assignment directions, and grading criteria, and request an appointment if you have questions about what you have earned.
Deadlines	If you have any issue with a deadline, speak to your professor before the due date. If you have an emergency that prevents you from completing an assignment, contact your professor as soon as possible.
Contraversial topics	Remember that your university courses are supposed to challenge you thinking. Think about how the controversial topic can enrich your understanding of others and yourself. Always speak to your professor privately far serious concerns.
Conflicts, with Other Students	
Workload on team projects	Communication is key to managing conflict with group work. Be sure to clearly communicate individual expectations and responsibiities throughout the entire project, and work through conflict immediately.
Dating/personal relationships	Work through any conflict while dating with honesty and communication, but seek out help from a counselor if the conflict is more than you can manage.
Roommates	Roommate conflict may be best managed with clear expectations and immediate communication about issues. A resident advisor can help with tools for keeping communication lines clear.
Conflicts with University Staff	
Financial aid	Manage conflict with financial aid when you are calm and level-headed. Focus on what you need and what you can do to move forward rather than rehash the issues that led to the conflict.

GRIT GAINER™

GRITIFY YOUR RELATIONSHIPS   You can strengthen your GRIT by joining with diverse others to achieve your goals. Relationships take effort. Don't expect it to be balanced or fair. Take the lead. Ask yourself, "What relationships do I need to invest more effort into to bring them back to full strength?" Then go do it. Everyone will benefit.

4 things future professionals need to know about relationships and diversity

your ability to get along well with others can't be faked

If you don't have all the skills or experience you need to fully meet the qualifications of the job, an employer might still choose to hire you because they can probably provide some on-the-job training to help you address those deficiencies. But if you don't have a good track record of getting along well with others, working well in teams, or resolving conflicts, most employers won't take a chance on you, because they'll conclude that there's little they could do to improve you.

savvy employers know how to uncover your relational skills

Employers who regularly recruit at your university have a vast network of connections with faculty, students, staff, local employers, and others who, in some way or another, will know something about you. Developing and improving your ability to work well with others and maintain healthy relationships should be a top priority in your quest to get in, get through, get out, and get paid.

meaningful relationships in college are a top predictor of lifelong success

The ability to relate well with others is a lifelong skill with lifelong effects. A 2014 survey conducted by Gallup and Purdue University showed that college graduates who had a meaningful relationship with at least one professor were twice as likely to be engaged at work and were also twice as likely to thrive in all aspects of their well-being after college (www.gallup.com/poll/168848/life-college-matters-life-college.aspx).

don't burn bridges or you will have short-lived success in any career

You never know when you might meet someone again in a future stage of your life, so it's always best to avoid ending relationships on a bad note. Someone you know in college could reappear in your life at any time as a co-worker, boss, or customer. If you choose to move beyond a particular relationship, you should do so in a kind and respectful manner.

59

THE G R I T ADVANTAGE

Diversity is a powerful and essential force for you to tap as you broaden and strengthen your perspective on life. Optimizing diversity requires all facets of GRIT. Ask these four questions to put it into practice:

Growth. Whom don't I know that I probably should know better?

Resilience. Who makes me the most uncomfortable, or whom do I most dread approaching, who could actually be a tremendous resource for me as I strive for my goals?

Instinct. How could I better approach any key relationship(s) I may have given up on?

Tenacity. What existing, past, or potential relationship deserves a few more tries?

HOW GRITTY ARE YOU?

Now that you've completed this chapter, how committed are you to:

1. Putting forth the effort to get to know a more diverse group of people?

Zero Commitment 0 ———————————————— 10 Fully Committed

2. Doing what it takes to start and build relationships with the right people?

Zero Commitment 0 ———————————————— 10 Fully Committed

3. Working relentlessly to be more open and sensitive to people you don't understand and/or people who make you uncomfortable?

Zero Commitment 0 ———————————————— 10 Fully Committed

4 Time and Money

Chapter goals to help you get in, get through, get out, and get paid:

In order to get in, get through, get out, and get paid, you will need to become an effective manager of both your time and money. This chapter will help you develop time and money management strategies, as well as the kinds of habits that work best for you and your efforts to keep your life in balance.

To meet those goals, this chapter will help you:

- Establish time management habits and a plan that help you achieve your goals
- Exercise "smart **GRIT**" to put your time, energy, and money to optimal use
- Establish a connection between time management and energy management
- Develop a money management strategy that is a good match for your personal circumstances

MyStudentSuccessLab™

Log in to MyStudentSuccessLab.com to deepen your **GRIT** mindset and build the skills you'll need to get through the college experience.

Laura's Story

© MONKEY BUSINESS IMAGES/SHUTTERSTOCK

Pouring her fourth cup of coffee at 11:00 P.M., Laura searches for her history paper assignment. It's due at 9:00 A.M. tomorrow. She sinks into her chair to go through her backpack one more time and debates whether to call a classmate for help.

Laura doesn't normally procrastinate on her school work, but her middle child has been sick for two days and she's been home caring for him.

Three hours later, Laura's paper is finished. As she prints her final copy, the printer begins to screech loudly and stops. Frantic, she rips the page from the printer. When she presses "print" again, the first three words barely appear on the page before the ink completely disappears.

The only thing she can do is to save her paper to a thumb drive and hope that tomorrow provides her with a solution.

Before her head reaches the pillow, she remembers a flyer she found for the campus computer lab, which opens at 7:00 A.M. Because she gets to campus early, she is able to print off the remaining page in the computer lab—thanks to some help from the lab assistant.

"I will return your papers next week," says her professor. "In the meantime, you may want to get started on your next paper assignment on Greek culture."

Now, what do you think?

- What would you do if you faced a technical glitch right before an important assignment was due?
  a. Explain to my professor why I couldn't get it in on time and plea for more time
  b. Come up with a Plan A and Plan B for first thing in the morning to make sure I get my assignment in no matter what
  c. Pull out my schedule and make some tweaks to make sure I don't end up in the same spot on my other assignments
  d. Reach out to a fellow (good) student to either 1) help me get it printed so I can sleep better, or 2) work together on future assignments so we can help each other through any challenges

- If you wanted to be sure that you are not in the same predicament again, what would you do?
  a. Do the same thing as I did before, because this was a one-time event
  b. Make sure that next time I don't create unnecessary stress by waiting until the last minute
  c. Start working earlier on my assignments so that personal and technical challenges do not make me stumble
  d. Work on assignments with a classmate so that we can rely on each other if we run into challenges

Your Terms for success

when you see . . .	it means . . .
Academic calendar	The college's calendar that provides important dates throughout the semester, including due dates for tuition payments and dropping classes
Add/drop dates	The dates in your academic calendar when you can add or drop a class from your schedule; usually occurs within the first week of classes
Class schedule	Your schedule of classes for the semester
Course calendar/ course outline	Your instructor's calendar that provides important dates throughout the semester; may include due dates for projects and tests
Daily calendar	A calendar that shows one day at a time
Due date	The day that an assignment must be completed and turned in
Energy zapper	An activity or person that lowers your energy levels
Finals week	The week scheduled in the academic calendar in which final exams will be held; your class meeting time may change during this week

Monthly calendar	A calendar that shows one month at a time
Office hours	The hours your intructor is in her office and is available to meet with students; can be found in the syllabus
Procrastination	The act of delaying an activity
Re-energizer	An activity or person that increases your energy levels
Student study day	The date in the academic calendar in which no classes or final exams are held; intended for students to have a day of studying before the week of finals begins
Weekly calendar	A calendar that shows one week at a time
Withdrawal date	The date in the academic calendar that is the final day that you can withdraw from all of your classes; when you withdraw from classes, a "W" will be added to your transcript next to the classes from which you withdrew

Time Can Be on Your Side!

When asked, the number one issue and biggest challenge college students say they face is *time management*. Why?

- **The college experience adds new and different responsibilities to an already busy life.** Even before you stepped onto campus, you probably felt like your life was busy. Now you are a full-time college student on top of a full-time life.

- **The college experience brings high expectations.** Whatever your past level of motivation, college will likely require more. Even if you are a highly motivated, success-oriented person, you're already placing high expectations on yourself. Now, in addition to your own expectations, your professors, advisors, parents, and other people who care about you will place their expectations on you to succeed.

- **The college experience includes a wide variety of responsibilities.** As a full-time student, you're taking three to five different classes—each with its own requirements and schedule—and you may be involved in clubs or other student organizations, working, and juggling family and social responsibilities as well.

- **The college experience puts you in charge.** You have far more autonomy to make decisions about how you spend your time in a college setting than you did previously in high school or work. This freedom can be exciting, but it also brings a new level of responsibility for managing your time without direct supervision from either your parents or an employer.

- **The college experience is academically demanding.** A lot of assignments are bigger, tougher, more complicated, may require a lot of group work, and take longer than what you may have been required to do up until now.

To face the time management challenge, you need to not only develop the skillset, you need to develop a gritty mindset, growing the discipline, resilience, and tenacity to get the important things done, and done right. This chapter will help you with both your time management skillset and mindset.

An effective time management strategy will help you complete more tasks in a timely manner. It will minimize the stress that comes from both procrastination and excessive multitasking, as well as earn you that satisfying feeling of accomplishment. A huge part of resilience and

© MICHAL POPIEL/SHUTTERSTOCK

■ Getting organized and staying organized will help you manage your time well.

Growth

Before we introduce the skillset—the tools and how to use them—it's important to point out that it is your mindset that will determine how well you put these tools and tactics to use. GRIT applies to everything you care about in life. But it is particularly important to time (and life) management.

being a gritty student is proactively and consistently owning, taking charge, and staying on top of your schedule. Managing your time effectively will give you that deep sense of being in control of your life. Growing your GRIT will help you both respond well when things go wrong and stay on track, no matter what.

A key part of being a gritty student is becoming more resilient. That's why your time management strategy should include three key components—resources, resilience, and routines. Resources are what you need to *have* and routines are what you need to *do* in order to manage your time effectively. Resilience is responding effectively when things go wrong.

Calendars, Lists, and Work Space

Many a good student has fallen victim to "assignment amnesia." This occurs when otherwise smart students believe they can remember all of their assignments and appointments without writing them down and without consulting their syllabi or course outlines. Fortunately, there are measures you can take to prevent an attack of assignment amnesia: using a calendar to keep track of important deadlines and events and maintaining a list of prioritized tasks that you need to complete.

The best time managers and students relentlessly plan and spend their time on the right things: those that are most critical to fulfilling their main goals. They refuse to be pulled off course by the countless distractions and time wasters that spring up in the course of a normal week. Tools can show you how to make stuff fit. But your success depends on bringing a decent dose of GRIT.

If you use a paper calendar, you have many different types from which to choose. Once you determine the type that works best for you—a monthly, weekly, or daily calendar—make a habit of writing down your tasks, no matter how big or small. Here is an example of a typical list of a day's activities for a student like Laura:

Thursday

- Make appointment to have oil changed
- Pick up medicine for Mom
- Turn in housing deposit for next semester
- Study for history quiz on Friday
- Write essay for English Composition
- Turn in student club membership application

A typical monthly calendar, shown in Exhibit 4.1, allows you to see several weeks at once so that you can remain aware of upcoming events, but often there is little space on a monthly calendar to write down detailed lists such as the one above.

A weekly calendar allows you to glance at one week at a time. A benefit to a weekly calendar is that you can have room to write out details of each activity; however, a drawback to a weekly calendar is it is difficult to anticipate what you must do the next week.

Daily calendars, such as the one in Exhibit 4.2, usually provide the most space to write your day-to-day tasks and appointments. This kind of calendar may be the most difficult to work with if you need to plan ahead. Because you cannot see the rest of the week or month, you may overlook important events or be surprised by them. Use a daily calendar if you are

EXHIBIT 4.1 Monthly Calendar

Sunday	Monday	Tuesday	Wednesday	Thursday	Friday	Saturday
					1	2
3	4	5	6	7	8	9 Picnic— noon
10	11 Work late	12	13	14	15 Pay bills	16
17	18	19	20	21 Play rehearsal 7:00	22	23
24	25 Nutrition exam 10:00	26	27	28	29	30 Birthday party 2:00

extremely organized and can plan ahead effectively, or use it in addition to a monthly calendar. Exhibit 4.3 shows a typical student's work and school schedule.

If you have reliable Internet access in your home, apartment, or dorm and access to computers while on campus in computer labs, you may want to consider using a web-based electronic calendar system and to-do list. Most computers and electronic devices have a pretty slick calendar system included. These calendars allow you to quickly toggle between views of your day, week, and month, and can separate your school demands and personal life.

Electronic calendars allow you to set up events to automatically repeat themselves (e.g., calculus quiz every Thursday; Dad's birthday on March 18th), rearrange priority lists without having to rewrite them, set up reminders and alerts to prompt you about upcoming deadlines and events, and share your calendar with others so that you can coordinate team projects and family responsibilities. The added benefit of a web-based system is that you can access it anytime and anywhere you have Internet access. Google's calendar service is a popular choice among college students. Even with these electronic systems, you can always print a copy of your calendar and to-do lists to have readily available during class or other times when you

EXHIBIT 4.2 Daily Calendar

Friday March 15, 2013	
7:00	Wake up, shower, get ready for school
8:00	Drive to school, arrive early and study in the library
9:00	College Algebra
10:00	English 2
11:00	Study for Biology exam
12:00	Eat lunch and review notes for College Algebra
1:00	Biology—EXAM!!
2:00	Drive to work
3:00	Work
4:00	Work
5:00	Work

EXHIBIT 4.3 Student's College and Work Schedule

Responsibility	Contact Hours Per Week	Outside Hours Per Week	Total Hours Per Week
College Algebra	3	6–9	9–12
Composition 101	3	6–9	9–12
U.S. History	3	6–9	9–12
Reading	3	6–9	9–12
Work	25		25

TOTAL HOURS EACH WEEK: 61–73 HOURS

don't have Internet access. Whatever system you choose—electronic, paper-based, weekly, monthly, daily—pick a system that works best for you and keeps you on track.

Once you've chosen a calendar system that works best for you, find your university's academic calendar on the campus website or catalog and add the following deadlines to your schedule:

Instinct

The reality is, you may not always have an ideal learning or work space to accomplish your tasks. Things and people unexpectedly intrude. Sometimes you have to either agilely adjust the situation (like go somewhere else, rather than just suffer) or dig deep and do whatever it takes to achieve your goal.

- Deadlines for registering and filing financial aid forms
- Date for the beginning of classes (or instruction)
- Drop/add dates for changing your schedule
- Due dates for tuition payment
- Withdrawal dates for leaving college before the semester is over
- Registration dates for the next semester
- School holidays or breaks

There is no doubt that the most effective people—those who get the most done in the least amount of time—make constant and immediate use of their own calendars. They persistently plan. They use their calendars to be more resilient, adjusting plans to stay on track as factors change. Every time anything pops up (a new appointment, a changed date, a test or assignment), whip out your calendar and add a reminder, now! Life is fluid. And it feels great to stay on top as things unfold.

The ideal calendar and to-do list are first steps to managing your time well, but there is more you can do. To manage your time effectively and efficiently, create a quiet, clutter-free space where you can study and complete assignments. If you don't have a place in your house or apartment that you can call your own and a comfortable chair or seat at the kitchen table is all that you can spare, make sure it is comfortable and quiet and has adequate space for books, notebooks, and other supplies. It has to be a place where you *want* to be or it will be difficult to go there to stay on task. See Exhibit 4.4 for an example of a typical busy student's calendar.

■ Schedule time to work with your classmates and talk with faculty and advisors outside of class.

© FUSE/GETTY IMAGES

Daily Reviews and Back Planning

With an effective calendar and to-do list in place, you can now start to establish a time management routine that helps you stay on track and maintain control over your life. For your calendar and task list to be

EXHIBIT 4.4   Laura's Weekly Calendar

Monday	Tuesday	Wednesday	Thursday	Friday	Saturday	Sunday
6:30–7:30 Get ready for school	6:30–7:30 Get ready for school	6:30–7:30 Get ready for school	6:30–7:30 Get ready far school	6:30–7:30 Get ready for school	7:00–10:00 Clean house, shop	7:00–10:00 Study
7:30–7:45 Travel to work	7:30–7:45 Travel to work	7:30–7:45 Travel to work	7:30–7:45 Travel to work	7:30–7:45 Travel to work	10:00–11:30 Soccer	10:00–11:00 Go to church
8:00–12:30 Work	8:00–12:30 Work	8:00–12:30 Work	8:00–12:30 Work	8:00–12:30 Work	11:30–12:15 Lunch with team	11:15–12:30 Lunch with parents
12:30–1:15 Eat lunch and run errands	12:30–1:15 Go to doctor's appt.	12:30–1:15 Eat lunch with friend	12:30–1:15 Eat lunch and walk 1 mile	12:30–1:15 Eat lunch and study	12:15–2:00 Run errands	12:45–3:45 Study
1:15–4:45 Work	1:15–4:45 Work	1:15–1:45 Work	1:15–4:45 Work	1:15–4:45 Work	2:00–6:00 Go to library and do research	3:45–5:45 Do yard work
4:45–5:00 Travel	4:45–5:00 Travel	4:45–5:00 Travel	4:45–5:00 Travel	4:45–5:00 Travel	6:00–7:00 Fix and eat dinner	6:00–7:00 Eat dinner
5:00–5:45 Eat dinner and study	5:00–5:45 Eat dinner and study	5:00–5:45 Eat dinner and study	5:00–5:45 Eat dinner and study	5:00–7:00 Eat dinner with friends	7:00–9:00 Study	7:00–8:00 Walk 3 miles
6:00–9:30 Classes	6:00–9:30 Classes	6:00–9:30 Classes	6:00–9:30 Classes	7:00–9:30 See movie	9:00–10:00 Answer email and watch TV	8:00–10:00 Do laundry, get ready for next week
10:00 Go to bed	10:00 Go to bed	10:00 Go to bed	10:00 Go to bed	10:00 Go to bed	10:00 Go to bed	10:00 Go to bed

effective, you need to establish a daily routine of reviewing and updating this information. Take a few minutes every evening to review what you've accomplished and check those items off your to-do list (this will be a very satisfying experience!), add new tasks that came up that day, and then review tomorrow's calendar and to-do list so you can anticipate tomorrow's goals.

Knowing what to expect for the day will make surprises less likely. Also, if you know that you have an early start tomorrow, you can make special preparations such as preparing a lunch the night before, getting your backpack organized, making sure you know where you have to go by reviewing a map, and setting your alarm (and backups, if you tend to hit the snooze button a lot!). Stressful mornings tend to get you on the wrong track for the day, and they can typically be avoided with some thoughtful planning the night before. See Exhibit 4.5 for an example of how you can plan your day.

The second element of your time management routine that can help you manage your stress, keep you resilient, and put you in control of your schedule is a strategy called *back planning*. The basic premise of back planning is to look ahead at a deadline

G R I T
Resilience

Expect the unexpected. Don't be thrown off if you are forced to change your plan. Gritty students know and mentally prepare for the unexpected. When something threatens to throw you off, ask yourself, "How can I get back on track as quickly as possible?" Then adjust your schedule accordingly.

EXHIBIT 4.5 Time Log Example

Time	Wednesday's Activities
7:00 A.M.	Get ready for classes; eat breakfast
7:30 A.M.	Review nates for business class
8:00 A.M.	En route to school
8:30 A.M.	Business Communications
9:00 A.M.	Class, continued
9:30 A.M.	Class, continued
10:00 A.M.	See advisor to plan next semester's classes

for a task, estimate the amount of time it will take to complete the task, and establish a starting point for the task based on both. For example, if you know that you need to write a 20-page paper for English composition, and you expect that all of the research, writing, editing, formatting, and printing will take two weeks, you know that you'll need to start the project at least two weeks before its deadline. Back planning also works for shorter term planning. If you know that your morning class starts at 8:30, and it typically takes 45 minutes for you to complete your entire morning routine and find parking, then you know that you need to be walking out the door of your dorm or apartment no later than 7:45 to be on time for class. Establishing these short- and long-term milestones will help you stay on track to meet deadlines and reduce the stress that's often associated with running behind in your schedule.

Perhaps the most important benefit of back planning is that it attacks one of the biggest threats to student success—procrastination. Procrastination is the tendency to delay starting a task until the deadline is very near. Activities such as cramming for quizzes and exams, pulling all-nighters to finish a paper or project, and missing work or other classes to finish an assignment on the due date are all evidence of procrastination. These types of last-minute, hurried efforts to meet a deadline tend to yield relatively poor academic performance and generate a tremendous amount of emotional, physical, and social stress. Worst of all, these desperate strategies are avoidable! With effective back planning, you can alleviate the need to stay up all night before an exam or miss other classes to finish an assignment. An example of back planning for an important assignment can be seen in Exhibit 4.6.

The single biggest obstacle you need to overcome to avoid procrastination is *starting* the project. Procrastination typically occurs when we (yes, professors sometimes procrastinate, too) are confused, intimidated, or overwhelmed by an assignment or task. Our fears get the best of us, and we choose to forget about the assignment for a while instead of trying to get started. Once we do get started on a project, the fears tend to dissipate, and we discover that we're making more progress than we expected. The problem with procrastination is that if we wait a long time before starting the project, the fear of missing the deadline and being late begins to creep in and we lose our ability to be creative problem solvers. That's not a very gritty approach.

If you've ever tried to remember a phone number, locker combination, or some other mental note, you've probably discovered that it's more difficult to think clearly and solve problems when you're in a hurry or panicked. In the same way, it's difficult to be thoughtful and creative when you're trying to study for an exam or write a paper under excessive time pressure. The good news is, the grittier you become, the more you will flourish under pressure, and the less stressful it will feel.

We could have addressed procrastination at some other time. But we thought it simply couldn't wait, because it's such a common phenomenon in college. We regularly see our students suffer significant and unnecessary consequences by putting things off. Show some GRIT. Refuse to fall into that abyss.

When you are assigned homework, projects, or papers, take time to use back planning and clearly establish your start date for the project, as well as important milestones along the way (e.g., first two chapters by September 15). Build those milestones into your calendar system, set time aside for the work, and dig in. If you can establish a solid routine of regularly reviewing your calendar and to-do list and using back planning, you'll be taking control of your time and developing skills that will serve you well both in college and throughout your life.

EXHIBIT 4.6   Back-Planning Time Management

Sunday	Monday	Tuesday	Wednesday	Thursday	Friday	Saturday
		1	2	3	4	5
6	7	8 1:00 P.M. Receive paper assignment	9 6–7:30 P.M. Choose paper topic; brainstorm or freewrite on topic	10 9–10:30 P.M. Reread brainstorming list; create a draft outline	11	12
13 3–5:00 P.M. Write first draft of paper	14	15 11–12:00 noon Visit writing lab for assistance with paper	16	17	18 8:30–10:30 P.M. Write second draft of paper, incorparating tutor's advice	19
20 3–4:30 P.M. Write final draft of paper	21	22	23 8–9:00 P.M. Edit paper; print out on quality paper; place in backpack	24 2:00 P.M. Turn in paper	25	26
	27	28	29	30		

GRIT GAINER™

BEAT THE CROWD   There's an old saying, "The task expands to fill the time." So, you can shrink the time by shrinking the task. There are two kinds of GRIT: dumb GRIT and smart GRIT. Dumb GRIT is when you keep doing what everyone else does. Crowds are slow. Smart GRIT is when you do it quicker and better than almost everyone else.

- Be the first in line for everything. 15 minutes early is better than 60 minutes in line.
- Plan the ideal, quickest route between classes and other appointments. Get there faster and sooner; it can save you hours.
- Get the resources (books, people, supplies, etc.), answers, and specific requirements for each assignment now, so you can save time later.
- Plan persistently. Don't live by the question, "How long will this take?" The moment anything changes in your schedule, adjust and ask yourself, "Where, how, and when can I get this task done as efficiently and effectively as possible?"

the unwritten rules
about Time Management

- **Projects, midterms, and finals will all tend to collide at the same time each term.** The best way to not only survive but succeed each term is to start early on your projects and assignments and review your notes and class materials each week so that studying for midterms and finals will not require as much time or effort.

- **The best opportunities for accomplishing the important items on your priority list may occur between terms.** Look for opportunities during spring break, holiday breaks, summer, and even three-day weekends to get some solitude and quiet and to revisit the important-but-not-urgent items on your list, like your personal mission statement, SMART goals, and career plan.

- **No matter how well you think you can work under pressure, professors can detect procrastination from a mile away.** You'll be at a disadvantage as soon as the professor sees the evidence of procrastination. Most importantly, if you wait too long to start or complete an assignment, you forgo the biggest advantage of getting an early start— the opportunity to get helpful feedback from your professor on preliminary drafts of your work.

- **Even with today's technology, it takes time to learn.** In his comprehensive study of student success chronicled in the book *What Matters in College*, Alexander Astin (1997) found that the amount of time students spend practicing what they are trying to learn, or "time on task," is the single greatest predictor of academic success. It takes a lot of GRIT to succeed. You have to dig deep and stick with it. Sorry, no shortcuts here.

Manage Your Energy

Just as important as managing your time is managing, and ideally optimizing, your energy. Think about this scenario: You have all weekend off from work and your spouse has taken the kids to visit the grandparents. Therefore, you have 48 hours of complete solitude to write a research paper that is due on Monday. Sounds ideal, doesn't it? But what if you have the flu for those two days? Does the time mean anything when you don't have the energy to do the work? What if, instead of having the flu, you pulled two double shifts and haven't slept more than five hours in two days? Will you be able to use your free 48 hours productively working, or will you need to pause to take care of yourself?

Time is only valuable if you have the energy to use it well. Energy includes both physical and mental stamina, strength, sharpness, and focus. Everyone experiences variations in how "sharp" he or she feels throughout the day. Researchers sometimes refer to this as our *circadian rhythm*. The key point is to understand yourself well enough to know when you are at the peak of your mental and physical alertness and when you're not. To determine at which times of the day you feel most sharp, place an "X" in the appropriate column for each time of day in Exhibit 4.7. If you work nights and sleep during most of the day, create your own box with the times that you are awake.

In addition to the time of day, your energy levels rise and fall during the week. Do you find yourself tired on Monday mornings, but full of energy on Fridays? Or do you feel worn out by Thursday evenings, but rejuvenated on Sundays? Depending on your work, school, and personal schedules, you will find that you have regular bursts of energy at certain times of the week. To determine which days of the week you feel most energetic, write an "X" in the appropriate columns in the box in Exhibit 4.8.

Once you've identified the hours in the day and the days in the week when you tend to be at your best, you can build your schedule to maximize your productivity during those times and

EXHIBIT 4.7   Time of Day Energy Levels

Time of Day	High Energy	Neutral	Low Energy
6:00 A.M.			
8:00 A.M.			
10:00 A.M.			
12 noon			
2:00 P.M.			
4:00 P.M.			
6:00 P.M.			
8:00 P.M.			
10:00 P.M.			
12 midnight			

EXHIBIT 4.8   Day of Week Energy Levels

Weekday	High Energy	Neutral	Low Energy
Sunday			
Monday			
Tuesday			
Wednesday			
Thursday			
Friday			
Saturday			

schedule activities that don't require as much effort or concentration during times when you aren't at your peak. Activities such as writing papers, solving complex math problems, and reading articles and books for class assignments should be reserved for those peak times. It's during these times that you will also most need your quiet, uncluttered work space.

Make that time sacred. This will require some discipline and advanced planning, because you'll be tempted by other tasks and distractions. Take advantage of your mental and physical sharpness during these peak periods to perform activities that will clearly help you get through, get out, and get paid. It will save you time. Most students are at or near the peak of their mental alertness shortly after waking up in the morning. If that's also the case for you, commit yourself to tackling the most important task of the day first thing in the morning. Consider signing up for early morning classes.

What should you do during those times when you aren't at your peak? First of all, recognize that it's OK to have some

G R I T
Growth

It takes GRIT to find a way to do what you have to do when you're tired, your energy is low, and the last thing you want to do is school work. The gritty reality of school and life is sometimes it's messy and tough. But the best students are not usually the ones with the highest IQs. They are the ones who plan their time and energy intelligently, then refuse to make excuses when things don't go their way. They get it done.

Tenacity

Build the energy flywheel. GRIT takes and generates energy. Sure, it takes time to exercise. But exercise gives you energy, and energy makes you more productive and efficient, which saves you time. You have to schedule the time to invest some energy in order to gain more energy and greater GRIT.

periods of time when you take a break from working hard. In fact, it's actually more productive to take breaks than to try to work hard all day. The good news is that you can still get a lot accomplished, even during times when you don't feel mentally or physically sharp. During those times, you can accommodate the common "time zappers" that can rob college students of their time:

- Reviewing and sending emails
- Making phone calls
- Running errands
- Preparing meals
- Talking with roommates

One way to help yourself manage your energy is by becoming aware of what activities relax you when you are stressed and what activities allow you to refill your energy reserves. In Exhibit 4.9, place an "X" in the appropriate column next to each activity. If the activity does both, place an "X" in both columns. If the activity neither relaxes nor energizes, then leave both columns blank. Use this chart when planning your time. If an activity rejuvenates you and helps you recharge, you may want to schedule times to do it when you need more energy. If an activity helps you wind down, you may want to schedule it after you have completed major tasks.

Avoid the "Black Holes" of Television, Videogames, and Social Media

Often portrayed in science fiction movies or scientific documentaries, black holes in space absorb everything around them, including light. From the perspective of time and energy management, television, videogames, and social media have the potential to be virtual black holes in your life

EXHIBIT 4.9 Time and Energy Zappers and Re-energizers

Activity	Zapper	Re-energizer
Watching television		
Spending time with family/friends		
Pleasure reading		
Doing housework		
Exercising (light to moderate)		
Gardening		
Talking on the phone		
Writing		
Cooking		
Shopping		
Napping		
Participating in a hobby		
Surfing the Internet		
Organizing closets, drawers, files		
Enjoying a nice meal		

that can consume far too much of your time and energy. If you plan on watching TV or connecting with friends online for only 10 minutes, it's really easy to discover that you're still sitting in front of the screen two hours later, and you've accomplished nothing during that time.

Videogames have the capacity to be even more time consuming because of their interactive nature. Social media like Facebook and Twitter have emerged as another potential black hole of your time, consuming both your time and attention by feeding continual distractions to you throughout the day. As you establish your time and energy management strategy for the college experience, we urge extreme caution in your screen time. They are popular activities among college students, certainly, but if they aren't consumed in careful moderation, they can absorb your time and energy and leave you with little in return for your academic pursuits.

© DIGITAL VISION/GETTY IMAGES

Scheduling time to relax and recharge is just as important as scheduling your class work.

Multitasking Should Be Used in Moderation

The process of multitasking—simultaneously managing several tasks or devoting your attention to more than one activity at a time—is often lauded as an admirable and even necessary skill. In fact, many people believe that you can get more done and be more productive while multitasking. However, the scientific evidence doesn't support that premise. The brain cannot actually multitask. It switches between tasks. This means you have to turn off one thing to do the other thing. Research shows multitasking wastes time and produces inferior results.

If you have a tendency to check your emails, respond to text messages, monitor your Facebook status, and listen to music while attempting to write, study, or organize your calendar, you are undermining your ability to perform well because these simultaneous tasks are sapping both your time and energy. Take a moment to shut down the peripheral activities and stimuli to focus on the primary task at hand and you'll find yourself accomplishing far more than you expected.

G R I T
Instinct

You can let your distractions own you, or you can own them. Let "screen time" (or whatever your vice) be your reward at the end of a gritty, productive day. Save your lowest energy hours for those activities, and your prime energy hours for those things that create real momentum toward your goals.

integrity**matters**

Sometimes doing what is easiest, even if it's not the right thing to do, seems like the best way to manage time effectively. For example, a student who does not have enough time to finish a paper may be tempted to download one from the Internet, use someone else's previous work, or ask someone else to write it. Such a shortcut actually shortchanges the educational process. A student who saves time by not doing her own work for a class risks more than not learning from the assignment; she may find herself in serious academic jeopardy when the professor confronts her with the evidence she did not do her own work.

YOUR TURN

In 250 words, describe how you have saved time by not doing something or not doing it right. Discuss how you felt about not completing the task or by not completing it to the best of your ability. What have you learned about acting with integrity and managing your time?

GRIT GAINER™

T + E = M   Most students passively and half-heartedly put in long hours hacking away at their assignments, until, hopefully, they are finally complete. You can get two or three times more out of your day and your life if you apply the formula, Time + Energy = Momentum. Here's how:

1. Plan prime time. For any task that helps you achieve your goal (get in, get through, get out, get paid), schedule undistracted, focused time during the prime energy of your day. You'll get twice as much done in half the time.

2. Refuse distractions and temptations. Turn everything off. Lock yourself away. Be like a swimmer going the length of the pool underwater. Don't come up for air until you've touched the finish line and accomplished your task.

Money Matters

Instinct

Get gritty with your money by finding ways to get what you need for less. Some costs, like tuition, may be fixed. This applies to everything from the big stuff, like rent and a car, to smaller items like supplies, gas, clothes, and food. Some costs that appear fixed aren't. Shop the best deals and always ask for student discounts to get more for less.

One of the greatest challenges for students isn't meeting the academic expectations of college; it is handling the financial issues that come into play when you get there. Some students choose to go to school full-time and not work, whereas others juggle a job—either part-time or full-time—while going to school. No matter what their financial situation, many are adding the expense of going to college to their other obligations, or they are using grants, loans, or scholarships to cover costs.

As you know by now, investing in your future takes more than courage; it also takes some cash. Unfortunately, the costs of college continue to rise and will likely increase with each passing year. So what can you do?

The first step is to become financially literate. There are many resources available that help you learn more about how to become financially fit. The next step is to create a plan and develop the personal GRIT to stay on a budget while anticipating future expenses. The following section provides you with a brief overview of both steps.

Estimate Your College Costs

Tenacity

Most students end up spending money on things they don't need. The harder you work, the more tempting it becomes to buy yourself little indulgences along the way. If cash is tight, use your GRIT to focus your funds on what matters most. It will save you money and enhance your sense of accomplishment.

Estimating what you are going to spend in college for your education is a great first step to understanding your financial situation, and it will help you with budgeting. Because this is your first time in college, it will be helpful to see what you can expect to spend as you work on and complete your degree. Unfortunately, college tuition and fees are only part of the costs involved in earning a degree. No matter what you pay for tuition and fees, you will pay only a fraction of the actual costs of educating one student. Colleges make up the difference through taxes, state and federal money, and gifts and donations.

To determine your estimated costs, you will need to get very specific about what you will need during the semesters or quarters you plan to attend. The following list is only a suggestion of possible supplies: textbooks, notebooks/binders, computer/laptop, backpack, notebook paper, printer paper, pens/pencils, calculator, computer software, flash drive, stapler, hole punch, ruler, and other specialized supplies for labs or certain classes such as photography or drawing. For specialized programs, you may have other materials that you will need to purchase. Create a list of what you know you will need and then write down how much you think each item will cost. You will use this estimate when you create your budget.

In addition to supplies and tuition, you may also find other costs associated with going to college. For example, your transportation costs may increase as you go from home or work to campus and back. You may also discover that you need regular, reliable Internet access that will create an additional monthly cost. Unexpected costs such as these can be an awakening to the investment of money and time that wasn't covered during new student orientation. The following is just a suggested list of possible additional expenses that you may encounter: daycare or baby-sitting services, transportation (gas, car maintenance, tolls, bus pass), parking, and Internet services. You will want to talk with students who have been at your college for a few terms or recent graduates to determine what else may be needed. These same students may also provide you with some cost-saving ideas.

GRIT
Resilience

The fewer sources of income and the smaller the funds you have, the less resilient and the more vulnerable your situation becomes. If a lake is fed by one tributary, the lake is in danger when that creek dries up. If it is fed by two or more, its chances of survival dramatically improve. It may not be easy, but strive to create more than one source for your school funds. And whenever possible, build in a little padding, so you can weather the storm and stay in school.

Create a Budget

In order to manage these costs while balancing your other financial obligations, creating a budget will help you stay on track. A budget doesn't have to be a headache. In fact, it is relatively easy to create a budget. The hard part is following it. First, you need to create a customized budget sheet. Exhibit 4.10 shows a sample budget form that you can start with. In the first column, you will estimate your income and your expenses. The middle column will be used to record your actual amounts of income and expenses. Record any differences in the marked column by subtracting the actual amount from the estimated amount. For example, if you estimate that you earn about $1,000 a month, but this month, you earn $1,092, your difference is $92. If you earned $997, then the difference is –$3. Exhibit 4.10 provides a sample of what you need to write down each month.

Once you determine the categories that fit your lifestyle and requirements, you will need to gather all the bills and paystubs that you have and add up your expenses and income. It is a good idea to review at least three months of bills to get an accurate picture of your expenditures. If you have any bills that are paid less frequently than once a month, then you will need to convert them to a monthly expense. For example, if you pay $240 for car insurance every six months, your monthly expense is $40 ($240 divided by 6).

One key to an accurate budget that helps you track your spending is to be honest about your expenses. That means you must write down everything you spend, even the money you spend on snacks or supplies. You may find that you spend $25 a week ($100 a month) on items that are unnecessary. The more you can track unnecessary items, the better you can control your spending.

Set Financial Goals

After you get an accurate picture of your income and expenses, you can start setting short-term and long-term financial goals. Because you are in college and probably trying to keep expenses to a minimum, you may

■ Budgeting your money for college expenses will be crucial to your staying in college and being less stressed.

© ROB MARMION/SHUTTERSTOCK

EXHIBIT 4.10 Sample Budget Form

Category	Estimated Amount Per Month	Actual Amount Per Month	Difference
Income			
Source 1 (wages/salary)			
Source 2 (scholarship, financial aid, etc.)			
Source 3 (alimony, employee tuition reimbursement, child support)	300.	300	
Total Income			
Expenses			
Mortgage/rent			
Utilities	94.00	93.03	206.31
Car payment/transportation			
Insurance	64	63.95	142.42
Groceries	100	100	42.42
Household items			
Clothing			
Gas			
Car maintenance			
Cellular phone	116	115.64	-73.22
Eating out	50	50	-123.22
Entertainment			
Health care (medications, doctor's visits, etc.)			
Credit cards or loans	80	80	-203.22
Total Expenses			503.22
Net Income (Total Income minus Total Expenses)			203.22

think that creating and working toward financial goals will be a difficult undertaking until you have a job with a steady income and secure future. However, you can start setting small short-term goals now. For example, your first short-term goal could be tracking your monthly budget and consistently spending 5 percent less than you earn. Another short-term goal could be to save enough money to pay for your study abroad experience next year. Meeting these two goals will help you reach larger goals down the road.

You should also write down your long-term financial goals. One of these goals could be to start your own business. However, in order to reach that long-term goal, you will need to make a list of other goals and start working toward them.

Don't Take Credit

Credit cards can be very tempting when you are in college because they are so easy to use and the offers pour in just about every day. The reality of credit cards, however, is that they can cause big financial problems, ones that are sometimes difficult to pay off. Think about this: You don't want to start a new career after college that pays a good salary only to send a substantial portion of it to a credit card company.

In case you are still enticed to use a credit card, think about this sobering information. If you were to charge $1,000 on a credit card that charges 17 percent interest and you pay $100 a month, you will be accruing more in interest than you will be paying each month. And that is only if you do not charge anything else!

Exhibit 4.11 shows that paying twice as much—$200—each month for six months only reduces the balance by $276.21—after paying $1,200. Unfortunately, some students have many more thousands of dollars of credit card debt, and with the current interest rates, it is no wonder that students can find themselves in an endless cycle of charging and paying minimums. If at all possible, put the cards away until you are out of college, and then use them wisely.

GRIT Growth

Employers value students who worked hard and sacrificed a lot to put themselves through school, and students who put themselves through college feel a tremendous sense of accomplishment. Harder can be better.

Practice Good Financial Habits

A good financial plan is only good if you stick to it. The following tips can help you increase your financial literacy muscles, especially if you exercise them regularly.

- Balance your checkbook and other accounts every month. Online tools can be helpful, if you're comfortable managing your finances using a computer.

- Compare your financial statements with your own recording of expenses and income. This will help you catch any unauthorized charges on your accounts or bank fees that were inappropriately posted to your account.

- Separate your bills from other mail and create a schedule for paying them. Your paper-based or electronic calendar system is ideal for this purpose. Most bills are due on the same day each month, so you can set up a recurring reminder.

- Sign up for online payment plans if available and if it is easier to pay in this way. Just be sure that you have reliable Internet access and use a consistent email address so you don't lose track of these transactions.

EXHIBIT 4.11 Credit Card Payments

Month	Previous Balance	Interest (17%)	Balance + Interest	Payment	Remaining Balance
Month 1	$1,000	$170	$1,170	$200	$970
Month 2	$970	$164.90	$1,134.90	$200	$934.90
Month 3	$934.90	$158.93	$1,093.83	$200	$893.83
Month 4	$893.83	$151.95	$1,045.78	$200	$845.78
Month 5	$845.78	$143.78	$989.56	$200	$789.56
Month 6	$789.56	$134.23	$923.79	$200	$723.79

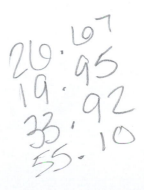

It's in the
syllabus

Look at your syllabus to help determine what you need for class.

- What are the supply requirements listed in your syllabus for each class (e.g., textbook, notebook, graphing calculator)?

- What are the supply requirements that are needed but not listed in your syllabus for each class (e.g., printer ink, copy paper, thumb drive)?

- If you have a credit card, use it for emergencies only.

- Put a small percentage of your income each month in a separate savings account for unexpected expenses. For example, for every $100 you earn, put $5 (5%) in an emergency savings account. Create a goal to increase your savings percentage.

- Check the university website every semester for updates about changes in tuition and fees.

Protect Yourself

Budgeting and creating a plan are not enough to make sure that you are on firm financial foundation—you will also need to protect yourself from scams that can do more harm than just draining your bank account. If anyone you do not know contacts you through email or by phone to ask you to send money or provide a bank account number, delete the email or hang up the phone. Thousands of well-meaning people get scammed this way by providing access to their bank accounts, only to find out that their money is gone and their credit is ruined. If the information sounds too good to be true or doesn't seem right, it is quite possibly a scam.

Another risk that you have to manage is identity theft. Keep your bank cards in a safe, secure place at all times, and never, ever write down your ATM PIN on a piece of paper. Also, be very cautious any time someone asks you to provide your Social Security number. Never provide it in an email, and make sure that any form requesting this number is from an official authority like your university's financial aid office or the registrar.

Learn More

There are numerous resources available for you to explore financial matters further. There are many local, state, and federal government programs that can provide free information and counseling if you are interested in getting your finances on track. The best defense is good information about your situation and your possibilities. For starters, you can—and should—request a free credit report. A request form from the Federal Trade Commission is available at www.ftc.gov/credit. You can also find a lot of useful resources online from not-for-profit organizations that have been established specifically to help college students better manage their money, such as 360financialliteracy.org and cashcourse.org. Remember that the best way to protect your financial future—and to secure the hard work that you are doing in college to get a better job—is to empower yourself with the knowledge of what you have and what you want to do with it in the future.

GRIT GAINER™

YES AND NO One of the most powerful ways to get gritty with your money is to make a list of those things that are utterly required to fulfill your goal of getting in, through, out, and paid. Ask yourself, "What is the minimum amount of money it takes for me to have/buy each of these items?" List those numbers. Say "yes!" to those items.

Next, make a list of all the things you know you spend money on that you do not absolutely need. You may really want them, but that doesn't mean you need them. Every dollar wasted on a want is a dollar less to nurture your needs. Say "no" to those items, at least more often than you do now.

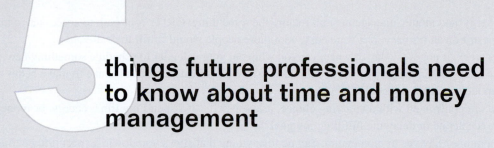

5 things future professionals need to know about time and money management

you'll be starting your career with habits you developed in college

College students, particularly those nearing the point of graduation, often allow themselves to slip into unhelpful habits like sleeping in late, studying less, and exercising less frequently because they get the false sense of security that it's a good time to kick back and relax before stepping into the "real world."

no matter how busy you felt in college, you'll feel even busier in your career

Students who are juggling classes, a job, club activities, and a social life might think that life after graduation is going to be a lot simpler and less busy. We hate to be the bearers of bad news, but that won't be the case. A whole new set of expectations and responsibilities will come your way, and you'll quickly discover that you're even busier after college than you were in school.

there is no such thing as partial credit in the workplace

In college, if you managed your time poorly and procrastinated, you may have missed some assignment deadlines and turned in your work late. Depending on how lenient your professors were, they may have given you partial credit for your late assignments and work. In a competitive work environment, there is no partial credit. If you miss a deadline or meeting, there's no second chance to make up for what you lost, and the mistake could actually cost you your job.

there's a big difference between your annual salary and your take-home pay

It is certainly exciting when you get a job offer that includes an annual salary that's more than you ever made in your life. Approximately 30 to 40 percent of your annual income will be deducted from your paycheck for income taxes, health insurance, retirement, and other deductions. So, before you run out and buy a new car or rent an expensive apartment, make sure you have an accurate estimate of your actual take-home pay.

your energy and health will become even more strongly connected

In this chapter you learned how important it is to manage your energy in the same way you manage your time. You need to recognize when your mind is at its peak performance to accomplish the most important opportunities of the day. Getting enough sleep, exercising frequently, and establishing healthy eating habits will directly contribute to your mental sharpness and stamina.

THE G R I T ADVANTAGE

Successful time, energy, and money management all require the same thing: GRIT. Your path to success is in many ways simple. But that doesn't mean it's easy. If it were easy, a lot more people would fulfill their dreams.

At least once a week, if not every day or whenever you whip out your calendar to schedule something new, ask yourself this question to keep you on the gritty path to your success: "What adjustments can I make to make better use of my energy, time, and money to fulfill my goals?"

Whenever you are confronted with a tempting choice, ask yourself, "If I spend my time, energy, or money on this, will it help or hurt, accelerate or delay me fulfilling my goal?"

Is it a plus or a minus? Say yes to momentum. Say no to anything that slows you down. Expect it to be tough. Pause and appreciate when it's not. And know, the tougher it is, the more accomplished you'll feel.

HOW GRITTY ARE YOU?

Now that you've completed this chapter, how committed are you to:

1. Taking charge—owning your time, owning your schedule, and owning your decisions?

   Zero Commitment 0 ——————————————————————— 10 **Fully Committed**

2. Not letting distractions, excuses, laziness, or competing demands get in the way of what you need to do?

   Zero Commitment 0 ——————————————————————— 10 **Fully Committed**

3. Saying yes to the right stuff and no to things that hinder your goals?

   Zero Commitment 0 ——————————————————————— 10 **Fully Committed**

4. Planning and managing your money so you can reduce your stress and enhance your college experience?

   Zero Commitment 0 ——————————————————————— 10 **Fully Committed**

5. Seeking advice on the stuff you don't know, so you avoid some costly mistakes?

   Zero Commitment 0 ——————————————————————— 10 **Fully Committed**

5 Stress and Health Choices

Chapter goals to help you *get in, get through, get out, and get paid:*

As you pursue your goals to get in, get through, get out, and get paid, it's a certainty that you'll experience stress. Stress can't be avoided, but it can be managed and even harnessed.

To meet those goals, this chapter will help you:

- Define stress and where it can appear in your life
- Take a gritty approach to stress, using it to fuel your performance
- Reduce damaging forms of stress and minimize stress-related illnesses
- Determine which health issues are important to consider while you are in college
- Develop a personal approach to maintain balance in your overall health

MyStudentSuccessLab™

GRIT

Log in to MyStudentSuccessLab.com to deepen your **GRIT** mindset and build the skills you'll need to get through the college experience.

Evan's Story

© MONKEY BUSINESS IMAGES/SHUTTERSTOCK

Evan is a student by day and a kickboxer by night, usually competing several times a semester. Sometimes he wonders if he can do both and be successful in and out of the ring. A few years ago, he saw a doctor because of depression, and he feels the symptoms creeping up on him again.

"Evan, man, you're a little late today," his coach says. "What gives? You are usually early to practice."

"Hey, Coach. Had too much homework to do," Evan replies.

"Evan, I know you are committed to college. That's great, but you have to do your time at the gym."

The words sting Evan. He is highly competitive—you have to be, in this sport—and he prides himself on his athletic ability even though he has started to pack on the pounds from too much studying and eating poorly.

Then, there is college—another goal that he wants to achieve. When he registered for college, he really thought he could do both kickboxing and college and succeed at both. Evan packs his sweatshirt into his gym bag, stretches, and thinks about the homework he still has to complete before going to bed tonight, which will be around 2:00 A.M. if he gets home by 11:00. A few energy drinks and a protein bar will be needed to keep him awake to get his work done.

"I've got some extra drills we need to work on tonight," his coach says. "Can you stay another hour after you get your workout in?"

Evan hesitates. He has to finish a paper, and now he will need to stay up all night to get it done even though that will mean sleepwalking through his classes and maybe even his workout tomorrow.

"Sure, Coach," Evan says, and reassures himself that worrying about what he has to do won't make it any better.

Now, what do you think?

- If you needed to ensure you had the energy to complete all your goals, what would you do?
  a. Create a balance between what I want to accomplish and taking care of myself physically and emotionally
  b. Give up all but my most pressing goal so I can ensure I can complete it
  c. Use stimulants such as energy drinks and supplements to maintain high energy at all times

- How would you deal with the stress of college demands if you were struggling?
  a. Figure out a way to manage stress on my own
  b. Seek help for managing my stress in the healthiest way
  c. Admit to myself that I cannot do everything and decrease my obligations

Your Terms for success

when you see . . .	it means . . .
Acquaintance rape	See date rape
Active lifestyle	Maintaining regular exercise
Alcohol abuse	Using alcohol excessively or using it to the impairment of your senses
Balanced living	Finding balance in your personal, academic, and professional life that provides you with a sense of well-being
Date rape	Rape, or forced sexual contact, between two people who know each other or who are dating
Mental abuse	Harmful treatment of the mind or intellect
Mental health	The condition of one's mind or mental processes
Physical health	The condition of one's body
Sedentary	Sitting in one place, not active
Sleep deprivation	The act of not getting enough sleep

Spiritual health	The condition of one's religious or spiritual outlook on life
STIs	Sexually transmitted infections
Stress	A physical and psychological response to outside stimuli
Stress-related illness	An illness that is caused by the body's reaction to stress
Verbal abuse	Harmful treatment of someone through yelling, name-calling, or insults

Stress Is a Response to What's Happening in Your Life

Stress is a physical and psychological response to outside stimuli. In other words, just about anything that stimulates you can cause stress. Not all stress, however, is bad for you. For example, the stress you feel when you see someone get seriously hurt enables you to spring into action to help. For some students, the stress of an upcoming exam gives them the energy and focus to study. Without feeling a little stressed, these students might not feel the need to study at all.

How You Handle Stress Is What Matters

Resilience

Not everyone handles stress the same way, and what is a stressful situation for you may not be for someone else. How we handle stress depends on our genetic makeup, past experiences, and the stress-reducing techniques that we know and practice. There are ways to reduce stress or change our reaction, both physically and psychologically. First, though, it is important to be able to identify causes of stress. The list in Exhibit 5.1 is not exhaustive, but it can start you thinking about different ways that you experience stress.

Each of us has certain triggers, such as the ones listed in Exhibit 5.1, that stress us out. Usually, however, the same

> Stress is determined less by the cause and more by your response. A big part of GRIT is resilience, your capacity to respond to adverse or stressful events in ways that strengthen and improve you. Step 1: focus on your response. That's where your power lies.

EXHIBIT 5.1 Possible Causes of Stress

Self-doubt	Pressure to succeed (from yourself or others)
Fear of failure or the unknown	Speaking in public
Congested traffic	Lack of support—financial, physical, or psychological
Uncomfortable situations	The demands of a job, such as a promotion/demotion, deadlines, and evaluations
Life experiences, such as the death of a loved one, having a child, getting married, and moving	Too many activities, and not enough time to complete them
Waiting in lines	Computer problems

Resilience

Stress or adversity is when you predict or experience something bad happening to something or someone you care about. This explains why what's stressful to you may or may not be to someone else. It's all about how bad you think it will be and how much you care. The more important it is, and the worse it is, the more stressed you become—unless you create a resilient, gritty response.

situation doesn't stress us out the same way each time we are in it. Take waiting in line at the bank. One day, you might be extremely angry to be waiting 15 minutes in line to cash a check because you are late for a job interview. The next time that you are in the same line waiting the same amount of time, you may be calm and relaxed because you are enjoying a little quiet time to think while your mother waits in the car. Thus, it is not necessarily the situation or action that causes negative stress, but other factors that are involved.

When you are suffering from lack of sleep, you may be more likely to react negatively to people and situations that usually would not bother you. When you are feeling unsure of your ability to be successful in college, you may take constructive criticism as a personal attack. Being aware of times and situations that cause you the most stress is one step to helping manage stress better. If you realize that you are sensitive to others' feedback because you are feeling insecure, then you may be less likely to react negatively.

In Exhibit 5.2, place an "X" next to situations that are negatively stressful for you. Consider other situations or people that cause you to react negatively. The goal is to recognize a pattern of stress and then work to overcome it.

College Has Stressors of Its Own

Because you will find stress in college, at work, and at home, it is important to be able to identify the different stressors in each environment and work toward minimizing the negative stress in each area. Some weeks, you will have to contend with negative stress in only one area, but there will be times when it seems as though each part of your life is making you miserable. The more you understand what you can and cannot control, the more likely it is you will be able to work through stressful times and stay on track with your goals.

EXHIBIT 5.2 What Stresses You Out?

Situation	Stresses Me	Does Not Stress Me
Starting a big project		
Paying bills		
Being in a messy environment		
Receiving graded papers and exams		
Not getting enough sleep		
Taking a personal or professional risk		
Getting out of bed		
Not getting feedback on my work		
Being distracted by other people		
Thinking about the future		
Taking tests		

Stress in college is inevitable, but it doesn't have to be overwhelming if you know what you can do to minimize negative stress in the first place. There are several ways that students unknowingly cause themselves stress: failing to read the catalog and student handbook about course prerequisites and descriptions as well as degree program requirements; registering for more hours than they can handle; trying to do too much at work and home; missing deadlines; arriving late for class or appointments; and keeping the same social schedule despite increased academic demands.

The information in this chapter and others in this book should help you minimize your stress in college by providing you with information and strategies for accomplishing your goals. Even if you avoid the previous behaviors, you may still find that things don't go your way in college. If you realize that there will be times that you or others will make mistakes, then you will be more likely to bounce back from problems. Minimizing the negative effects of stress can include activities such as reading all information that you receive from the college; paying attention to flyers on doors, bulletin boards, and tables; and talking to your advisor, instructor, and counselor on a regular basis.

You will also want to regularly check the college's website for announcements and updates. Be sure, too, to read publications such as newspapers and newsletters that the college sends to the community. As always, ask questions when you are not sure of something and make an effort to get involved with campus organizations and clubs; people in these groups often know what is going on around campus.

© VLUE/SHUTTERSTOCK

■ We all sometimes feel overwhelmed by what we have to accomplish.

Your Home May Be a Source of Stress

Reducing stress at home will, no doubt, be the first step for minimizing your overall stress. Because your family and friends are likely to be your most important supporters, what they think of you and the demands they place on you will need to be discussed. Some family members may be unsure of what you are doing or worried that your school work will leave little time for them. Your friends may feel the same way, especially if they are used to hanging out with you after work and on the weekends. The key to minimizing stress at home is to communicate your needs. Talk to your loved ones about what you and they can expect when you are taking classes. Sometimes you'll need to have an honest conversation with your loved ones to explain that because of the demands of college, you won't be able to spend as much time with them as you used to. You may have to revisit your commitments and priorities and step away from some responsibilities that you can no longer manage. Most likely, the amount of free time that you enjoyed in high school will be far smaller in college.

GRIT
Resilience

More important than what you can or cannot control is the question, "What facets of this situation can I at least potentially influence?" Whenever you're stressed or stuck, ask yourself that question to get some immediate, positive, gritty traction.

Work May Also Be a Stressor

For some, stress on the job can be the most difficult to deal with because of the fear of performing poorly and being fired. Stress on the job can also be particularly tough to manage because you may feel uncomfortable confronting coworkers and being honest about your feelings.

Additionally, coworkers may be jealous of your success or they may misunderstand the arrangements you have made to work and go to school. You may also be concerned with completing your work tasks as well as your college assignments. The stress you feel on the job may make it seem overwhelming to balance both effectively.

Tenacity

> One way to take charge of your stress is to "enter the storm." Most people try to avoid or ignore stress. But some stressors or adversities are best handled by dealing with them now, head-on. Rather than worrying about a class, festering over a relationship or issue, or hating a professor, go right to the source and handle it in a constructive way. It beats losing more sleep!

Stress Can Lead to Illness

Stress can cause a variety of health-related problems, including sleep deprivation. Stress-related illnesses can vary from person to person, but by becoming knowledgeable about your stressors and practicing techniques for reducing stress, you can decrease the negative health effects. Although some of the following illnesses can be caused by other factors such as heredity and environment, they can be signs that stress is making you ill:

- Digestive problems including upset stomach, heartburn, constipation, diarrhea, and ulcers
- Severe headaches and migraines
- High blood pressure, heart attack, and stroke
- Muscle and joint pain
- Cold, flu, respiratory, and sinus infections

It's in the
syllabus

> Use your syllabus to determine what you will need to be aware of during the semester so that you can better manage your stress.
>
> - What parts of your professors' syllabi will cause you the most stress in terms of meeting the expectations?
> - What will be easiest for you to meet?
> - If you find yourself overwhelmed or confused by the expectations in your courses, what can you do to help eliminate your stress?

Eating well, exercising, and getting adequate sleep are all ways to stay healthy and help prevent stress-related illnesses. Be careful, especially at stressful times such as the beginning and end of the semester, that you do not neglect both your physical and mental health and make yourself more susceptible to stress-related illnesses that could keep you from doing well in college. It's common for college students to disrupt their daily sleep and exercise routine during finals week and other intense periods of academic activities, but the reality is that it's even more important to maintain healthy exercise and nutritional habits during these times because they will help you perform better.

You Can Manage Your Stress

No doubt you have felt stress since enrolling in college. You wouldn't be human if you didn't at least worry at the beginning of the semester how you will manage it all—family, work, college, and a personal life. Stress is normal, but for college students it can seriously derail them from achieving their goals if they cannot manage it successfully. Looking for ways to minimize—not eliminate, because you can't—stress and maximize balance in your life will make your college experience more enjoyable and successful.

Disarm the Negative Effects of Stress

Because you cannot eliminate all stress, you will need to develop methods for reducing the negative effects that your body and mind experience when they are stressed out. One of the quickest, easiest ways to reduce the negative effects of stress is to take a deep breath. You may have even told someone who was upset to breathe deeply in order to calm down. The breath is, as many cultures have known for thousands of years, an important part of life; in yoga, the ability to control the breath is essential to controlling the mind and body.

GRIT GAINER™

EXERCISE YOUR GRIT   Most students do exactly the opposite of what they should do when it comes to stress. They abuse their bodies with junk food, no exercise, poor sleep, and extra caffeine, or worse, right at the time when their bodies crave resilience. Take charge of your stress—funnel it like fuel. Use it to enhance your workouts and focus your mind. Own your stress. Eat healthier than ever, make sleep sacred, and pause for laughter and fun, so you can attack your stress with fresh energy.

Visualization is another method for reducing the effect that stress has on the mind and body. In order to visualize a more relaxed time and place, all you need to do is to find a quiet, comfortable spot, sit down, and close your eyes. Relaxation experts suggest that you visualize a place that makes you feel warm and relaxed. Many people think about a beach because the mood there is often relaxed and the sound of the ocean is comforting. You will need to find your own special place.

Once you decide where you want to go mentally, you should start noticing the details in your place. If you are at the beach, then you should feel the sunshine's heat. Next, listen to the waves crashing on the surf and smell the salty air. Depending on how long you need to visualize this special place, you may want to stick your toe in the water or lie down on the beach and soak up the rays—leave your stress in those designated beach trash cans. The goal in this method of relaxation is to stay there as long as you need to; when you mentally return to your present location, you should feel refreshed and renewed.

Sometimes physical activity can be a better stress reliever than mental exercises. Getting outside or to the gym to work out your frustrations is an excellent way of maintaining your health. By exercising, you can eliminate the physical side effects of stress while you take your mind off your troubles. If you do not usually exercise, take it slowly. Start with a 15-minute walk around the block or do some simple stretching exercises on the floor. Overdoing exercise can lead to more stress, so start small and increase the time you spend getting your blood circulating as you get stronger.

If you happen to exercise too much, you can look toward massage therapy to reduce your stress. Although it is a little less conventional than other methods of reducing stress, a massage can improve circulation and alleviate muscle soreness. You can seek professional massage therapy or ask a family member to rub your neck, shoulders, or feet. Massage therapy can give you the rejuvenation you need to tackle the rest of the week.

You have heard the cliché that "Laughter is the best medicine," and it is also an ideal way to eliminate stress. Have you ever been in a very stressful situation when someone made you laugh and you thought, "Boy, I needed that"? You probably felt all the tension melt away as you doubled over giggling. Surrounding yourself with people who make you laugh is one way to keep stress at a minimum. Other ways include renting comedies or reading funny books. Of course, good, old-fashioned acting silly can relieve stress and anxiety as well.

G R I T
Growth

Take a fresh approach to stress. Ask yourself, "What can I do in the next 30 seconds (or 30 minutes) to significantly reduce the downsides of my stress and put me in a grittier mindset?" Confront your stress rather than becoming its victim.

■ Find time to incorporate fun activities to help you manage your stress.

© RICHARD GREEN/ALAMY

Last, you can comfort yourself with familiar favorites to eliminate the negative effects of stress. A special meal or a visit with your best friend can put you at ease. Looking at old photographs, reminiscing about family trips, and watching your favorite movies can be great stress relievers. If you have enrolled in college in a new town or you have moved out on your own for the first time, you may find comfort in the familiar, whether it be an old pillow or a favorite movie. Make sure, though, that your methods of reducing negative stress are healthy. Drugs and alcohol may temporarily relieve stress, but they cause more problems in the long run.

Reducing negative stress that you experience on the job, at home, and in college will be easier if the lines of communication are open and you are committed to explaining what is stressing you out. On the job, you may want to talk to your supervisor (rather than coworkers, unless they can truly help) about what is causing you stress and how you can manage it. You may find that your boss can reassure you that you are supported as you juggle both work and college. At home, you may want to talk with your family members about what stresses you out and why. Explain that your college career is temporary and that adjustments that need to be made at home will most likely be temporary until you complete your degree. If you are experiencing stress in college, speaking with the professor or a counselor can help you reduce the negative effects of stress. Remember that the people who work at a university were students, too, and may have some good tips that helped them minimize stress when they were in college.

Instinct

Chances are you know people who deal with stress better than others. Ask yourself, "How would the grittiest, most resilient person I know deal with this situation?" Then give it a try!

Flexibility Can Help Minimize Stress

An important method of managing stress is to remain flexible. If you try to control too many aspects of your life, you will quickly discover you can't do it all. Although it is important to manage your time and mark your progress toward your goals, you still need to plan for the unexpected and be willing to make adjustments. Good time managers plan for problems by keeping their schedules loose enough to make room for adjustments. For example, if you have a doctor's appointment at 2:00, you shouldn't schedule a job interview at 3:00. Delays in the doctor's office or traffic problems could keep you from your 3:00 appointment and cause more stress. Instead, you should give yourself plenty of time in between scheduled tasks, especially if you will have to rely on others' time management skills. The idea is to build some margin in your life so you have a buffer to absorb the so-called "unexpected" events in our lives that we can actually expect. This margin can be in the form of time—giving yourself time to handle a traffic jam or a full parking lot to make it to class—or money—setting aside some money each

integrity matters

Have you ever promised someone that you would do something, only to break your promise? No matter why we break promises, the end result always causes us some stress in our lives because such actions, or inactions, can damage our relationships with others.

One way to eliminate stress and anxiety is to make integrity a top priority in your life. Only promise what you know you can deliver. Your negative stress will decrease when you maintain your integrity.

YOUR TURN

In 250 words, describe a time when you have let someone down by not delivering on a promise. Discuss how you felt about not honoring your word and how your relationship changed afterwards.

GRIT GAINER™

GIVE A SHOT OF GRIT   When an unexpected stress hits, immediately limit its negative impact by asking yourself, "How can I minimize the downside of this stress as quickly as possible?" A small dose of GRIT can contain a big dose of stress.

month for an emergency fund to cover the flat tires, lost books, and parking tickets that always seem to come out of nowhere. You can also build margin in your relationships by having some candid conversations with your friends, roommates, and loved ones about how you'll need their help and understanding when you're facing a lot of stress in your life. Simply forewarning your roommates that you have a challenging comprehensive exam next week can help them anticipate and effectively manage the situation if you seem more irritable or impatient than usual.

Seek Help for Your Stress If It Becomes Overwhelming

If you ever feel as though you cannot cope with the amount of work and responsibility that you have—despite attempts to reduce your stress—seek professional help. Excessive crying, difficulty breathing, inability to get out of bed, and suicidal thoughts are severe reactions to stress. Knowing when to reach out to other people will be crucial in your recovery.

When asking for help, find someone you trust and who will be objective about your experiences. Sometimes, close friends and family members can be your best allies to combat stress, but other times an outside party who will listen to what you have to say without judging can be extremely helpful. When you talk to someone, be honest about what you are feeling. Don't try to minimize any fear or anxiety. The more the person knows about what you are experiencing, the better able he or she will be to help. Most universities have professional counselors with whom you can meet to share your experiences. Check with your health center or student affairs office if you can't locate information on the college website.

Your Physical Health Matters a Lot in College

Think about this scenario: You have just bought a brand-new car and you are about to drive it off the lot. Before you do, the salesperson provides you with an owner's manual and begins to tell you how often you will need to fill the tank, replace the oil, check the brakes, and rotate the tires. You tell the salesperson you don't need to know any of that stuff, and you drive the car off the lot. Besides, you know that the car needs to be filled up whenever the light on the dashboard comes on. What else is there to know?

For those who own and drive cars, you can imagine what will happen next. One day, maybe in a few months or a few years, you will find the car stops working regularly or stops working at all. In some cases, the repairs are minimal; in other cases, major repairs must be made to get the car into shape. The costs could be astronomical, so much so that you find yourself without a car and without hope for getting another one any time soon.

Now, consider that the car is your body. You know when you are hungry and when you are tired, when you feel happy and when you are stressed, but do you know how to take care of yourself? Maybe you do know that exercising will improve your health and help you manage your stress, but you won't make the time to include fitness as a part of your weekly routine. Just as

G R I T
Resilience

Resilience is more than a mindset. You need physical, mental, emotional, and spiritual resilience to really grow your GRIT. Sacrificing your health to engage your mind is a short-term strategy at best, and a weak one, no matter what. Do the opposite. Engage your body to strengthen your mind, emotions, and spirit.

a car may drive well for a while without regularly scheduled maintenance, there will come a day that the neglect will keep it from running properly or at all.

Learning to take care of your physical and mental health is crucial to getting where you want to go. To continue the car analogy, you won't be arriving at your destination if the vehicle is not in proper working order. One of the benefits of higher education is that you learn to make better choices, and that includes making better choices about your health. You can do that by understanding what you can control and how to get information to stay physically and mentally healthy.

Nutrition Gives You Fuel

One key to living a healthy life is making it a priority to eat nutritious food. Getting the recommended daily allowances of fruits, vegetables, whole grains, proteins, and fats is a common-sense approach to healthy eating, but as a society, we are choosing less healthy foods that are quick and easy—and loaded with calories, fat, salt, and sugar. Some of the reasons for poor nutritional choices include lack of time, information, and access to healthy alternatives. Increased stress is another reason that students make poor food choices; they may choose comfort food over nutritious alternatives.

To make healthier choices, arm yourself with information. As with any aspect of your health, the more you know, the better choices you can make. Learn what healthy foods are and seek them out. Read about and pay attention to serving sizes; too much of even a healthy food can add unneeded calories and contribute to weight gain. Read and learn to interpret food labels and ingredient lists that provide information about what is in the food and how much of it represents recommended daily values. The U.S. Food and Drug Administration (2014) provides detailed information on their webpage "How to Understand and Use the Nutrition Facts Label" (www.fda .gov/food/ingredientspackaginglabeling/labelingnutrition/ ucm274593.htm). It provides helpful information about what percentages of fat, sodium, and sugars you should limit.

© UWIMAGES/FOTOLIA

■ Making good food choices is the foundation for overall good health.

Another way of getting nutritional information is to talk with a physician or a nutritionist to get a better idea of what kinds of food will be best for you to consume. Regular doctor visits will determine if you have any potential health risks, such as high blood pressure or diabetes, which will make your food decisions even more crucial to good health. Keeping chronic illnesses in check with monitoring and medication will not only help you feel better, but it will also keep you healthy for the long term.

Eating healthy means eating regularly. Most experts recommend eating smaller meals more frequently rather than heavy meals five to seven hours apart. At the very least, start the day with a healthy breakfast, even if you don't have enough time to sit down and eat a full meal. You will feel more alert and energized throughout the early morning. However, what you eat for breakfast is just as important as eating something. Powdered doughnuts and a sugary, caffeinated soda will not provide you with the nutrients you need to be at your best. A piece of fruit and a cup of yogurt would be a better choice if you have to eat on the run. In addition to smaller, frequent nutritious meals, drinking plenty of water throughout the day has numerous health benefits, including regulating body temperature and assisting digestion. You should also consider drinking juices to get more nutrients.

G R I T
Resilience

Think of food as your climbing fuel, what you use to propel yourself forward and up along your ascent toward your goals. Would you put polluted fuel in your car, especially when it really needs to perform? Go for high-octane foods that optimize your focus and energy.

Avoiding fad diets is another strategy for staying healthy. Although they may promise increased energy and weight loss, the results may be short-lived and potentially harmful. A better approach to eating healthy is to stick to the recommended guidelines from the Food and Drug Administration or a health expert. Be aware, too, of the potential for eating disorders such as anorexia and bulimia. Anorexia, a condition in which people strictly control how much food they eat, and bulimia, a condition in which people cycle between overeating (binge eating) and purging (through vomiting or abusing laxatives), are two eating disorders that can cause serious physical and psychological harm. Students who suffer from anorexia or bulimia, or believe they do, should see a health professional as soon as possible. The website National-EatingDisorders.org provides definitions of eating disorders as well as a helpline for those who need to talk to an expert.

Why should you be concerned about what you eat and how much? One benefit of eating healthy is that it improves your body's functions. You may find that eating better improves your ability to sleep or reduces the fatigue you feel by the end of the day. Eating well also improves your mental abilities. Studies have shown that eating certain foods, such as fish, can improve your test-taking abilities. Finally, healthy eating and avoiding overeating help keep stress under control, which in turn keeps stress-related illnesses at a minimum. See Exhibit 5.3 for ideas for eating healthy in college.

Exercise Gives You Energy and Relieves Stress

We all know that making good choices about nutrition and exercise is part of a healthy lifestyle, but busy students often find it difficult to squeeze in time to work out. Take into consideration that as a student, you will spend many hours sitting down studying or working on the computer. Even if you have had a regular exercise routine, you may find that you have to make studying a higher priority.

Because you may have less time for exercise, it will be even more important that you find time to include some exercise in your busy schedule. At the very least, getting regular exercise will help you relieve stress.

G R I T
Tenacity

Health clubs make their money off broken promises. They count on the majority of people who pay to sign up not showing up. It takes tenacity to stick to your promises and build your health. Think of yourself as an academic athlete, conditioning for the mountainous marathon required to get through, get out, and get paid.

EXHIBIT 5.3   Tips for Healthy Eating in College

Find and read reliable information about health issues.

Eat consciously and take time to appreciate the nourishment you are receiving from healthy foods.

Plan your meals *and* snacks ahead of time so that you are not susceptible to last-minute, poor choices.

Take bottled water in your backpack, and drink it throughout the day.

Take healthy snacks with you to eat between classes to avoid making unhealthy choices at the vending machines, or at the student union.

Pay attention to serving sizes, and eat what you need to stay healthy, not the amount that you want to eat.

Make wise choices at vending machines by avoiding food that is high in fat, caffeine, sugar, and salt content.

Make any changes gradually; think long-term health, not short-term results.

Regular exercise can lower blood pressure, increase your metabolism, improve muscle tone, and lessen your chances of suffering diseases that are directly related to a sedentary lifestyle. It can also improve your mood and your self-confidence. Experts vary on how much exercise is ideal, but most agree 30 minutes of sustained activity three or four times a week will provide you with health benefits.

If you have trouble getting started or staying in an exercise routine, consider setting fitness goals that are reasonable and achievable. Reward yourself whenever you meet your goals, and don't get discouraged if you fall short now and then. Exercising regularly should be a lifestyle, not a short-term activity, so think of your progress as part of a long-term plan to live better. As with any exercise program, see a doctor before you begin and start gradually if you are not usually physically active.

Some students feel like it's not worth the time to work out if they can't be in the gym for an hour or more. Once their schedules get busy, especially during midterms and finals, those one- and two-hour time slots quickly disappear. The truth is that even if you only have 20 minutes, you can engage in a worthwhile physical activity that can improve your health and relieve stress. You can also do interval training, such as incorporating short bursts of running into your walking. Varying your workout activities, length of time, and intensity will keep boredom at bay and help you keep it up. Exhibit 5.4 provides tips for including exercise into your daily college routine.

Sleep Recharges Your Batteries

Getting an adequate amount of sleep each night is as important to maintaining good health as what you eat and how often you exercise, but most Americans, especially college students, do not get enough sleep to maintain their health. Experts say that adults should get seven to nine hours of sleep a night to function normally throughout the day, but millions regularly get six hours or less. While you are in college, you may believe that six hours a night sounds like a luxury. For sure, there will be times that, because of circumstances, you will not be able to get enough sleep, but those times should be few and far between. Maintaining a regular schedule of going to bed and getting up will help you get the amount of sleep you need. Despite the myth of what college life is like, pulling all-nighters to study for tests or complete assignments is strongly discouraged, because it will make you less likely to perform well the next day.

For some students, the idea of keeping a regular sleeping and waking schedule seems impossible because of other factors that limit their ability to sleep. The reasons for many students' sleep deprivation are varied, but include health problems such as breathing obstructions and stress. If you believe your lack of sleep is the result of medical problems, consider seeing

---

EXHIBIT 5.4   **Tips for Exercising in College**

Take a physical education class at your college.

Use the exercise facilities and equipment on your campus.

Take advantage of walking trails or paved walkways on your campus.

Park farther away from the buildings and get extra steps in.

Join a gym and go regularly.

Ask a friend to exercise with you.

Incorporate short sessions of exercise into your studying routine by taking walking or stretching breaks in between reading or writing papers.

Learn how to play a new sport, or investigate a new form of exercise.

the unwritten rules
of Managing Stress and Health

- **Everyone in college is under some kind of stress; each person just handles it differently.** Students tend to think only about the stress they face, but the professors, staff members, and administrators on campus are also trying to manage stress. Everyone on campus has a shared responsibility to help each other manage stress and to try to avoid contributing to the stress that others experience.

- **Your choice of peers will dramatically affect how stressful your life is and how well you manage stress.** Face it—some people just seem to create more drama and stress than others. It might be funny and entertaining for a while, but after time it can wear on you and actually draw you into the stress. Steer clear of "drama queens" and "drama kings" and spend time with people who have healthy outlets for stress through laughing, exercising, and engaging in healthy and enjoyable recreational activities.

- **Maintaining good physical health in college requires more discipline than your earlier years.** You won't always feel like exercising, so there are times when you will have to just gut it out and go to the gym. You'll also be tempted to eat sugary snacks and drink sodas instead of a nutritious meal and a healthy beverage, but it's a matter of making good choices more often than you make poor ones. The reality is that your body becomes less forgiving of your poor choices as you get older.

- **We need to help each other.** If you see a friend or classmate clearly struggling, reach out to him or her and support the person's efforts to get the help he or she needs. You don't have to be a counselor, just encourage and help the person get an appointment with a counselor. Wouldn't you want someone to do the same for you?

a health care professional. For stress-related sleep problems, practicing the stress-relieving strategies discussed earlier will help alleviate the symptoms; however, if you find that relaxation techniques do not improve your ability to sleep well, then consider seeing a general practitioner or mental health professional.

What you put into your body can affect your sleeping habits. Eating high-fat and high-sugar foods near bedtime can slow you down, even if they seem to speed you up at first. Good sleep can also elude you if you consume alcohol and caffeine—even in small amounts—close to the time that you go to bed. Drugs, including medications for common illnesses, can deprive you of sleep or make you feel sluggish after you take them. Avoid consuming food, drink, or medications that overstimulate you right before bedtime. Never abuse prescription or over-the-counter medication, or illegal drugs to stay awake.

In addition to what you put into your body, what you do to it will affect your ability to get a good night's rest. Exercising too close to your bedtime will make it harder to fall asleep. However, too little physical exertion during the day can also contribute to difficulty falling and staying asleep. Experts suggest exercising early in the day—an activity as easy as walking for 30 minutes will suffice—in order to sleep more productively at night. Regular exercise will also help you alleviate the negative

GRIT
Tenacity

Lack of sleep saps your energy, effort, and GRIT. One of the secrets of high performers is that, no matter how busy they are, they make sleep sacred. Be tenacious about getting good quality rest, so you can refuel your GRIT and your momentum.

effects of stress. If you find, though, that you cannot "shut off" your mind because thoughts overwhelm you, consider writing down your worries—anything you may stay up thinking about after the light is off—in a journal, which will help you unwind and put away your day's thoughts.

Because sleep deprivation can contribute to irritability, depression, and physical health problems, it is important to make getting enough sleep a priority throughout the semester. If you have difficulty sticking to a regular sleep schedule, treat it like any other goal and write down what you want to do. Make it easier to achieve your goal by keeping your bed and bedroom free of clutter and by avoiding using your bed as a place to do homework or watch television. In other words, creating a sanctuary in your bedroom, a place where you can truly relax, may alleviate stress and anxiety that contribute to sleeplessness. Finally, avoid taking naps during the day, even on weekends, because they can throw off your sleep schedule. If you have an irregular schedule because of working different hours each day of the week, find a system that is relatively regular and that works for you. You may have to be creative about how you get enough sleep each evening or day.

The bottom line is that sleep deprivation can be dangerous. How little sleep you get should not be a medal of honor that demonstrates how much you work or how dedicated you are to meeting your goals. Getting enough sleep is a necessary part of living well, enjoying what you *do* accomplish, and being enjoyable to be around when you are awake.

Drugs and Alcohol Can Quickly Derail Your Health and Life

There are some habits that we know are potentially hazardous to our health, and yet some people still do them. Smoking and using tobacco products, taking drugs, and consuming too much alcohol are known risks, but college students sometimes pick up these poor health habits because of peer pressure, a desire to fit in, and a need to find a way to relax or escape.

According to the American Heart Association (2008), about a quarter of Americans smoke, and people with the least education (9–11 years in school) are more likely to smoke than people with more education (more than 16 years in school). Smoking or chewing tobacco carries with it increased risks of heart disease, stroke, high blood pressure, cancer, and emphysema. The more educated you become about the health risks that are associated with smoking and using smokeless tobacco, the more it will be obvious that using tobacco products can cause serious health consequences. There are a variety of methods for quitting. It is worth investigating what your college and community offer if you are a smoker or a user of smokeless tobacco. Your college may provide information, support groups, or physician referrals for students who want to quit.

Alcohol and drugs are two other health issues that affect college students—sometimes even before they get to college. Having parents, partners, or friends who have abused drugs or alcohol is one way students can be affected. They may feel that they have to take care of others who drink too much or take drugs, which can take a toll on their time and emotional well-being. Students may also suffer from abusing drugs and alcohol while in college—and the effects can be far-reaching. According to the website CollegeDrinkingPrevention.gov, a quarter of college students claim that they have had negative academic consequences because of alcohol use.

Being drunk or high can have grave consequences, the least of which is that you will do something you later regret. You increase your risk of having an unwanted sexual experience and causing physical harm to yourself and others. Death from overdosing on drugs and alcohol can happen even for those who are first-time users. Whether they are consumed for recreational purposes or because of other, more serious health reasons, abusing drugs and alcohol should not be a part of your college career

GRIT
Resilience

Drugs and alcohol are used to avoid adversity and stress, rather than deal with it. The stronger your GRIT, the less you need or even want drugs, excess alcohol, or any escapes. Instead, use life's daily stressors as fuel to stay challenged and engaged.

EXHIBIT 5.5   **Tips for Avoiding Drugs and Alcohol in College**

Educate yourself about the effects of abusing drugs and alcohol.

Cultivate relationships with people who have healthy habits.

Avoid situations in which you know drugs and alcohol will be present.

Take walking breaks instead of smoking breaks.

Find other ways to relax that are healthy, free, and legal.

Talk with a counselor or health care professional if you feel you are about to make a poor decision regarding the use of drugs and alcohol.

Appeal to your vanity, if all else fails: Drugs, alcohol, and tobacco make you look and smell bad.

---

because you will find it difficult to reach your educational and personal goals. See Exhibit 5.5 for ways you can avoid drugs and alcohol while you are in college.

In addition to abusing alcohol and illegal substances, using medications for purposes other than for what they were prescribed can have grave consequences, including death. Excessive use of medications that contain amphetamines and narcotics may seem like a good idea if you have trouble staying awake or going to sleep, but using them for a longer period than they have been prescribed can lead to dependency.

Yes, We Do Need to Talk About Sex

A discussion of health issues would not be complete without talking about sexual health. Most colleges and universities strive to educate their students, especially those who are recently out of high school, about sexual responsibility, sexual assault, and common sexually transmitted infections (STIs). Many experts and college officials have been alarmed at the recent statistics that show 73 percent of students report having unprotected sex while they are in college. More disturbing is that 68 percent of those having unprotected sex do not consider themselves at risk (Gately, 2003). This last statistic points to a major reason why students, despite sex education in high school or elsewhere, continue to engage in risky sexual behavior. Because most STIs lack immediate visible or physiological symptoms, students who are at risk for contracting a sexually transmitted disease rarely ask to be screened for signs of infection.

Risky behavior, which includes having sex with multiple partners and having unprotected sex, opens the door to possible infections and illnesses such as chlamydia, gonorrhea, genital herpes, HIV, and AIDS (see Exhibit 5.6). Some diseases can be transmitted in ways other than sexual intercourse. Hepatitis B and C are both diseases that can be contracted through shared razors, toothbrushes, body piercing, and tattooing.

If you are sexually active, it is important to be screened regularly for STIs even if you do not have symptoms. Your long-term health and the health of those you come in contact with are at risk if you do not. As with any health issue, educate yourself with the facts about risk factors and symptoms. Then, monitor your behavior, practice safe sex, and see a doctor regularly to maintain good health.

Sexual assaults in the university environment are a troubling phenomenon that you shouldn't ignore. Some of the most common incidents of sexual assault are related to excessive consumption of alcohol and date rapes. The Rape, Abuse, and Incest National Network (RAINN) provides numerous resources that students can use to educate themselves about the risks, consequences, and preventative actions. Some important tips for reducing your chances

EXHIBIT 5.6 Common Sexually Transmitted Infections

STD	Symptoms	Treatment
HIV and AIDS	May have no symptoms; extreme fatigue, rapid weight loss	No cure, but prescribed medication can keep the virus from replicating
Chlamydia	May have no symptoms; abnormal discharge, burning during urination	Antibiotics
Genital herpes	May have no symptoms; itching, burning, bumps in the genital area	No cure, but prescribed medication can help treat outbreaks
Gonorrhea	Pain or burning during urination; yellowish or bloody discharge; men may have no symptoms	Antibiotics
Hepatitis B	Headache, muscle ache, fatigue, low-grade fever, skin and whites of eyes with yellowish tint	No cure, but prescribed medication can help guard against liver damage

of being involved in such a tragedy and for helping others avoid risky situations include the following:

- Be aware of your surroundings at all times. This means taking out earphones and avoiding talking on your phone when walking as well as paying attention to where you are hanging out and who is there.
- Walk tall. Act confident and self-assured when you are moving from one place to another. RAINN calls it "walk[ing] with a purpose."
- Listen to your "little voice." If you feel uncomfortable in a situation or environment, remove yourself. You often know best when something is not right.

Instinct

A vital part of GRIT is listening to and honoring your instincts about what is right, good, smart, and healthy, and what is ultimately damaging, especially in the face of temptation. Be clear, strong, and unwavering on your most important goals, and be unwilling to do anything that can compromise your ability to get there.

One particular type of unhealthy relationship that occurs most frequently among traditional college students is date or acquaintance rape. Simply defined, date rape is a forced sexual act in which one party does not actively consent; often, the two people involved are not complete strangers—hence the terms "date rape" and "acquaintance rape." Both men and women can be victims of date rape, although women are more often victims. Alcohol or a "date rape drug" such as Rohypnol may be involved in the incident. Many experts warn college-age women and men about the risk factors for date rape and encourage them to get to know whom they are going out with, not getting intoxicated, making sure their food or drinks are not handled by others, and communicating loud and clear if they find themselves in an uncomfortable situation.

Depression and Suicide Are Sad, but Real, Occurrences in College

The pressures to succeed and juggle multiple priorities can lead to negative stress and feelings of being overwhelmed. Many times, feeling a little stressed during the semester is normal, but there are times that students can feel as though they are in over their heads with no hope of getting out. It is no wonder that one of the most common mental health issues on college campus is depression.

GRIT GAINER™

GRIT BUILDS HEALTH GRIT fuels health, and health fuels GRIT. Being a gritty student means making the right but often tough choices, and sacrificing short-term pleasures for your long-term goals. One way to really build your GRIT is to commit to and stay true to the right and best path forward.

Problems with depression often start before students enroll in college. Signs of depression include loss of pleasure in activities, feelings of hopelessness, inability to get out of bed, increased use of alcohol or drugs, changes in appetite or weight gain or loss, changes in sleep patterns (sleeping too little or too much), extreme sensitivity, excessive crying, lack of energy or interest in participating in activities, and lack of interest in taking care of oneself.

Suicide is another mental health issue that is associated with depression. With the startling statistic that 25 percent of college students have contemplated suicide, it is no wonder that college health and counseling centers strive to educate students about the signs of severe depression and potential suicide attempts. Thoughts of ending your life should always be taken seriously and you should seek help immediately. Call a college counselor, an advisor, a hospital emergency room, or 911 if you are thinking about committing suicide. If one of your friends or roommates exhibits any behaviors or says anything that implies suicidal thoughts, do everything you can to put the person in contact with professionals on campus or at the local hospital who can help.

Healthy Living Is a Choice You Make for Life

There is more to life than just eating well and exercising. Healthy living is a practice that involves all parts of your well-being: physical, mental, and spiritual.

A Balanced Life Is a Healthy Life

Living a balanced life means paying attention to and improving all areas of your life—from relationships to cardiovascular health to your inner peace. If one area is overdeveloped, then the other areas will suffer from the lack of balance. There will be times that you will need to put in more hours at work and school, throwing the balance off slightly, but be careful that you make some time for the other areas that have been neglected.

A great way to stay balanced is to strive to create relationships with people on campus. Having healthy relationships with professors, advisors, and classmates will not only enable you to stay connected with your college work, but it will also provide you a personal support network in case you feel as though you need help with the stresses of being in college.

Balancing your life to eliminate stress also entails evaluating your values and priorities whenever you begin to feel stressed. You can then identify areas in your life that are getting out of balance and put those areas higher up on your list of priorities. For example, if you value exercise and are stressed because you realize that you have been spending most of your time at work or at school, you can make working out a higher priority, creating better balance in your life.

Relationships Affect Your Health

Maintaining healthy relationships is as much a part of your good health as eating nutritious foods and exercising, but there are some issues that are signs of unhealthy, even dangerous, relationships. One type of unhealthy relationship issue is abuse: physical, mental, verbal, and sexual. Being in a relationship with someone who is abusive is not healthy. Although the previous statement seems like common sense, take time to think about it. No one deserves to be hit, controlled, or humiliated, *ever.*

Although we know that someone who makes us feel bad physically or emotionally can prevent us from being our best, studies find that abused men and women find it difficult to get out of abusive relationships. One reason people stay with abusive partners is that the abusers are—at first—charming, attentive, and loving. Usually, abusers begin to show subtle signs that something is not right; they may be extremely jealous, verbally insulting, and focused on your every move. Victims may also be dependent financially or emotionally on their abusers, which makes eliminating their influence difficult at best.

Maintaining a healthy relationship takes time and energy, but there are many ways to make sure your relationships are positive experiences. For example, get to know people well before spending time alone with them. Learn to communicate your wants and needs effectively. Say "no" loud and clear when you do not want something to happen. Watch for signs of abusive and controlling people; sometimes, people show you signs of their true selves in smaller, subtler ways early in a relationship. If a situation makes you uncomfortable, get out of it immediately. Last but not least, do not abuse alcohol and drugs, which can impair your ability to judge situations. If you feel as though you have no options in removing yourself from an abusive relationship, seek professional help.

For most of your relationships, communication will be the key to balance and satisfaction. Whether it is your family, friends, roommates, or significant others, you will want to be an advocate for your own feelings and needs and to express them in a respectful manner. Learning to listen actively and critically will also help you strengthen relationships as you will be able to hear what others need. Good, solid relationships are built on honesty, communication, and a healthy respect for others' physical and emotional well-being.

◾ Incorporating regular exercise into your routine will help you alleviate some of the negative effects of stress.

© TYLER OLSON/SHUTTERSTOCK

Getting Help When You Need It

An important part of making good choices and staying healthy is to get regular checkups and to see a health professional whenever you experience pain, difficulty, or even uncertainty about a health issue. Your college may provide access to a health clinic or health fairs. Free screenings, health seminars, and dispensing of over-the-counter medications are possible services that your college clinic may offer. Take advantage of these types of services, such as blood pressure checks or information about handling diabetes, because they may provide you with life-improving or life-saving information. If your college provides only limited access to health services, then you will need to find other ways to monitor your health. Regular checkups are part of taking care of yourself both in the short term and the long term.

GRIT GAINER™

GET THE GRIT GANG TOGETHER One way to protect and grow your GRIT is to deliberately seek out and surround yourself with gritty people. Spend less time with those who implode when stress strikes and more time with those who rise up and are at their best in the face of adversity. Pick your own GRIT gang.

4 things future professionals need to know about stress

stress will be a
lifetime companion

Although the sources of your stress might change, you'll face some form of stress throughout your life. The skills and techniques you develop in college for managing stress effectively will establish habits that you'll use well beyond college. If you develop unhealthy coping mechanisms for dealing with stress, the consequences of those behaviors will become more severe later in life, so it's crucial that you establish effective habits now.

stress is an
outstanding differentiator

Stressful situations are like truth serum—they reveal someone's deepest feelings and fears. If you can be the person who manages stress effectively while others around you are having a meltdown, you're going to differentiate yourself in a positive way. Your peers will see it, your professors will see it, and eventually your employer will see it. And it will pay off.

journaling is a great way to
identify predictors of stress

If you develop a habit of keeping a daily journal, you'll be able to look back on your journal entries and see the events and circumstances that preceded the most stressful periods of your life. This observation can help you anticipate when stress is coming your way. For example, your journal might chronicle some periods of time when you were in conflict with others, and then a week later your journal might show that you caught a cold or the flu, which led you to miss class, which led you to perform poorly on an exam. As you look back on the chain of events, you'll realize that you might have been able to avoid some of the stress by proactively managing difficult circumstances or conflict when they first emerged.

employee health has become a
big deal to employers

With the trends in health care, including the high costs associated with obesity, substance abuse, and depression, employers recognize the importance of supporting their employees' health. Demonstrating a healthy lifestyle, including effective stress management skills, will make you more attractive to potential employers.

THE G R I T ADVANTAGE

Upgrade your overall GRIT and your CORE Response to any stress by asking one of these CORE Questions™:

Control: What are the facets of the situation I can potentially influence?

Ownership: How can I step up to improve this situation as quickly as possible?

Reach: What can I do to minimize the potential downside and maximize the potential upside of this situation?

Endurance: How can I get past this stressful situation as quickly as possible?

HOW GRITTY ARE YOU?

Now that you've completed this chapter, how committed are you to:

1. Owning your health, resilience, and how you respond to stressful events?

Zero Commitment 0 ——————————————————————— 10 Fully Committed

2. Digging deep and doing what it takes to remain healthy and strong?

Zero Commitment 0 ——————————————————————— 10 Fully Committed

3. Using your stress to motivate you to greater things?

Zero Commitment 0 ——————————————————————— 10 Fully Committed

6 Learning, Memory, and Thinking

Chapter goals to help you *get in, get through, get out, and get paid:*

The college experience is, above all, about learning. In college, you learn about yourself, others, the world around you, and about specific disciplines that relate to your major. At this point, you may think of yourself as an effective learner, or you may have some doubts about your ability to learn. Regardless of your starting point, this chapter will help you improve your ability to learn, and, in turn, complete your classes, finish your degree, and start a great career.

To meet those goals, this chapter will help you:

- Progress through the stages of learning to achieve mastery of a skill
- Develop strategies that support active learning
- Use mnemonic devices to improve your memory
- Identify different types of thinking
- Describe techniques for both creative and analytical thinking
- Use **GRIT** to solve problems better and faster

MyStudentSuccessLab™

Log in to MyStudentSuccessLab.com to deepen your **GRIT** mindset and build the skills you'll need to get through the college experience.

Michael's Story

© MONKEY BUSINESS IMAGES/SHUTTERSTOCK

Michael can hike 12 miles in a hot sandstorm with 30 pounds of equipment on his back. What Michael can't do, he believes, is understand algebra.

Inside the student center, Michael sits back down on a chair and he opens his math notebook.

"The order of operations is F-O-I-L: first, outer, inner, last. But after that, I don't know what to do," he thinks to himself.

If his professor would just slow down and allow students to get it before moving on to the next unit, he wouldn't feel so stressed.

"Isn't teaching me algebra *his* job, not a tutor's?" Michael asks.

Michael finds it difficult to seek help on his own. By the time he got to high school, he was able to slide by, and in the military his superiors ordered everything he did.

Before he decides to leave, his girlfriend Michelle calls him.

"Michael, do you remember when I struggled through biology? I wanted to be a nurse so much, but I struggled," she says.

"Yeah, I do. I remember helping you study before tests."

"Do you remember how much better I did after I went to the tutoring center? I found someone who helped me take better notes."

"You're right," Michael says. "I need to get over myself and see what kind of help I can get."

Michael walks into the tutoring center.

Now, what do you think?

- If you found yourself struggling in a class, what would you do?

    a. Worry about my ability to succeed, but keep doing what I have always done

    b. Find someone to help me because I know that I cannot do it all by myself

    c. Just try harder

- If you were uncomfortable asking for help when you needed it, what would you do?

    a. Nothing; it is not someone else's responsibility to help me succeed

    b. Approach it carefully, find the most comfortable way to get some initial help, then ask for more help if I need it

    c. Put aside my ego and ask anyway

Your Terms for success

when you see . . .	it means . . .
Acronym	An abbreviation in which the first letters create a word (for example, AIDS is an acronym for acquired immune deficiency syndrome)
Acrostic	A mnemonic device in which the first letter of each word in a sentence stands for information or a process (for example, Please Excuse My Dear Aunt Sally is an acrostic for the order of operations: parentheses, exponents, multiplication, division, addition, and subtraction)
Analytical thinking	Breaking apart information and examining its parts
Cerebellum	Region of the brain that controls sensory perception and motor skills
Chunking	A method for remembering information by grouping it together in small chunks
Creative thinking	Thinking that involves generating ideas
Critical thinking	Thinking that involves reviewing information for accuracy, authority, and logic before considering it useable
Dendrite	The branch at the ends of neurons
Long-term memory	Memory stored for longer than a few days
Metacognition	Thinking about thinking
Mnemonic device	A method of remembering information

Neuron	A cell in the nervous system
Prefrontal cortex	A region at the front of the brain where complex thinking is believed to occur
Roman Room	Another term for the loci method
Short-term memory	Memory stored for a few hours or days

Learning Is a Process

It seems like there are dozens of bumper stickers and t-shirts that broadcast what people are born to do: "Born to Run," "Born to Shop," "Born to Boogie." But could you add "Born to Learn" to the list? All of us, researchers say, are indeed born to learn. Babies do it without giving the process any thought. The process is simple: The more you do something, the more you create connections in the brain that not only help you remember how to do something, but also help you get better at it. This process is called *growing dendrites,* or *hardwiring.* Dendrites are the tree-like structures on the ends of neurons (nerve cells in the brain). The more you practice something, the more those dendrites grow, improving the connections between the neurons in your brain (Exhibit 6.1).

Learning is a six-stage process that begins with being curious and motivated to learn something new, moves to practicing and refining the new skill, and then ends with mastery of the skill (Gunn, Richburg, and Smilkstein, 2007). If you think about anything that you are good at, you should recognize the same process that you went through to get better and better at it. We often recognize the need to practice sports and musical instruments, but sometimes we don't make the same connections with other skills such as writing, reading, and math. Michael would feel more confident about seeing a tutor if he realized that learning algebra is

EXHIBIT 6.1 Dendrite Growth

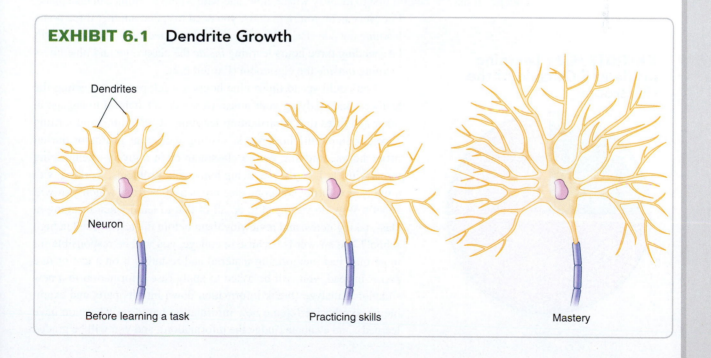

Dendrites

Neuron

Before learning a task   Practicing skills   Mastery

It's in the
syllabus

By rereading your professors' syllabi and by considering your experiences so far, determine how much time you will need to spend outside of class to meet the goals of each course you are taking. Which classes will require the most amount of time? How will you be spending that time?

G R I T
Tenacity

Focus and intensity matter. Research shows that hardwiring happens 100 times more effectively when you focus intensely and put your full energy into what you're doing, compared to when you try half-heartedly. Use your GRIT to up your game.

a process that requires time for practice. How much time is needed will be different for different people, but your skills will increase just as your dendrites will grow.

Your Mindset Matters!

What happens when you can't get motivated to learn a new skill and make it past the first stage in learning? People who lose interest when learning gets too challenging are described as having a "fixed mindset," whereas people who thrive when they are being stretched have a "growth mindset." Growth is the first core element of GRIT. People with a fixed mindset believe that they are either born smart or not, that there is no changing their fixed state of intelligence. People with a growth mindset, on the other hand, believe they can develop talents and skills; even if they fail at a task, they see it as an opportunity to learn more and improve on what they know about the task.

In the story at the beginning of the chapter, you learn that Michael knows how to do many things, which no doubt came from a belief that he could improve on his skills; however, he seems to have a fixed mindset about algebra. Sometimes one bad experience can influence how we see ourselves as learners and masters of a skill. Believing in our ability to learn will result in learning and mastery of whatever task we set our "growth" minds to.

We Learn Best When We're Active

How does the information about brain research and learning translate to what you are doing in college? It may be helpful first to identify where, how, and with whom learning can take place.

For every hour you're in class, you need to spend another three hours learning outside class. Therefore, for a three-credit-hour class, you will be spending three hours learning *inside* the classroom and nine hours learning *outside* the classroom (Exhibit 6.2).

You could spend those nine hours a week per class reading the textbook and studying your notes. However, it's helpful to engage in other activities that contribute to learning. Researching and writing papers, completing homework, visiting with your professor during office hours, studying with a classmate or in a group, memorizing terms with flash cards, practicing homework problems, working with a tutor, or tutoring someone else are activities from which you will benefit. Why do you need to do all of that to learn when listening in class, taking notes, and reviewing them before the test worked in high school? The answer is because in college, you will be responsible for more than just memorizing material and restating it on a test or in a paper. Instead, you will be asked to apply (use information in a new situation), analyze (break information down into its parts and examine it), synthesize (create new information based on what you have learned), and evaluate (judge the information), and you will be graded

EXHIBIT 6.2 **Learning Inside and Outside of the Classroom**

in class

out of class

on your ability to do all of those activities well. See Exhibit 6.3 for examples of the types of active learning you will be doing in your college classes.

Some research has reported that if you listen to a lecture you will remember only about 5 percent of the material. In other words, what you hear will be forgotten over time at an enormous rate! What does that mean for students whose instructors rely on lecture to convey information in class? It means that you will need to do more than just listen passively. You may need to record the lecture and listen to it again later, discuss the lecture with classmates, and help others understand it once you have mastered the material.

Of course, you may need to read, take notes, and rewrite them as well. The goal for you, regardless of your learning style preference, is to move from learning passively—merely taking in the information through listening or reading—to learning actively—applying, discussing, evaluating, and creating new ideas from the information you hear and read.

© PURESTOCK/ALAMY

■ Learning is often more engaging when it is active rather than passive.

EXHIBIT 6.3   Active Learning Strategies

Action	Definition	Example
Apply	Use information in a new way or to create a product	Demonstrate by writing and acting out a sketch about how a student may successfully transition into college culture.
Analyze	Break information down into parts and examine each part	Compare and contrast the different ways a student can finance a college education.
Synthesize	Create new information or examine two or more pieces of information	Examine two different views on how to choose a career by discussing each view.
Evaluate	Judge the information	Assess the effectiveness of each of three welding techniques.
Create	Produce, build, or craft a project or object	Design and execute a newsletter for incoming first-year students.

GRIT GAINER™

THE GRITTY TAKE CHARGE   Shift your mindset from "What are you doing to teach me?" to "What am I doing to learn what I need to master?" Shift from passive to active. Part of being a gritty student is taking charge of your learning and refusing to let anything get in the way of mastering the content. Own it. Then go get it.

Active Learning = Deep Learning

The good news that we've learned from brain research is that spending more time actively learning a subject can translate into deeper learning, and a gritty mindset toward challenging learning environments will enable you to learn more. Why? Because as you spend more time studying and engaged in active learning with a gritty mindset, you will remember more of what you have learned because you have moved it from your short-term memory to your long-term memory.

When you meet someone for the first time, you will keep that person's name and face in your short-term memory. In general, you can only store five to nine items in your short-term memory. If you try to put too many items in there, you will find that some of them slip away. Try glancing at the following list for 30 seconds. Then, cover up the list and write down the words you remember; the words do not have to be in the order that you see them.

cup	paper	pencil	magnet	ruler	scissors
spoon	towel	tape	apple	knife	straw

Instinct

Stop doing what doesn't work. Sure, memorizing takes some work. But exercise some smart GRIT by using the new, effective ways to memorize more in less time offered in this chapter.

■ Memory can be strengthened by participating in mental activities such as working on puzzles.

© SHOCK/FOTOLIA

How well did you do? If you remembered five to nine items, then you can consider your memory average. It takes some work, though, to transfer information from your short-term memory to your long-term memory, which is responsible for storing things like names and dates as well as skills such as tying your shoe. People can have well-developed memory storage for images (visual), sounds (aural), words (read/write), and processes (kinesthetic).

Modern technologies like computers, smartphones, and ebook readers make it easy for us to have a lot of information at our fingertips. With information so accessible, we might think that it's no longer necessary to memorize anything anymore. The truth is, however, that effective memorization skills are very important to be a successful college student. Quizzes, tests, and other types of examinations are often "closed book," meaning that you can't have your textbook or other materials available during the test. And because most exams and tests are timed, you wouldn't have enough time to search for information in a book to answer a question, anyway—you either remember the information or you don't. For these reasons, it's very important to develop effective memorization skills.

Mnemonic Devices Can Help You Remember

Mnemonic devices are memory aids or strategies that help you remember items, concepts, or a series of events. Usually, mnemonic devices are *not* used for deep learning, but there will be times during college that, for example, remembering the names of all the bones in the body or all the constitutional amendments must be conquered before deeper learning can happen. Thus, you may find yourself using mnemonic devices as part of your learning process.

DEVICE 1: THE ROMAN ROOM. Let's go back to the previous list and figure out how you could remember all of the items. Ancient Romans are credited with being able to remember significant amounts of information by using the Roman Room or loci method. This visualization technique can be useful when trying to remember a string of seemingly unrelated items or complex material that needs to be pulled together.

To create a Roman Room, visualize a familiar place, such as a room in your house. If your room is connected to other rooms, then you will have more "places" to put ideas. When you visualize your room, pay particular attention to the items that are already in the room, such as furniture or favorite pictures, and unique details, such as peeling paint. The more vivid the visualization, the better able you will be to remember the items you place there.

To see the Roman Room or loci method in action, take another look at the list.

cup	paper	pencil	magnet	ruler	scissors
spoon	towel	tape	apple	knife	straw

Can you place these items in your kitchen? Put the straw in the cup and place it in the cabinet. Tape the paper on the front of the cabinet. Place the towel on the counter next to the apple, spoon, and knife. Then, put the pencil, ruler, magnet, and scissors in the drawer.

Take 30 seconds to review this room above or visualize your own Roman Room with the items listed. Then, cover up both the list and the description of the room and see how many you can remember. Write the words on a separate piece of paper.

Did you remember more words this time? If not, then visualization strategies may not be the only type of mnemonic device you need to help you remember lots of information. There are other mnemonic strategies that may benefit different learning style preferences. Acrostic sentences and acronyms are two methods that may help students with a read/write learning style preference.

DEVICE 2: ACRONYMS AND ACROSTIC SENTENCES. Take the first letter of items in a series to form sentences that help you remember the items and their order—acrostic sentences. For example, music students remember the order of the treble clef staff, E, G, B, D, F, with the sentence "Every Good Boy Does Fine." To recall the order of biological groupings used in taxonomy, just remember "Kids Prefer Cheese Over Fried Green Spinach" (Kingdom, Phyllum, Class, Order, Family, Genus, Species).

Take the first letter of items in a series and spell another word to create acronyms. Here are a few examples of acronyms that we use every day: AIDS (acquired immune deficiency syndrome), SADD (Students Against Drunk Driving), REM (rapid eye movement), and SCUBA (self-contained underwater breathing apparatus).

Although there are too many words in the previous list to create an acronym, you can create an acrostic sentence (or two) with the letters of each word. Because the order of the items is not important, feel free to rearrange the letters to make your sentence(s).

C	P	P	M	R	S
S	T	T	A	K	S

DEVICE 3: RHYMES AND SONGS. Though a little more difficult to compose than acronyms and acrostics, rhymes and songs, which often appeal to aural learners, are another type of mnemonic device. Who doesn't remember, "Thirty days hath September . . . " and "In 1492, Columbus sailed the ocean blue"? Again, simple information works best for these memory strategies. It will take more work to remember the economic effects of Columbus' discovery of the New World.

When you have the time to explore the variety of memory strategies, try them out until you find the one that works best for the subject matter and your learning style. However, many students who need a memory strategy need it to work quickly as they are cramming before a test. Those students may be successful in remembering it when they get to the test the next day, but the possibility of their remembering it weeks, months, or even a year later is slim. That is why professors and tutors discourage cramming—it may work some of the time, and it is better than not studying at all for a test, but it often produces more anxiety and stress, and the material is less likely to be in your long-term memory when you need it later.

DEVICE 4: CHUNKING. With that warning, there will be times, nonetheless, when despite your best intentions, you will need a fail-safe memory technique to help you remember key concepts in a short period of time. One method, called *chunking*, is similar to the Roman Room or loci method in that items are grouped together to allow the brain to make connections with the items. This will make it easier to recall the information later.

To see chunking in action, consider the following 10-digit number:

5114796210

It may be easier to chunk the numbers the way a phone number is divided:

511–479–6210

You probably don't realize that you chunk any time you memorize a phone number or Social Security number. In other words, you are taking the seemingly random numbers and putting them together in groups. The goal in chunking is to reduce a large number of items into only five to nine items. To practice this mnemonic technique, use the following list of key terms: acrostic, acronym, chunking, cramming, loci method, long-term memory, mnemonic device, rhyme, Roman Room, short-term memory.

First, make sure that you know the definitions of each term. Record your definition next to each term below:

Acrostic _____

Acronym _____

Chunking _____

Cramming _____

Loci method _____

Long-term memory _____

Mnemonic device_____

Rhyme _____

Roman Room_____

Short-term memory _____

Next, group the items together logically. Then complete the chunking with the remaining terms.

For example, one way to group some of the terms could be:

Mnemonic devices are strategies for remembering items and they include **acrostics, acronyms, rhymes , and Roman Rooms.**

GRIT GAINER™

YOU HAVE TO CRAWL TO WALK   Chances are you didn't crawl to school today. Yet you fell countless times when you first tried to stand. Why did you persevere? Because you knew it would pay off. Life is better walking than crawling. Same deal applies to memory devices. It's hard. Show some GRIT and keep going. Your memory will be off walking and running soon.

How else could the terms be grouped together? Use a separate sheet of paper to group them.

Thinking Is a Skill You Can Develop

Think about it. Those are three simple words that you have been asked to do before, but have you ever thought about how you are thinking? The term for thinking about thinking is *meta-cognition,* or the act of being aware of your own thought processes. So far in this book, you have thought about what you value, how you spend your time, what college culture is, and how you relate to others. You have also been asked to think about what you are reading and learning, whether it has been through the reflection and critical thinking exercises or the end-of-chapter questions and ideas for further research. In fact, this book has been designed so that instead of passively taking in the information, you are actively engaged in thinking it through and creating knowledge.

The same activities that have brought you to this point in the book are the ones you are currently practicing in your classes as well. You are moving beyond only taking information in to send it back out in the same form for a test or paper. Instead, you are building creative, analytical, and critical thinking skills with each course.

Strong critical thinking skills will set you apart in the classroom and the workplace: You will be better informed, because you will know to seek out the information you need; you will make better choices, because you have thought through all the possibilities; and you will continue to improve on your chosen solutions, because you will understand that evaluating your solution is the key to making better future choices.

Creative Thinking Helps You Build Ideas

Creative thinking, or the act of creating ideas for solving problems, is an integral part of education. Without creative thinking, there would be no inventions, new formulas, breakthroughs in technology and science, new art movements, advances in design and architecture—the list is endless. Without creative thinking, there would be no electricity, no indoor plumbing, no automobiles, and no zippers in our clothes. Just getting to your classes would be a totally different experience.

Creative thinking is a skill, a process, and an attitude (Harris, 2002, pp. 1–2). In other words, creative thinkers are not born with special powers of the imagination; they just use their imaginations more regularly than others. The good news is that you can learn to think creatively by following some basic ideas in Exhibit 6.4.

Robert Harris states, "Creative thinking creates the ideas with which critical thinking works" (p. 5). To improve your

G R I T
Resilience

Guess what predicts who solves problems better and faster than everyone else? *GRIT.* Research shows that as your grow and show your GRIT, you will be even more innovative and work through sticky problems more quickly and effectively.

EXHIBIT 6.4   Creative Thinking Strategies, Definitions, and Activities

Strategy	Explanation	Activity
Improve your imagination each day	Find ways to keep your mind sharp and your imagination flourishing. Turning off the TV and picking up a book is an easy way to stimulate your imagination. If you enjoy kinesthetic activities, create something to get your mind active.	Participate in one thinking or imaginative exercise each day, whether it is doing a crossword puzzle or Sudoku puzzle, constructing an object, or listing the plusses and minuses of the healthiness of what you ate for breakfast.
Ask what would someone else would do	Looking at a problem from a different perspective can provide more creative ideas.	Determine what issue you want to generate more ideas for. Then, choose two people—such as Oprah Winfrey or Walt Disney or your mother—and write down the different ways they would approach the issue.
Suspend judgment	For creative thinking, evaluation is not necessary—save it for critical thinking and problem solving.	Make a list of 50 ways to use a paper clip, and do not delete or edit the list in any way. Share your list with others.

critical thinking and problem solving abilities, you will need to consider the previous guidelines, find ways to practice them, and maintain your curiosity and a gritty mindset.

■ Analytical thinking can help you in classes that require you to learn processes.

© NATALIA D/SHUTTERSTOCK

Analytical Thinking Helps You Break Ideas Down

Analytical thinking involves breaking down a subject and examining its parts. Students who learn about computer processing or automotive technology use analytical thinking so that they can understand how a machine works. When they master how the parts work together, they are able to diagnose problems that may occur within the processes. The same is true for students learning about the processes in the body: They use analytical thinking to determine what how muscles work or how the lungs are supposed to function. Students of literature will use analytical thinking to break apart short stories or poems to determine what effect the setting has on the characters or what effect language has on the tone of the text.

Anyone who has tried to figure out why an event has happened (e.g., How did I run out of money before payday?) has used analytical thinking. Just as any skill, however, it takes practice to become better at seeing the parts of a process or a whole unit and determining how the parts work together to create a unified result. To develop your analytical skills, you can follow these guidelines:

- **Break down a whole into its parts.** Ask yourself, "What are the pieces that create the entirety?" For example, if you work at a sandwich shop, you can break the sandwich-making process into its distinct parts, such as taking the order, cutting the bread, etc.

- **Examine each part for a unique function.** After you identify every step in the sandwich-making process, examine each one to determine its function, such as fulfilling the purchase transaction or putting condiments on the sandwich.

- **Organize parts by function.** What elements can be grouped together? How did you determine what groups to create? You could put all the steps in the sandwich-making process that have something to do with the purchase transaction in one group and all the steps in gathering the ingredients in another.

- **Explore the meaning behind the parts.** If possible, find out more information about the meaning or function of each part. You might discover that keeping track of how many sandwiches you make is an important piece of information for the restaurant owner to manage inventory.

- **Re-examine the whole in light of its parts.** Look back at the whole and determine what you have learned from examining the parts. Do you have a better understanding of how all the parts work together? You can now understand how each step in the sandwich-making process contributes to the success of the restaurant as a whole. You can also appreciate how your individual contributions make a big difference for your employer.

Growth

Change your angle on the problem. A key element of GRIT is mental agility. This means looking at problems from fresh perspectives, with fresh ideas and fresh eyes. Ask yourself, "How would the world's greatest problem solver, who knows nothing about this situation, approach this problem?"

Critical Thinking Helps You Evaluate Ideas

The term *critical thinking* is difficult to define, but it has a long tradition. Critical thinkers such as Socrates and Thomas Aquinas, to name only two, have had a tremendous effect on the way we think about the world. But what makes them critical thinkers? What is a critical thinker? A critical thinker is "someone who uses specific criteria to evaluate reasoning and make decisions" (Diestler, 1998, p. 2). Someone who thinks critically does not take information at its face value; instead, he or she carefully examines information for accuracy, authority, and logic before using it.

To illustrate the importance of using critical thinking skills, consider this first scenario: Michael receives an email from a friend who claims that she has sent him a virus unknowingly. Her message instructs him to search for the offending file and delete it immediately. Unaware of any problems that are usually associated with viruses, he searches for the file and finds it, exactly where his friend said it would be on his computer. Michael's friend is a trustworthy person and he values her advice, so he deletes the file. He gets an email the next day from her that says she is sorry that she sent him a hoax. Thus, he has deleted a perfectly normal file on his computer.

integrity matters

You can't be a true critical thinker without maintaining integrity in the process. To think critically with integrity, you will need to be fair in your judgments and represent others' views as accurately as possible. Critical thinkers know that every viewpoint has a counterargument that is equally valid, and critical thinkers with integrity acknowledge those other viewpoints without misrepresenting them.

Critical thinkers who have integrity also do not shortcut the process of examining and judging an idea. The reward is the assurance that their final conclusions are fair.

YOUR TURN

In 250 words, explain how you would handle the following situation: Your professor asked you to write a paper on affirmative action in which you defend the practice, although you do not agree with that position.

G R I T
Resilience

To grow greater GRIT and resilience, ask yourself, "What do I want life to look like on the other side of this problem? What's the smartest way to get there?" And, "What can I do, beyond what I've already done, to get there as quickly as possible?"

Now, consider this second scenario: Juanita sends Evan a link to a pop-up blocker because she knows that he hates those annoying intrusions while surfing the Internet. Because Evan has been deceived by free software before, he decides to search several reputable sites that are devoted to reviewing new software. Evan finds that the pop-up blocker is a fraud; instead, if he were to click on the link that Juanita has sent, his computer would have been overrun with pop-up advertisements of questionable origins.

In the first scenario, two people, at least, have been deceived by what appears to be legitimate and helpful information. Who doesn't want to rid his or her computer of a potentially dangerous virus? Unfortunately, Michael and his friend did not question the information. In the second scenario, however, Evan has encountered false claims before and realizes that he must check out every piece of information that comes to him, regardless of the friendly source. Evan applied critical thinking to the situation. Thinking critically allowed him to review the information he was sent and search for authoritative sources that provided reliable information so that he could make a decision about what action to take.

As the Information Age evolves, critical thinking skills are not just advantageous; they are essential. Not only do you need to practice these skills, but you also need others to practice them so that you will not constantly have to evaluate every piece of information that you receive. Can you imagine a world in which everything that you read is suspect and there is no sure way of finding out what is true and accurate and what is not? For people who do not think critically, that imagined world is a reality.

Problem Solving Brings It All Together

Although not all critical thinking leads to solving a problem, problem solving relies on critical thinking as well as creative and analytical thinking. In order to think critically to solve a problem, you will need to go through a process within a group or as an individual. Remember that the more minds are working on a problem, the more likely that all sides of the problem can be addressed, which may make the solution better. You may not always have an opportunity to work in a group on a problem, but you may be able to ask others for their advice during the process.

Once you have your gritty mindset in place, here are the basic steps for using critical thinking to solve a problem:

■ You use problem solving and critical thinking skills every day to make decisions.

© STEFANOLUNARDI/SHUTTERSTOCK

- Clearly identify the problem or goal.
- Generate several possible solutions to the problem or goal.
- Critically evaluate each possible solution.
- Choose one of the solutions and develop a plan for putting it in action.
- Evaluate the solution after it is in place.

STEP 1: IDENTIFY THE PROBLEM OR GOAL. Sometimes a problem is obvious, and other times we may make an incorrect assumption about the real problem. Either way, it's important to take some time to clearly identify the problem before moving on to possible solutions. For example, if you're constantly late for your first class every morning you might assume it's because you're not getting up early enough. After examining the situation more closely, however, you discover that you're spending too much time trying to find a parking spot before class. The problem may be a transportation problem and not a problem with your sleeping habits. Or, instead of a problem, we may be trying to

the unwritten rules
about Critical and Creative Thinking

- **It won't always be obvious when you will need to practice critical thinking.** You'll need to be an alert and vigilant information processor when you're in college, and almost every decision you face will require careful consideration. For example, during a meeting with your study group, one of your classmates might tell you that the exam will only cover the first five chapters of the textbook. You may not want to take one person's opinion at face value in this kind of situation, because the consequences would be significant. If you walk into class on exam day and discover that Chapters 6 and 7 were also on the test, you'll have no one to blame but yourself.

- **Too much stress, fatigue, and time pressure can kill creativity.** A little bit of stress might help to get you motivated, but too much of it will typically cause you to shut down. If you have a project or assignment that requires creative thinking, it's best to give yourself some time to work on the project in advance. Some research suggests that your mind actually develops creative solutions when you're asleep, so give yourself a few days to generate ideas before the project deadline.

- **Some of your best ideas will come when you least expect them.** Successful entrepreneurs and inventors often refer to thoughts that occur to them while they're in the shower or when they are engaged in an activity completely unrelated to the problem they're trying to solve. Keep a notepad and pencil handy wherever you are so that you can put your ideas on paper when they occur and reduce the chances of forgetting really good ideas when they come.

- **Failure and mistakes can help you become a better thinker.** Some students are so focused on getting perfect scores and all A's that they resist taking chances that might lead to failure. This approach might lead to a high GPA, but it can stifle your ability to generate creative solutions. If you make mistakes or fail, review the circumstances and your decision making process, and use the experience to help you generate new ideas and solutions.

accomplish a particular goal. For example, you might set a goal to save an extra $200 over the next six months so you can buy an ebook reader.

Identifying the problem's cause is the first logical step before you can begin to solve it. If you do not identify the cause—or at least eliminate possible causes—before starting the next step, either you won't solve the problem or you might create a whole new problem to solve.

STEP 2: GENERATE POSSIBLE SOLUTIONS. This is the step where creative thinking will kick in. When you generate ideas, there are no rules except not to eliminate any ideas because they are too far-fetched or too odd. The goal for this step is to get a lot of ideas on paper. The more you can think of, the more likely it is you'll come up with a really creative solution that comes from "outside the box"—a phrase that describes ideas that aren't readily obvious.

When generating ideas, consider creating a list of your possible ideas and role playing (if you are able to work with another person) to get ideas flowing. This is a good time to take advantage of your learning style strength to stretch your imagination. For the "late for class" problem, you

GRIT Tenacity

Gritty problem solvers become excavators. They dig underneath by asking, "What's the problem underneath this problem (or the issue underneath this issue)?" Getting to the bedrock will help you build a solution that stands strong.

GRIT GAINER™

SLOW DOWN TO SPEED UP   Problem solving requires you to really pause, focus, think, analyze, and solve. Go beyond "good enough" and strive for the best possible solution, especially on the ones that count, by asking yourself these questions:

1. What would be an even better way to solve this problem?

2. If I had to solve it faster and/or more completely, how would I do it?

3. If there were a tougher but better option, what might it be?

might identify some obvious solutions (e.g., riding bike to class instead of driving), but by giving yourself room to be really creative and open, you might come up with some less-than-obvious ideas, like packing your breakfast in a cooler and eating it *after* you find a parking spot.

STEP 3: CRITICALLY EVALUATE EACH POSSIBLE SOLUTION.   To *critically evaluate* means that you consider both the advantages and disadvantages, strengths and weaknesses, plusses and minuses of every option. Sometimes it's helpful to construct a chart or table that describes each solution in the first column, and the advantages, strengths, and plusses in the second column, and the disadvantages, weaknesses, and minuses in the third column. It's helpful to force yourself to fill in every square in the grid so that you are thorough in considering both sides of a solution, especially if you find yourself preferring one particular solution from the very beginning. This is also a time when the opinions of others can be very helpful. Your friends, parents, professors, and roommates can provide a critical perspective that can help you understand your options better than you could have done so yourself. For example, if you're considering the possibility of getting a part-time job to make the money you want to save for your ebook reader, your trusted advisors might help you discover some of the drawbacks of adding work to your weekly schedule because of their own personal experiences with similar circumstances.

STEP 4: SELECT AND IMPLEMENT YOUR SOLUTION.   Some people have a tendency to make decisions too quickly before giving careful consideration to all the possible alternatives and potential outcomes. Other people, however, spend too much time considering all the alternatives and agonizing over the possible outcomes, and they have trouble making a final decision. The best course of action, of course, is to be somewhere in the middle—giving careful thought to each potential solution and then making a final decision in a timely manner. Once you've carefully evaluated all of your possible solutions, you eventually need to make a decision. Evaluate each possible solution based on its plusses and minuses, pick the one that has the most plusses compared to minuses, and then move on to put the solution into action. It's one thing to decide to do something, but it's a far different step to put that decision into action. If you chose riding your bike to class as your solution to getting to class on time in the morning, you need to have a bike with a lock and know where you can park it near your classroom. You might also need to make a test run on a day when you don't have class to figure out how long it will take to get to your class using a different mode of transportation.

STEP 5: EVALUATE THE SOLUTION.   This is one of the easiest steps to overlook, and yet it's one of the most important. You can become a more effective problem solver and decision maker by revisiting the decisions you've made in the past and evaluating how they turned out in the long run. By examining several decisions over a six-month or one-year period, you'll see patterns, and if you practice the problem solving process described here, you'll see a gradual, steady improvement in your decision making and problem solving over time. By practicing this five-step process on a regular basis with relatively simple problems, you'll develop effective skills to tackle the really big problems when they arise. You'll have a lifelong habit that will serve you well.

3

things future professionals need to know about learning, memory, and thinking

regardless of your career path, critical thinking will be crucial

The skills and practices that you develop in college of critically evaluating the information you're given, evaluating the source and credibility of that information, and making decisions based on the information that passes muster will help you in every aspect of your life and career. You will be barraged with information, but not all of it will be useful or reliable. If you practice critical thinking in college and exercise some real GRIT, you'll have a stronger ability to critically evaluate all of this information to make the best decision for yourself.

the most common critical thinking challenge in your career is problem solving

Almost every situation you'll face in your career will be in the context of a problem that needs to be solved. If you regularly practice the problem solving process we describe in this chapter, you'll have great experience to tackle any of the problem solving challenges you're presented on the job. Your manager will be impressed if you are able to demonstrate very early in your career that you are comfortable with the process of defining the problem, creatively identifying several potential solutions, selecting the best solution, and knowing how to implement it.

the quantity and pace of learning in the workplace far exceeds what you did in college

College students sometimes think that as soon as they graduate, school is over and they won't ever need to take classes or study for exams again. Nothing could be further from the truth. Almost every job in today's knowledge economy requires advanced training, which means that you'll be given books and other materials to study and memorize, you'll continue to take classes, and, in many cases, you'll need to take and pass exams. For example, if you're a finance major and want to become a Chartered Financial Planner (CFP), you need to study a large quantity of materials, pass several exams that are very lengthy and challenging, and satisfy several other requirements. Most of the truly important challenges you face will require you to show GRIT—to dig deep and do whatever it takes—to get it done. As you progress in your career, you'll repeat that process to maintain your license and earn additional licensures. Learning is for a lifetime!

115

THE **GRIT** ADVANTAGE

Research shows that GRIT is the single most important factor when it comes to optimizing your memory, learning, and thinking. Challenge yourself with these questions to fortify your GRIT mindset and put this chapter into practice:

1. Based on all you've learned in this chapter, what is the one thing you would benefit from the most and might need to work hard to master?

2. If you really applied your best focus, effort, and energy, what would you like to hardwire to become a more effective student?

3. What problems are you facing right now that can be fixed by practicing these tips until they become hardwired?

HOW **GRITTY** ARE YOU?

Do a GRIT gut check, by (honestly) answering these questions:
Now that you've completed this chapter, how committed are you to:

1. Applying these techniques to become a more effective, efficient, and active learner?

Zero Commitment 0 ——————————————————————— 10 **Fully Committed**

2. Applying these tools to enhance your memory and performance in school?

Zero Commitment 0 ——————————————————————— 10 **Fully Committed**

3. Applying these tools to become better and faster at solving problems?

Zero Commitment 0 ——————————————————————— 10 **Fully Committed**

7 Reading

Chapter goals to help you get in, get through, get out, and get paid:

In order to get in, get through, get out, and get paid, you will need to read—a lot—and understand and remember what you read. This skill will be as important after you graduate as it is while you are in college. This chapter will help you develop reading strategies and habits that you can apply immediately.

To meet those goals, this chapter will help you:

- Justify the importance of reading effectively in college
- Break down a long reading assignment for better comprehension and understanding
- Identify methods for improving your reading skills
- Use different reading strategies to improve your comprehension
- Apply your **GRIT** to upgrade your reading skills, with all the rich benefits it provides

MyStudentSuccessLab™

Log in to MyStudentSuccessLab.com to deepen your **GRIT** mindset and build the skills you'll need to get through the college experience.

Evan's Story

© MONKEY BUSINESS IMAGES/SHUTTERSTOCK

To Do

- 54 pages of biology textbook
- 72 pages of aviation textbook
- 213 pages of autobiography

Even though he can bench press hundreds of pounds, Evan feels weak when he thinks about reading. Evan is discovering that college without reading is like kickboxing without sore muscles.

When he runs into Michael in the hall after class, he complains about what he has to do and why he doesn't want to do it.

"Evan, I know exactly what you need to do. I just got help with my algebra homework, and the tutor explained it in a way that I could get it," Michael says.

"It's not that I don't know what to do," Evan says. "I just don't like to read. It's boring."

Michael laughs. "It does seem boring at first," he says, "but you will get better at reading the more you do."

"I don't think I want to get *that* good at it," Evan jokes.

Despite his joking, Evan goes to the only place he knows can help him: the tutoring center.

Evan knows that, like sports, you only get better at reading with practice and by challenging yourself with harder exercises. But he also knows he has a long way to go to get better at reading.

Now, what do you think?

- What would you do if you did not want to read an assignment?
  a. I would dig in anyway and wade through it no matter how long it takes
  b. Not do it or reluctantly do it; I cannot make myself read something I am not interested in
  c. Break down the reading assignment into parts and start working on it a little at a time
- What strategies could you use make reading assignments more enjoyable?
  a. Just do it no matter what
  b. Learn how to use different reading strategies to read with less difficulty and more interest
  c. Give up; there are other ways to learn material other than reading about it

Your Terms for success

when you see . . .	it means . . .
Active reading	Reading to remember and understand; reading with a purpose
Bibliography	A list of books or other sources
Comprehension	The ability to remember and understand
Context clues	Hints of a word's meaning by how it is used in a sentence
Critical reading	Reading to evaluate and to question
Dyslexia	A learning disability that makes it difficult for a person to read, spell, or listen effectively
Introductory material	The information that appears at the beginning of a work; often contains background information on the material or the author
Index	An alphabetical list of subjects or terms that appear in a book; appears at the end of a book
Information literacy	The ability to determine if information is needed; to access the information; to assess the usefulness of the information; and to incorporate the information ethically and responsibly
Introduction	The beginning paragraph or pages of a text
Section titles	The titles that appear within the sections of a chapter
SQ3R	A reading strategy that stands for survey, question, read, recite, and review
Subvocalization	Sounding out individual words while reading

Reading Is Crucial for College Success

If death and taxes are unavoidable parts of life, then reading is an inevitable part of college and lifelong learning. Fortunately, reading is more enjoyable and more profitable than death and taxes. The bottom line is that you will not be a successful student if you do not read assigned and supplemental material regularly. Likewise, it will be difficult to practice lifelong learning after college without reading on a regular basis. As previous chapters have mentioned, reading class handouts and college publications as well as your textbooks is essential to success in college. The reasons that reading is important to your college education and lifelong learning are many, but here are just a few incentives for making reading an integral part of your daily college work:

- Reading provides you with basic information that you can use to create knowledge of a subject.
- Reading improves your understanding of others and the world around you by exposing you to new viewpoints, ideas, and cultures.
- Reading provides you answers to and strategies for life's biggest questions and challenges.
- Reading helps you understand yourself, which will assist you in making better life choices.

Professors would be ecstatic if all their students read well and enjoyed all the assigned reading material. However, it must be acknowledged that some students just do not enjoy reading because of bad experiences in school or because of learning difficulties. More often, students find some reading dull and difficult to comprehend, and they long to read something "exciting." Thus, for some college students, reading can be a challenge to academic fulfillment. The not-so-good news is that until you get into classes that pertain to your major or career choice, you may feel that the assigned reading is uninteresting, but the good news is that there are ways to improve your comprehension *and* enjoyment of the reading assignments.

Tenacity

Remember, a big part of GRIT is finding ways to achieve your goals in spite of the frustrations, obstacles, and struggles along the way. Decide to dig deep and do whatever it takes to learn what you need so you get what you want.

In addition to the subject matter that you will encounter in college reading, you will also find the reading load to be larger than it was in high school or for your job. If you are taking four three-credit-hour classes and each professor assigns a chapter from the textbook, you can expect to read more than 100 pages a week. This number does not reflect full-length novels, supplementary articles, required periodical subscriptions, reserved library materials, online resources, and your own notes from class—all of which may be part of your weekly reading load. You will also be held accountable for reading, comprehending, and thinking critically about all of this material.

Information Literacy

Along with the increased reading load, your professors will also expect that you are an information-literate student. That means that you not only know how to read well, but you also know how to find information and use it effectively and ethically. You will learn more about how to research a topic in another chapter, but we'll introduce the concept of information literacy in this chapter as well. Information literacy is the ability to:

- Determine what information you need
- Locate the information you need
- Critically evaluate the information and its source(s)
- Add the information into your existing knowledge
- Use the information effectively, legally, and ethically

the unwritten rules
about Reading

- **You cannot multitask while reading material for your classes.** If you have music or the television on while you're reading, or if you're constantly checking your phone or computer for emails, texts, or calls, it will take you at least 30 percent longer to read the material, and you'll remember less of it. Find a quiet place of solitude for reading and you'll have far better results.

- **Reading online is very different than reading a physical book.** Students are increasingly using laptops and tablet computers and other hand-held technology for reading. You will more likely be reading physical texts—books, journal articles, and handouts—in the majority of your classes, so good reading (and annotating) skills will give you an advantage over other students who only read (and perhaps only skim) material online.

- **Reading expectations continue to be raised.** The more progress you make toward your degree, the more you will be expected to read, comprehend, analyze, and evaluate. The reading load may or may not get heavier, but how you use what you are assigned to read will be more important.

- **Critical readers are successful in college and beyond.** Good reading skills not only get you through college more successfully, they also set you apart in the job market. Employees who can read large quantities of information quickly, determine the meaning, and use that information effectively are extremely valuable to any company or organization.

To become truly information literate, you will need to become proficient at finding information, reading that information thoroughly, assessing the value of the information, and using it effectively in a presentation, paper, or other assignment.

How to Successfully Complete a Reading Assignment

The majority of your reading assignments in college will most likely be assigned by your instructors. When you first get a reading assignment, you will need to spend a little time preparing to read, which will help you maximize the time that you have to complete it. No doubt, in the first week of classes, you will be given handouts, syllabi, and chapters to read in your textbook. How do you manage it all without getting behind and overwhelmed at the start of the semester? Follow these steps to help you successfully complete your assignments:

- **Assume all assigned material is important.** Before you begin any reading assignment, remember that all written material that your professors give you needs to be read. You will be held responsible for it; therefore, you will need to create a process for reading and remembering what you have read.

- **Treat the reading assignment seriously.** No matter how big or small the assignment, make a conscious effort to read and remember important information. A positive attitude about the reading assignment will help make the other steps easier to complete.

- **Organize assignments according to size, importance, and date of completion.** Before you begin reading, you will want to start with the most important or urgent assignments first, and then work your way down the stack. A shorter assignment can be completed first unless its due date is far off.

- **Schedule reading time as you would any important appointment.** To increase your chances of reading effectively, set a definite time and place to read, preferably at the same time each day. Finding a comfortable, quiet area to read is also important because it will put you in the mood to focus on what you are reading. Equally important to setting a definite time is to establish routine breaks from reading. Get up, walk around the room, get a drink of water, and get the circulation going in your legs again. Taking breaks in which you physically move around the room will help your concentration and keep you from falling asleep.

- **Establish a clear purpose for reading.** Setting purposes for reading will make the assignments easier to comprehend and complete. For example, if your reading purpose is to improve your understanding of networking, then when you sit down with the textbook for your computer networking administration class, you are in the right frame of mind to absorb this specific information. Conversely, if your reading purpose is to be entertained when you read a chapter in economics, you may be disappointed and less receptive to remembering what you have read. One method for helping you set a purpose is to start a reading log. Exhibit 7.1 provides a method for reading effectively as well as critically. The first two questions at the bottom of the log support active reading; the last two ask you to think critically about what you have read.

G R I T
Growth

When it comes to reading, most students focus on quantity over quality. This is a mistake. Instead of putting in longer hours reading more, use the tools in this chapter to read and comprehend better, maybe in less time. It's not how much you read, but *how* you read that matters.

- **Stay healthy.** Finally, take care of yourself throughout the semester as you do your assigned work. You won't be able to read effectively if you are tired, hungry, or sick. Don't try to force yourself to read if physical or psychological issues distract you. Too much sugar and caffeine and too little sleep can make reading more difficult, as can certain medications and emotional distractions. If you cannot concentrate, return to the material when you are feeling better—but be sure to use this advice sparingly. Sometimes, you will just need to dig and get it done regardless of how you feel.

Reading in the Disciplines

The type of content that you'll be reading will vary by what kind of classes you're taking. Science and math classes have different reading requirements than English and psychology. The following strategies for reading in the disciplines are just a sample of what you may encounter in college.

MATH. Take your time to read both the written information and explanations as well as the visual representations of problems and steps for solving them. Reading assigned chapters before you get to class will help you follow what the professor is talking about and ask questions about content that you didn't understand.

LITERATURE. You may find you have more reading in literature classes—novels, short stories, plays, and poetry. Start early with these long reading assignments and take notes along the way. Depending on the complexity of the literature, you may need to read the work a few times, especially poetry, and sound each word out. Although sounding out individual words, or subvocalization, is often considered a reading difficulty (see "Reading Difficulties" section), it may be necessary to slow down and read short pieces of literature aloud. Also, pay attention to details when reading fiction and poetry.

LANGUAGES. The goal in reading in a foreign language is to improve your comprehension first. Use a dictionary the first time you encounter new vocabulary and work on improving your speed.

SCIENCES. Reading in the sciences will take time and focus as you encounter new concepts and processes. Look for visual representations of the content in your textbook or sketch your own in your notebook.

EXHIBIT 7.1   Sample Reading Log

Title of text or chapter _____

Number of pages _____

Author _____

Class _____

Instructor _____

Date reading should be completed _____

Estimated time to complete _____

Reading goals _____

Actual time to complete _____

Reading goals achieved   YES   NO

Skimmed   YES   NO   PARTIALLY

1. What is the reading about?

2. What did I learn from the reading?

3. What questions do I still have about the reading?

4. What difficulties, if any, did I have while reading?

New vocabulary words and their definitions:

Resilience

> Pick your most difficult subject, and do whatever it takes to master at least one chapter or one major concept. Once you do, you'll realize, "Gee, if I can master the toughest stuff, I can master almost anything!" Master the worst and enjoy a real burst!

SOCIAL SCIENCES. Large amounts of assigned material will be part of any social science class. Start reading the chapters early and look for key ideas. People and their theories or their actions (in history) will be key components of the reading. Learning the who, what, when, and where of the material will make it easier to remember. Remember trading cards from the days when you were young? You could use the same concept and develop summary profiles about the various individuals and events you read about in your assigned materials.

Reading Difficulties and How to Overcome Them

For some students like Evan, no matter how much they want to read well, the activity is difficult. Dealing with reading difficulties can make a short reading assignment seem like climbing Mount Everest and can make it hard to stay motivated. The following paragraphs describe some common reading difficulties that students experience. It is not intended as a comprehensive list, nor is it intended as a diagnosis for problems that you may experience. If you think you may have a reading difficulty or a learning disability, you should see your college counselor for a proper diagnosis.

Your college's counseling services should also provide you with resources to help you overcome the challenges you may experience because of a learning difficulty. Some reading difficulties are bad habits rather than disorders. The following list provides an overview of common reading challenges:

- *Subvocalization*, or pronouncing each word in your mind as you read, is one type of bad habit that some readers experience.

- *Regression,* or reading the same words or sentences over and over again, is another bad habit that some readers have. Improving your reading speed, or the rate at which your eyes move across the page, often eliminates the reading habits that slow you down.

- *Moving a finger, pen, or pencil across the page as you read* can also slow down your reading speed. Unless you are stopping to take notes along the way, eliminate the use of an instrument to keep your eyes moving.

- *Poor concentration* can negatively affect how quickly you read. In some cases, poor concentration is part of a larger issue that may be diagnosed by a health professional. If poor concentration is just a bad habit, then you can work toward improving concentration by eliminating distractions such as television and music and following the suggestions outlined in this chapter.

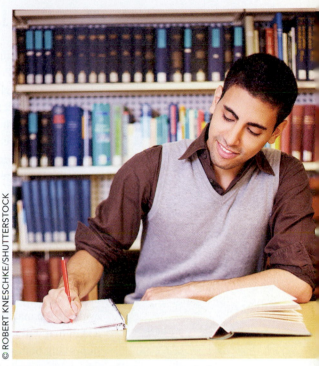

Use your college's resources to help strengthen your reading strategies and overcome any reading difficulties you may have.

- *Dyslexia* is a neurological disorder that makes it difficult for a person to comprehend and recognize written words; the person may also have trouble writing and spelling. Approximately 15 to 20 percent of all students have dyslexia, and most people with dyslexia have average or above-average intelligence (International Dyslexia Association, 2001). The good news about dyslexia is that many students have learned to cope with the disorder and have succeeded in college and careers. For example, Paul Orfalea (2007) struggled with both dyslexia and attention-deficient disorder his entire life, yet became a millionaire entrepreneur who founded Kinkos.

- *Attention-deficit disorder* (ADD) or *attention-deficit hyperactivity disorder* (ADHD) is a behavioral disorder in which a person has difficulty paying attention. Reading can become just another obstacle that someone with ADD or ADHD must overcome. In order to work through any difficulties that ADD/ADHD may cause, you will need to contact your counseling center. As with dyslexia, ADD/ADHD can be managed so that your reading skills get sharper.

- *Vision problems* may actually result in some reading difficulties. A regular eye exam can determine if your difficulties are caused by the need for corrective lenses. If you think your eyes are the reason that you have difficulty reading, get your eyes checked by a doctor. You may want to stop first at your college's health clinic, if one is available, for a screening. Also, take advantage of any health fairs that are offered on your campus where you can get a free screening that may pinpoint the problem.

GRIT GAINER™

READING TAKES GRIT   No matter what challenges or obstacles you may face, you can use your GRIT to overcome, even harness them, and become an effective reader. Some of the most famous people in history struggled with reading. But they persevered and found a way. Remember: "What's inside of you is stronger than what's in your way" (No Barriers USA motto).

Reading Is an Active Process

What do you picture in your mind when someone tells you that he or she has been reading for three hours? Perhaps you envision the person reclining in a comfortable chair with a cup of coffee. Although this may be an enjoyable way to read, the reality is that a lot of us would probably fall asleep if we sat in that kind of position for any length of time! When you read books, articles, and online content to learn and study, you'll have a lot more success if you make it a far more active process.

Active reading, a term that you may hear often in college along with *active listening,* means that you are fully engaged in reading by focusing your mind and body on the activity. Many first-time students read passively rather than actively and do not fully concentrate on the material. Just reading the words is not enough for college classes. Instead, you must be a part of the process by making sure you comprehend what you are reading.

Critical reading is another term that you will hear frequently in college. Some students may think that critical reading means having a negative reaction to what they have read, but it actually involves a series of steps to react and respond to the reading—either positively or negatively, depending on the material. Your end goal of critical reading is to question and evaluate the material, not to take it at face value. Critical reading, as well as active reading, is a skill that will take practice to develop. The following sections provide specific strategies for improving both skills.

Skimming and Scanning

You may already be familiar with the terms *skimming* and *scanning* as they pertain to reading. Skimming is reading material quickly and superficially, paying particular attention to main ideas; use this method of reading when you first get a reading assignment because it can help you get a feel for what the material is, how long it is, and how difficult it will be to read. In order to skim a text effectively, you should read the first and last paragraphs, the main headings of each section, and the first and last sentences of each paragraph; of course, if time is a factor, you can delete some of the steps or add more. Ideally, skimming should be done before in-depth reading. However, sometimes skimming may be the only chance you have to read the material. If this is the case, be sure to pay attention to the major headings of each section and the first and last paragraphs of the material. Don't be surprised, though, if you miss major ideas that are sandwiched in the middle.

Scanning is looking quickly for a specific item or topic as you would scan a website for a particular product or a dictionary for a particular word. Scanning also includes examining the table of contents and index of a book to help you find what you are looking for. Just as with skimming, scanning requires that your eyes move quickly over a page. However, the difference between scanning and skimming is that you know what you want to find and will slow down once you find it. Scanning is particularly useful when reviewing sources to use for a paper. You can determine rather quickly if the source pertains to your topic or not. Once you scan, you can then skim or read the text actively.

■ Improving your reading skills includes learning to read on a computer or with other forms of technology.

© GEORGE DOYLE/GETTY IMAGES

Breaking Down the Material

Part of skimming a text includes examining its parts. Certain pages of a book or article hold valuable information for deciphering its purpose. Students who want to hurry up and read the meat of the assignment often overlook some of the most important parts: The title, author, table of contents, chapter titles, introduction, section headings, footnotes, bibliography, and index are all informative components of a piece of writing. See Exhibit 7.2 for a complete list.

The process may seem time consuming and unnecessary, especially if you do not have much time to spend reading anyway, but the more you do it, the less time it will take because you will know what to look for. Also, your reading speed and comprehension will improve, which will mean that you can complete your assignments more quickly.

EXHIBIT 7.2   Parts of a Reading Assignment

Title	The title of an article or book will give you a clue as to what it is about. When reading, any material, take time to think about the significance of the title of the work you are reading, and go back to the title to look for additional meaning once you have completed the whole text.
Author	The author of a text can be just as important as what he or she has to say. Because of their reputations, some authors lend credibility to their words or they instantly make readers suspicious of their motives. If you recognize the author's name, then you should have a good idea of what the text is about. The more you read, the more you will encounter writings by certain people, and you will be able to expect certain viewpoints from them.
Table of Contents	Most books have a table of contents that shows how the book is organized. A table of contents lists the chapters as well as any subsections that appear in the chapters. Lastly, the table of contents contains the beginning page number for each chapter or section. Familiarizing yourself with the table of contents will make it easier to find information when you need it.
Introduction	Sometimes overlooked, the introduction can provide all the information you may need to determine if a particular book is what you want. When researching a topic, you can decide whether a book will be a good source for you by reading the introduction. The introduction typically tells the reader what the whole book is about, what unique features you will find, and what viewpoint is supported.
Chapter Titles	The titles of chapters are a good indication of what you can expect to read within the book. Chapter titles also help you locate information more quickly. Can you imagine trying to find information from a book about taking notes without any chapter titles? You would have to scan each chapter until you found the information you were looking for.
Section Headings	Section headings work in the same way as chapter titles; they indicate how the material is organized, and they give you a sneak peek of what is to come.
Introductory Material	Introductory text appears at the beginning of a section or before an essay and explains or briefly summarizes what you are about to read. It can provide biographical information about the author or can indicate the essay's main points.
Bibliography	A bibliography, or list of references or works cited, usually appears at the end of an article or a book, right before the index. Literally, a bibliography is a list of books that the author has read or used in preparing the text. This section of a book or article is often overlooked, but it actually contains a wealth of information for the reader. If you want to learn more about a topic that the author briefly mentions, you can look at the bibliography to see what other books are listed about the subject.
Index	One of the last elements of a book is its index, which is an alphabetical list of major ideas or words that are keyed to the pages on which they appear. If you need to find information on note taking, for instance, you can use the index to pinpoint the exact page it is on. Indexes, (or indices) are especially helpful in research when you are evaluating sources to see whether they contain material about your subject.

Critical Reading

Once you have actively read assigned or researched material, your next step will be to read it critically. In most cases, this will mean rereading the material, especially if it is short. Be sure to allow yourself plenty of time for this activity. At this point in the critical reading process, you do not necessarily need to answer the questions you raise—you will just want to look for places within the material where you want to know more, want clarification, or disagree with the author's conclusion.

Instinct

Because a key element of being a gritty learner is assessing and improving *how* you learn, not just how hard you work to learn, pick the tool that you think would give you the biggest benefit and put it to use immediately until it becomes hardwired and saves you time.

Questioning who the author is and his or her purpose in writing the material is the first place to start. If the material comes from a certain source, such as a magazine, newspaper, or blog, you will also want to question the purpose of that source. Questions to ask include: Is the author an authority? Is he or she credible? Is there an agenda or bias in the writing? By considering the source, you may ask, What is the purpose of presenting this material? If it comes from a newspaper, does the material aim to inform, persuade, present one side of a debate? If the material comes from a blog or an anonymous website, does the material intend to serve as reliable information, or is it only someone sharing his or her observations with no intention of providing accurate information? Writing these questions in the margins of the text or using a notebook for your questions is a good start to reading critically.

Another important element of information literacy is evaluating what you have read for its usefulness. Just because a book, article, or other content mentions a particular topic that you're studying doesn't mean that it's a relevant source. You need to review the content to determine if it helps you answer the specific questions you have. For example, if you have to write an essay explaining *why* the Congress of the United States includes both a Senate and the House of Representatives, a website that lists all the members of Congress won't be helpful for your assignment. Furthermore, if your assignment requires you to argue in favor of a certain law or legislative act, you need to evaluate the material you read to determine if it provides supporting information.

In the era of Google searches and Wikipedia, it seems easy to find a lot of information about virtually any topic you need to study. The challenge is to evaluate this information for both

integrity matters

Reading in college is not optional; rather, it is crucial to success. When you make the commitment to enroll in college, you must also follow through with that commitment by tackling the reading that is part of the experience. You will also need to demonstrate integrity when you do not read—be honest with your instructor, if asked, and be honest with yourself that your progress (or lack of) is related to how well you are preparing for class through active and critical reading.

YOUR TURN

In 250 words, describe a time in which you were confused in class because you did not prepare by reading the assignment beforehand. What was the experience like? What did you learn from the experience?

credibility and relevance. These skills are crucial for your information literacy, and they will serve you well both in college and throughout the rest of your life.

Reading Is a Skill You Can Develop

The great news about reading is that it's a skill you can develop and improve over time. If you struggle with reading, there are a number of activities you can practice that will improve your reading comprehension and efficiency.

Building Your Vocabulary

Ever notice how some people just seem to know the right words to say in any situation, while others struggle to think of what to say? Increasing your vocabulary is a great benefit to reading regularly. Some students get sidelined when they read because they encounter unfamiliar words; few students take the time to look up words that they don't know, and they subsequently miss out on learning new ideas or understanding the intent of the author. It is well worth your time to look up words when you read, but there are some methods you can use to decrease the time you spend flipping through your dictionary.

The first method of learning new vocabulary words is to look for context clues in the sentence. Many times you can figure out what the word means by how it is used in a sentence or by the words that surround it. Consider the following sentence:

Students often use context clues to *decipher* the meaning of unfamiliar words.

If you didn't know that *decipher* means to figure out, you could still understand the meaning of the sentence by the words around it and by considering that students are using something (context clues) in order to do something to (decipher) the unfamiliar words. You could deduce, then, that students are making the unfamiliar words more familiar by using context clues. Now, try this sentence:

It was not until we traveled to Beijing that we realized how *ubiquitous* American fast food was. On every street corner we saw a McDonald's or a KFC restaurant.

If you are not familiar with modern-day Beijing, you may not know that American restaurants are plentiful; in fact, you may believe that China has very little American food. Thus, to understand the meaning of *ubiquitous,* the second sentence provides the context clues.

It's in the
syllabus

Review your syllabi and determine how many pages (approximately) you are required to read each week for all of your classes.

- Do some classes require more reading than others? Which ones?
- Are some of the reading assignments harder than others? Which ones?
- How do you plan to handle the reading load this semester?
- Do you expect to keep up with the readings? Why?

GRIT GAINER™

READ MORE, BE DIFFERENT   One way to set yourself apart and increase your chances of successfully getting through, getting out, and getting paid is to become competent or strong at the thing others lack. In an era when all of your friends read and exchange micromessages, learning to really read and fully comprehend is a huge advantage.

With the phrase "On every street corner" from the sentence that follows, you should realize that *ubiquitous* means "everywhere."

Although context clues will allow you to make sense of most unfamiliar words, there will be times when you cannot rely on the other words in the sentence to help you. For example, can you tell what the words *amenable* and *obsequious* mean in the following sentence?

Charles was *amenable* to going out to eat with Sheila's *obsequious* mother.

In this case, if you don't know what the words mean, the sentence offers little assistance. Does Charles want to go out to eat or doesn't he? Is Sheila's mother someone who is enjoyable to be around or isn't she? To answer these questions, you may need to look up the words. Here is what you would see if you were to look up *amenable* in a dictionary:

a·me·na·ble (∂ m' n∂ b∂l) *adj.* 1. responsible or answerable 2. able to be controlled; submissive— a·me'na·bil'i·ty *n.*—a·me'na·bly *adv.*

Now, look up *obsequious* for yourself and see if you can decipher the sentence.

Another way to figure out what words mean is to know some common Latin and Greek root words, prefixes, and suffixes. For example, if your professor calls astrology a *pseudoscience* and you know that the Greek root *pseudo* means "false," then you will be able to understand that your professor is claiming that astrology is not a true science. In order to learn the common roots of words that we use every day, you will need to study words' origins. A college reading class or looking up words in the dictionary regularly will help you learn to recognize the roots in other words. More tips for building your vocabulary are listed in Exhibit 7.3.

GRIT
Growth

One way to build your GRIT is to become a voracious (look it up!) learner. Putting out the extra effort to figure out new words and read more difficult subjects will help you grow stronger and better.

EXHIBIT 7.3 **More Tips for Building Your Vocabulary**

Purchase or borrow discipline-specific dictionaries when you begin a class that contains a large amount of terminology (e.g., medical or scientific dictionaries, foreign language dictionaries, and glossaries for literary terms).

Before asking your professor or classmate what a word means, look it up.

Don't be afraid to look up words, even the same word multiple times. You will eventually be able to recall their meanings.

Use new words in conversation to "try them out." Using them regularly will help you remember what they mean.

Write new words on 3 × 5 index cards, and jot down the books and pages where they appear. Look up the definitions when you have time and write them on the cards. Take the cards with you and review your new words when waiting in line or stuck in traffic.

Buy and browse a thesaurus, a book that contains synonyms for words. A thesaurus is handy when you are searching for a word that is similar to another.

If you have an email account, subscribe to a word-a-day service that sends you a new vocabulary word each day, or buy a word-a-day calendar.

Subscribe to magazines that challenge your reading skills: *The Atlantic Monthly, The New Yorker,* and *Harper's* are examples of print magazines that provide interesting and challenging material.

Increasing Your Reading Speed

Knowing how quickly you read is helpful in planning time for reading and in marking your progress. The goal is to increase your speed *and* your comprehension. In order to calculate your reading speed, time yourself while you read. Go back to the first two paragraphs under "Critical Reading" and reread that section. It is 250 words in length. To calculate your reading speed, divide the number of minutes that it took you to read the passage into 250 to get your reading speed. For example, if it took you two minutes to complete the passage, then (250/2) you read at a rate of 125 WPM (words per minute).

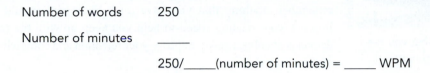

Number of words	250
Number of minutes	_____

250/_____(number of minutes) = _____ WPM

Average readers read between 200 and 250 words per minute, but that does not reflect their comprehension of the material. Techniques for improving speed are worth learning and practicing. For example, instead of carefully processing every word in a sentence, skim the sentence to capture its meaning. This is similar to what you may have learned in typing class—not focusing on each individual letter, but on the entire word. Another effective reading technique is to keep the key elements of a sentence (e.g., the subject and verb) in the foreground, and other elements of the sentence (words like *the, and,* and *to*) in the background. Other techniques for improving your reading speed are listed in Exhibit 7.4. Your college may also offer a speed reading class, or you may be able to find more methods in websites and books.

EXHIBIT 7.4 **More Tips for Building Your Reading Skills**

Get comfortable	Make sure your reading space is comfortable and favorable for concentrating, but avoid tackling reading assignments in bed!
Stay focused	Find a time of the day when you are most focused to read and your energy levels are high.
Skim when you can	When the reading is not as important or complex as other assignments, learn to skim quickly. At the very least, skim before reading more closely.
Learn new words	The more words you know, the easier some reading may be.
Avoid overhighlighting	If you want to emphasize an important section, it may be better to mark it with a summary and a short explanation of why it is important rather than merely highlighting or underlining it.
Use a strategy	Use a comprehensive strategy such as SQ3R to help you read both actively and critically. A good strategy will involve skimming, questioning, and reviewing what you have read.
Take a class	If your university offers reading classes, even speed reading classes, take advantage of them.

© ISTVÁN CSÁK/SHUTTERSTOCK

■ Check your understanding of what you read before moving on to more reading material.

Checking Your Comprehension

The most important aspect of reading is comprehending and remembering what you have read. If your textbook has questions at the end of each chapter that will help you reinforce what you have learned, get in the habit of answering them when you finish a reading assignment. Even if you just answer the questions in your head, you'll understand the material better. If your textbook does not have questions, write a short summary of the chapter in your own words. To reinforce what you have learned, trade summaries with a classmate.

A high WPM reading speed means very little if you do not remember anything that you have read. Your goal should be to improve your reading speed to help you keep up with the reading demands of college and to improve your retention and comprehension of the material.

Improving Your Reading Attention Span

Resilience

A big part of GRIT is resilience. As a reader, this means refusing to let frustrations and failures hold you back or beat you down. It means working through the tough patches so you can enjoy the rich rewards of taking on and busting through adversity.

Each semester will get more demanding in terms of reading because you will be advancing in your degree program and will be encountering new, more challenging content. Therefore, the more practice that you have in reading effectively, the easier it will be to complete larger reading assignments. If you find that your reading attention span is not long, then you can work on lengthening it.

First, you will need to figure out how many pages you can read comfortably without getting distracted or tired. Write down the number in your reading log, a notebook, or in a calendar. Each time that you sit down to read an assignment, notice how many pages it is. See if you can beat the number in the previous reading session. The more you read and the more you challenge yourself with reading, the better you will get. Just be patient.

Reading Strategies Can Help

As you have read so far, the act of reading is more than just moving your eyes along a page of words. Instead, reading in college requires that you use a reading strategy that will help you retain the information and think critically about what you have read. The following sections provide different types of proven strategies for both printed and electronic books that can help you read more efficiently and effectively.

GRIT GAINER™

BUILD GRITTY READING SKILLS   Here's a great GRIT challenge:

1. Pick the toughest section of any textbook.

2. Time yourself on getting through.

3. Ask yourself, "What are the three most important lessons in that section?"

4. Repeat steps 1–3, and make it a goal to get faster and better.

Practicing Strategies for Printed Books

Printed (or traditional) textbooks, novels, nonfiction, and articles may be becoming a relic of the past, but it is likely that you will still be reading printed material in your classes. Taking notes as you read, either in your textbook or in a notebook, is an excellent way to remember what you have read and to begin the process of critical reading. Writing down key ideas, terms to look up later, and questions that you have as you read helps you stay focused and improves comprehension. Highlighting is also useful; however, avoid highlighting large sections of text. Excessive highlighting defeats the purpose of noting only key or very important information. If you can write in your textbook, create one- or two-word summaries of each paragraph or section. If you need to keep the text clean, then use your reading log exclusively. Otherwise, you may want to use it in conjunction with in-text notes.

Practicing Strategies for Ebooks

Electronic books, or ebooks, have been gaining popularity with students, professors, and libraries, and they certainly can be more convenient than printed sources. For example, you may be able to download an ebook on your computer or other handheld device and read it without having to go to the library to check it out. Also, some ebooks can cost less than their traditional counterparts. Nonetheless, there are some drawbacks to using ebooks rather than printed books. They are dependent on a student having access to technology, and students cannot sell them back as they can printed texts. You may want to test one out—either borrowing a friend's or using a library ebook reader—before committing to purchasing an ebook reader for a class.

Strategies for reading an ebook are similar to a printed text in that you can preview the overall reading by examining the table of contents and chapter headings, looking for main ideas, and questioning the authority and accuracy of the text. However, ebooks have additional tools that can make reading actively and critically easier. Some ebooks allow you to search for certain terms and will highlight them in the text. This can be useful if you are trying to find a specific section in the text. Ebook tools may also include highlighters and notes that you can use to mark important information and record your own ideas. Often, these can be saved while you have access to the ebook. A print function may also be included in some ebooks—although printing the entire book may not be possible, it should allow you to print pages that you need.

Practicing the SQ3R Reading Strategy

One of the most popular reading strategies, SQ3R, was originally developed in 1946 and is still used today (Pleasant, 1970):

(S) Survey: Before reading your text closely, start by examining the headings, subheadings, graphics, charts, and references (if included).

(Q) Question: After you look for these major organizational signposts, you can either think or write questions that you have. One way to generate questions is to turn headings and subheadings into questions. For example, the subheading "SQ3R Reading Strategy" can be turned into the question "What is the SQ3R reading strategy?"

(R1) Read: Read each section at a time, making sure you are concentrating on what you have read.

(R2) Recite: At the end of each section that you have read, say aloud what the section was about and answer the questions that you asked during the Question stage. You may also want to write your answers on note cards to review later.

Tenacity

Do you know why practice typically fails? Because most people quit. Not you. You know that a huge part of GRIT is trying over and over until you get better. Expect to be weak at a new skill the first time. It only gets more fun from there.

Figure out where you can squeeze in a little time to complete your assigned reading.

(R3) Review: Anytime after you have completed the first four steps, you will be ready to review what you have read. Some experts suggest reviewing within 24 hours of reading; others recommend reviewing what you have read in short sessions over a period of time.

Connecting Your Reading to Your Life

One of the most difficult reading obstacles that every college student faces, no matter how well he reads, is generating interest in the material. If the material you're reading seems boring, take a few minutes to consider how the content you're reading might apply to careers or societal issues that are relevant to you. For example, if you're reading a textbook about chemical reactions, take a few minutes to surf the web to figure out what chemical reactions occur in hydrogen-powered vehicles or what it's like to have a career as a chemist. You'll enjoy reading more and you'll better comprehend what you're reading if you can make a connection between the reading material and your own personal interests.

Another way to connect your reading with your life is to seek out pleasurable reading yourself. If you have favorite authors or types of writing, go to the library, pick out a favorite book, and give yourself some time to read for fun. Or, if you're interested in a particular sport or recreational activity, find blogs or online interest groups and read those regularly. Make an effort to find reading that is interesting, stimulating, and even fun. Reading or browsing through a magazine or newspaper a week will help your reading skills. The habit of reading will also make it easier to stick to the schedule you have set for reading class material. If you have a good book on your table, it can serve as a reward for completing less exciting reading assignments. Once you create good reading habits, you will find yourself reading—and enjoying—even after classes are over. You will soon discover that you are curious to learn new things, and reading will satisfy your thirst for knowledge.

GRIT GAINER™

BUILD GRITTY READING SKILLS   To become a grittier reader, try this challenge:

1. Pick a tool from the previous list that you think will help you the most.

2. Commit to trying it, with your best effort, at least three times in a row.

3. Rate yourself on a scale of 1–10 on how well it worked each time.

4. Compare the first time to the third time.

   You'll be amazed how fast your gritty brain can hardwire new habits!

3 things future professionals need to know about reading

in college, life, and career, those who read have an edge

In every class, in every meeting, in every situation in life, you'll encounter people who have opinions, who make decisions, and who act without carefully reading material that could have helped them do each of these things well. Some will succeed, but most will not. You can be the exception, the standout, and the sole survivor if you devote the time and attention it takes to read relevant material before your class, before your meetings, before making decisions, and before sharing your opinion with others.

effective reading is primarily about attention and focus

Some students stubbornly try to convince themselves that they can read well while listening to music, while the TV is on, or in the midst of a noisy and busy environment. In most cases, they simply lack the discipline to unplug from the world around them for the block of time it takes to really read and understand something. You don't have to practice this kind of self-deception. Put the electronics away, find a quiet and secluded place, and go deep into your reading. You'll get results, guaranteed.

the quantity of reading will expand as you progress in school and your career

Learning to read effectively in school is so important not just because it's a major factor that determines your academic success, but also because it develops your capacity to consume even more reading material after you graduate and as your career develops. As you trace the path of successful people whose careers expand and progress, one of the most important elements of their success is to be well read, so that they understand the world around them, the issues they face, and how to lead their organizations and families.

THE G R I T ADVANTAGE

Engage your GRIT to get great results by taking on this challenge:

1. Pick the reading assignment you dread the most.

2. Answer this question: If the person that knows you best in the whole world were coaching you on how to get the most out of that assignment, a) specifically what tool(s) would that person suggest you use, b) how would he or she recommend you do it, and c) in what setting (place, time, etc.) would that person recommend you do it to give you the best chance of success?

3. Apply your own wisdom to every assignment and use your GRIT to keep trying until you prove to yourself it works.

HOW GRITTY ARE YOU?

Now that you've completed this chapter, how committed are you to:

1. Enduring discomfort and frustration to learn better ways to read?

Zero Commitment 0 ———————————————————— 10 Fully Committed

2. Applying at least one new tool to read better and faster within the next 24 hours?

Zero Commitment 0 ———————————————————— 10 Fully Committed

3. Being willing to do whatever it takes to become a stronger reader?

Zero Commitment 0 ———————————————————— 10 Fully Committed

8 Listening and Note Taking

Chapter goals to help you get in, get through, get out, and get paid:

This chapter will help you develop effective listening and note-taking skills so you can get in, get through, get out, and get paid. To graduate, you need to complete all of the courses in your degree plan, and each of these courses will require you to listen well and take informative notes to help you perform well on quizzes, tests, and projects. You will also need to learn how to minimize distractions and work with your peers.

To get a great job, you'll need to listen well and take accurate notes so that you can learn the technical requirements of your job, complete the tasks you've been given, and solve customers' and work teams' problems. You will also need to identify when you need more help and how to access it.

To meet those goals, this chapter will help you:

- Practice methods that help you listen more effectively
- Identify barriers to listening
- Apply different note-taking strategies to each of your classes
- Apply **GRIT** to strengthen your capacity to stick with it and not give up until you get or learn what you need

MyStudentSuccessLab™

Log in to MyStudentSuccessLab.com to deepen your **GRIT** mindset and build the skills you'll need to get through the college experience.

Laura's Story

Laura settles in her usual seat in the front row of her world civilization class.

"The clip we are about to watch," her professor says as she pushes the play button, "discusses the ancient library in Timbuktu."

"I love it when she stops lecturing and shows us these videos," her classmate whispers. Laura misses some of the information.

"Hey? Do you have an extra pen?" her classmate whispers again.

"You have the material that was assigned for reading, the information I cover in the lecture, and then anything else that I bring in. All of this should be studied for the test," the professor says as the lights come back on.

"And she's not lying," says Laura to herself. Even with help from the tutor in the learning assistance center, Laura has her work cut out for her: The information in the book is arranged chronologically, but her professor lectures on causes and effects in history. Then there are the tests that cover major themes. Laura has struggled in this class to find the right note-taking method.

"Any other questions?" her professor asks and pauses for a few seconds. "Okay, if you realize you do have questions after class, be sure to email me or come by my office early next week." She heads for the door.

Now, what do you think?

- What would you do if you missed hearing important information because someone or something was distracting you?
  a. Not worry; I will figure it out on my own
  b. Ask someone else after class what I missed
  c. Panic that I missed something important
  d. Immediately email the professor, concisely explain my concern and strategy, and ask for any advice on how to make sure I've filled any gaps so I can do well on the test

- If you felt you needed extra help improving your listening and note-taking skills, what would you do?
  a. Go to a tutoring lab to get assistance
  b. Talk to a friend who also has difficulty
  c. Just try harder.
  d. Nothing; if I cannot do it on my own, I will just deal with the consequences

Your Terms for Success

when you see . . .	it means . . .
Active listening	Listening with focus and a purpose
Annotating	Taking notes within a text
Cause/effect	An arrangement of information that connects the cause of an event to its effects
Chronological	An arrangement of information by time
Compare/contrast	An arrangement of information that connects the similarities and differences of two subjects
Cornell System	A note-taking strategy that involves dividing your paper into an upside-down T
Critical listening	Listening to evaluate the information
Least important/most important	An arrangement of information that lists points based on their importance
Listening barrier	An obstacle, either physical or mental, that keeps you from listening effectively

Outlining	An arrangement of information that is ordered by how the information is presented
Shorthand	A note-taking strategy in which shortened forms of words and symbols are used
T-System	Also known as the Cornell System

Listening Is More Than Just Hearing

Listening, remembering, and note taking all have something in common: You need them to learn, make decisions, and act on those decisions. You will not be able to make it successfully through your classes, get your degree, or pursue a successful career without doing all three.

A Prepared Listener Is a Better Listener

Active listening is a term that you may hear in college classes; someone who listens actively is fully concentrating on what is being said, refusing to be distracted, and taking steps to remember the information. The following tips are intended for those who want to listen actively and effectively.

Growth

The first step to effective listening is to prepare to listen before you get to class. You will need to read the assigned pages or chapters ahead of time so that you know what the lecture or discussion topic will be. If you have read the chapters ahead of time, you will be familiar with new words and concepts. Preparing to listen also includes reviewing your assigned readings before you get to the classroom. If you have a few minutes between classes or on the bus, pull out your book and skim the major headings, boldfaced terms, and text boxes that appear in the margins. Build time into your schedule to arrive a few minutes early so that you have time to review the course material before class begins. This will help you keep pace with the professor when class starts.

> To be an active listener, you must decide that listening is a worthwhile activity and that important information will be shared. You have to show some GRIT and commit.

You will need to sit up front, move away from a talkative person, and put away textbooks for other courses, cell phones, and other distracting items. Your best defense against interruptions is to clear your desk of anything except your textbook, a pen, and paper. Stow other items in your backpack or underneath your desk or table.

If you need to get anything out during class, such as a dictionary, minimize the disruption by being as quiet as possible. If you find yourself next to a chatty classmate or one who likes to write notes to you, simply move. Even if you are politely listening or reading her messages, you will be guilty of disrupting the class by association. Talkative classmates make it difficult for you and others to listen, and they distract you from taking good notes.

Instinct

> How you listen matters. To listen effectively while in class, avoid in-class distractions. Dig deep, turn off the noise, and get focused.

Another good way to listen effectively is by maintaining a positive mindset about the class. Once you're in college and taking classes, it's easy to start taking your classes for granted and viewing them as a boring waste of time, especially when the content doesn't seem relevant to anything in your life.

Remind yourself that your decision to attend college is critical to your long-term success in life. Remember, your goal is to get through this class (and earn a good grade in the process), graduate, and get a great job. Keep your eye on the big picture. Also, take some time to consider how the topic you're listening to may someday be relevant to your career, or how it might help you understand an important issue that society is facing today. Finally, consider the possibility

Resilience

that at any moment, you could learn something new. That's an exciting perspective that can keep you engaged in the class, no matter what the topic or how it's being discussed.

Minimizing out-of-class distractions is another method of keeping a positive and resilient mindset. There will be times that you have to work late, stay up all night with a sick baby, or help a friend who has just had a crisis. If not handled well, these stressful experiences could affect your performance in class.

Finally, prepare for class psychologically by preparing physically. Make sure you have eaten something before each class so that you won't be interrupted by a growling stomach or hindered by weak focus. Try dressing in layers in case the room is an uncomfortable temperature. Nothing is more distracting than being too hot or too cold. Getting plenty of sleep the night before class will also help you pay attention and listen effectively. Although adequate sleep may be a luxury if you work a late shift or if you get up in the middle of the night to take care of a child, be sure you make an effort to get a good night's sleep as often as possible. You won't be able to maintain high concentration and retention or even good health without adequate rest. See Exhibit 8.1 for tips on preparing to listen in class.

> Your response matters. It's not about whether you face adversity, but how you handle it. That's GRIT. Remember, successful students and effective listeners don't typically do well because everything in life is perfect. Usually it's the opposite. They find ways to stay focused and do well in spite of the unexpected hardships and ways life may conspire against them.
>
> Some students who encounter personal problems will use those problems as an excuse to miss class or allow themselves to be distracted during class. Not you. You instinctively know how important each class is toward the achievement of your goals in life. So, you'll stay focused and press through those challenges. You commit yourself to attending each and every class session, adjusting your strategy or approach for capturing the important information from the class along the way, so you can earn good grades and your degree.

To Listen Critically Is to Listen Well

Active listening, much like active reading, involves focusing on the task at hand and concentrating on what is being conveyed. Another part of listening effectively is listening critically, or processing and evaluating what you have heard.

EXHIBIT 8.1 Tips for Preparing to Listen

Tip	Explanation	Example
Prepare ahead of time.	Read all pages from textbooks, handouts, and extra material that your professor assigns or mentions.	Before the lecture on the American Dream in Arthur Miller's *Death of a Salesman*, read the entire play.
Minimize in-class distractions.	Make sure that you have few if any items or people near you that can get your attention.	Turn your phone to silent made and stow it in your backpack before walking into class.
Maintain a positive attitude.	Stay positive about a class no matter what others have said negatively about it or what you have experienced so far.	On your way to class, think about five positive aspects of the class that will help you achieve your ultimate academic or career goal.
Minimize out-of-class distractions.	Your situation and thoughts can get in the way of concentrating on what is being said. Work to focus on the present, not the past or the future.	If there is something on your mind, write down your concerns before going to class and promise yourself to think about it after class is over.
Prepare physically.	Take care of yourself by getting enough rest and food or drink before you go to class. Wear appropriate clothing so that you will be comfortable.	Grab your jacket, an energy bar, and a bottle of water before you go to your classes.

Listening critically will help you make decisions about what is important and what is not, what is objective and what is subjective. Listening critically is a skill that should be practiced regularly.

Your college professors will invite you to think critically and challenge your assumptions (that is learning!). As you get more comfortable with listening actively and critically, you will move from merely listening and taking notes that reflect what your instructors have said to listening to evaluate and ask questions of the notes you have taken. Here are some questions to consider as you work on listening critically:

Tenacity

Listening critically isn't always easy. It takes GRIT. Getting good at it means you have to persist and sometimes struggle through frustrations.

- **Speaker.** Is the speaker a credible source? How do I know? What possible biases does he or she have? What is his or her experience with the topic?

- **Message.** What is the speaker's purpose? What are the details he or she uses to convey the message?

- **Details.** Is the speaker using facts or opinions? How do I know? Which type of details work best for what the speaker is trying to convey?

- **Self-knowledge.** What do I already know about the topic? How does what the speaker is saying conflict with or support my beliefs and opinions? Do I feel I have learned something new?

- **Larger picture.** How does what the speaker is saying fit into the larger picture? How can I relate the message to something I already know about life or the world at large? Are there any connections between what I have heard and what I have experienced?

Answering some of these questions will get you started on the right path to listening critically. Even though you are listening critically and mentally asking questions of what you are hearing, you still need to tune in when you hear something that you don't agree with or don't understand.

Remember, too, that "critical" does not mean "negative." If you find that what you are hearing is not holding up to what you know about the subject or the speaker is not credible, you can still ask questions that are respectful and curious. Most people do not mind being politely challenged or debated.

Growth

Listening improves with effort. Exercise your GRIT to work through and get past barriers. Taking on, navigating, even busting through barriers is what separates the best from the rest. Each time you do, you will get stronger and better equipped to take on the next one.

There Are Barriers to Listening That You Can Overcome

Despite your efforts to prepare for class, you may find barriers to listening effectively that you cannot avoid no matter how well prepared you are. How you respond to those barriers is what separates success from failure.

For example, what should you do if your instructor talks too fast, has an accent that is unfamiliar to you, uses technical jargon or an advanced vocabulary, is disorganized, digresses from the lecture material (tells stories, allows too many irrelevant questions), or does not explain key concepts? Although you cannot coach your instructor in the art of speaking, you can ask him or her to slow down or define terms. Most professors do not mind repeating information or defining specialized language on the board because they want students to understand the material.

It's in the
syllabus

By looking at your syllabus, determine how the information will be presented in the course.

- Will it be presented by chapters, topics, units?

- What are the note-taking expectations for the class?

- Is that information in the syllabus or did you learn it from your professor or other students?

© RYAN MCVAY/GETTY IMAGES

■ Prepare for class in advance and get involved in class discussions so that your notes will be more meaningful when you go back to review them.

G R I T
Tenacity

Stick it out. Go past listening to remembering. Once you adequately prepare to listen in class and you remove any barriers that inhibit your ability to take in information, you will pour real effort into remembering what you hear in class.

G R I T
Resilience

These are perfect moments to employ your GRIT to get what you want. GRIT means digging deep, doing whatever it takes to make it happen or get what you need. Give it a go. Bury your doubts and raise your hand. It's a courageous step that will help you gain confidence. If it doesn't work the first time, adjust your approach and try again. That's GRIT in action.

It's neither your responsibility nor your role to tell the professor how to structure his or her discussion or class session. However, there are a few strategies you can use to build better structure around the content. First, ask your professor if he or she would be willing to share a copy of the lecture notes before class so you can review them beforehand. Also, you can take notes, build a structure of your own, and then take time to ask the professor for confirmation that you've captured the main ideas. For example, if the professor is explaining how photosynthesis works, but you're finding the discussion to be disorganized or confusing, take notes and try to describe the process from start to finish. Raise your hand and ask the professor if you can walk through the steps to make sure you understand them. This process will not only help you, chances are it will help other students in the class who are having a tough time following the discussion as well.

Besides getting enough sleep and sitting comfortably in class, there may be other barriers to listening effectively. If you have an unaccommodated learning disability or a hearing problem, you may not be able to listen productively. Talking to a counselor about learning or hearing difficulties can help you listen more effectively. A more common hindrance to listening is students' insecurities about their ability to do well in the course. It is not uncommon for a new student to feel, at first, intimidated by the course, the instructor, or other students in the class. The reason for the discomfort could stem from a student's feelings that he or she is not good enough or smart enough to be in college. A student also may feel that everyone else knows what to do, what to say, and how to act. This fear is common, and usually it subsides after the first week or two. It's also based on a belief that's rarely true. If you have a question about something the professor said or if you're confused about something, there's a very good chance that several other students are as well. The question is who will have the courage and leadership qualities to raise their hand and ask the professor to review or explain something.

Listening Is Just the First Step Toward Remembering

Taking notes, of course, is one way to retain information. However, there are some other methods that will help you recall information at a later date.

Participating in discussion and activities is an excellent way to remember key concepts. In fact, professors consider student participation as part of active, rather than passive, learning. You are more likely to remember a concept if you have incorporated it into your own thinking. There is a reason that students who participate in class discussions are usually the most successful. They have made the material relevant to them, which makes remembering easier for them as well.

However, participating in class discussion may be difficult if you are shy or feel out of place in the classroom. Some students refrain from asking questions because they don't want to look ignorant in front of their classmates. These fears are often based on false or ungrounded beliefs. "Everyone else understands this, and I'm the only one who's confused," "I don't belong in this class," and

GRIT GAINER™

GRITTY LISTENING   Now that you know even more about why listening matters and how to listen more effectively, it really comes down to what you do with whatever limitations you may feel you have. It's about how you handle the obstacles you confront when you're trying to really listen. Students showing weak GRIT give up. They make excuses. Not you. You can show strong GRIT to find a way to listen and learn, no matter what.

1. When you're especially tired or bored, try this: Bring out the Big Why, and your Best How. Ask yourself, "Why am I doing this, again? Why am I in this class, or even trying to get a degree?" Keep asking "Why?" until you clearly remember the highest, most powerful reason you are there. It may be to become a better person, to be more employable, to feed your family, or simply to learn. Once you recall the biggest Why, ask How: "How can I adjust my strategy or approach to learn more, getting what I need better and faster?" Then do it. Now.

2. Most people give up the moment listening becomes difficult. Not you. You know GRIT matters. GRIT pays off. Apply the T^3 formula. *Try* twice, then if you don't get what you need, *tweak* your approach. Try, try, then tweak until you get what you want.

"If I ask a question, everyone will laugh at me" are some of the natural thoughts that might run through your head when you're in class.

You'll quickly discover that other students had the same questions and confusion as you did, that your professor really wants to help you understand the material, and that you remember more about the topics covered in class when there is some class discussion about them.

Then, there is the other end of the spectrum from the silent student—the constant questioner. These students dominate the professor's time by asking questions that sideline the discussion or about material that has already been covered. Professors value the *quality* of a student's participation and not just its *quantity*. Don't be intimidated by a predominantly quiet classroom or by a student who asks the professor excessive questions. If you have a question, ask it. If you don't feel comfortable asking questions during class, visit with your professor after class or during office hours. Some instructors ask students to write questions down and pass them up before class is over. Take advantage of such a practice; you will be able to ask questions without the fear of speaking up in front of classmates.

Another method for remembering, audio recording lectures, is popular with students who have the time to listen. Listening to a recording will work best if you have a long commute or if you go over your notes as you listen. Be sure to ask permission before you turn the recorder on and make sure you have fresh batteries with you in case they run down. Some universities are using "lecture capture" systems to record the lectures for you to view on the web later. Ask your professor if such a service is offered at your campus and for his or her class.

Taking Notes Is Part of the Listening Process

There are numerous methods of taking notes for a class. Your goal should be to find the note-taking strategy that works best for you. Remember that you may have to adapt your note-taking style to each course, each teaching style, and each learning style strength. For example, outlining may work well in a history course in which the instructor writes key terms on the board and organizes her lecture around key ideas. If your professor prefers unstructured discussion, you will need to adapt your note-taking strategy to make the most of disorganized information.

Whatever you choose for the particular course, your learning style, and the specific situation, there are a few tips that you need to remember when taking notes.

- **Listen for the main ideas.** Relentlessly ask yourself, "What's the key lesson/idea I need to learn?" Instructors will slow down and emphasize information, terms, and definitions. They may even use verbal signposts such as "The most important thing to remember is," "This may appear on an exam," or "Two crucial points about . . . ." If the instructor writes or hands out an outline, you can be sure that it contains the main points of the lecture.

- **Leave plenty of "white space" (blank space on paper) when taking notes.** Don't try to fill your page with as much information as possible. You will need the white space to add more notes or to synthesize ideas once you have reviewed.

- **Review your notes as soon as possible after class.** Waiting two weeks to review your notes will ensure that you won't remember everything that you have written or how it all fits together. Most experts suggest that you review your notes within two days of the class.

Knowing How Information Is Presented Can Improve Your Note Taking

GRIT
Instinct

Play spy. Focus in and try to decode not just what's being taught, but *how*.

Learning to listen effectively is the first step to taking good notes, but you will also benefit from understanding how information can be presented during a lecture.

As you attend more classes, you will probably notice that professors have a certain way in which they present their material. Some will follow the textbook. Others will lecture only on new material that cannot be found in the textbook or other course materials. Others will present a combination of the two methods. Reading assigned chapters and materials before you attend class will allow you to determine which information in the lecture is new and which has been covered in assigned reading materials.

There are many different ways information can be organized. Recognizing the different ways material can be organized will help you stay organized in your notes and will provide you with strategies for revising and reviewing your notes when you begin studying.

the unwritten rules
about Listening and Note Taking

- **The ability to listen well is arguably more critical to your success than your ability to speak well.** Why else would you have two ears, but only one mouth?

- **By preparing for class, listening well, and taking good notes, you can actually reduce your study time.** Professors will be hesitant to suggest this, because they don't want anyone to reduce how much time they devote to studying, but the fact is that if you listen to, process, and organize information effectively the first time, it doesn't take as long to review and remember the information the second time.

- **Sitting next to your friends or other students you know in class might not be the best idea.** The probability of distracting activities and conversations increases when you are in close proximity to people you know. It might be socially awkward to tell your friend that you're not going to sit next to them in class, but your academic performance stands to gain from making wise choices.

- *Chronological:* Details arranged in time (first this happened, then this happened, etc.)

  Example of Chronological Lecture Notes

  1801: United Kingdom of Great Britain is created

  1803: Louisiana Purchase is made by Thomas Jefferson

  1815: Battle of Waterloo signals end of Napoleon's career

- *Cause/effect:* Details arranged by presenting a cause and then its effects or an effect and its causes

  Example of Cause/Effect Lecture Notes

  Cause: Civil War

  Effects: Slavery ended, industrialism began, the nation was brought back together, the federal government proved stronger than the states

- *Compare/contrast*: Details arranged by similarities and differences

  Example of Comparison/Contrast Lecture Notes

  Similarities between Robert Frost and Walt Whitman: They were males; they used nature in their poetry; and they were considered "poets of the people."

  Differences between Frost and Whitman: Frost's poetry is more structured, whereas Whitman's is open and loose; Whitman's speakers are more positive and upbeat than Frost's; Whitman lived during the 19th century whereas Frost lived in both the 19th and 20th centuries.

- *Most important/least important*: Details arranged in order of importance; the most important detail can come first with minor supporting details to follow, or the least important details can start a list that works to a major detail

  Example of Most Important/Least Important Lecture Notes

  Self-awareness (purpose of education)

  Values

  Goals

  Mission

  Personality type

  Learning style

Abbreviations Can Help You Take Notes Faster

As you take more notes in each class, you will find yourself using a few of the same words over and over again. These words are good candidates for abbreviating or denoting in symbols. You can then create your own shorthand. Shortened words such as *ex.* for *example,* *w/* for *with,* and *b/c* for *because* are abbreviations you probably already use in notes and email. Symbols that you may already use include % for *percentage,* + for *add* or *and,* and # for *number.* If you use a new abbreviation or symbol for a word, be sure to make a note of what it means; for example, "TR" could mean "theory of relativity" in a science course and "Teddy Roosevelt" in a history course. Exhibit 8.2 shows a list of other commonly abbreviated words and symbols.

Developing shorthand abbreviations that you can still understand will allow you more time to concentrate on what is being said. As you get more practice, you will become better at judging what information is worth writing and what is not, and your shorthand will become more efficient. Just remember

G R I T
Growth

One of the smartest and grittiest ways to deal with potential frustrations is to eliminate them before they happen. Plus, completing your abbreviations will reinforce your learning the material. It will help you grow.

EXHIBIT 8.2 Common Abbreviations

At	@
Between	betw, b/w
Decrease	decr
Department	dept
Does not equal	≠
Government	govt
Increase	incr
Equals	=
Example	eg, ex
Important	imp
Information	info
Regarding	re
Significant	sig

■ Find a note-taking style that works best for your learning style preference and each class you are taking.

© LAURENCE GOUGH/SHUTTERSTOCK

to read over your notes within a day or two so that your abbreviations are fresh in your mind. It is a good idea to complete the words or concepts at that point so that you won't struggle to remember what all the shortened words mean later in the semester.

Outlining Is an Effective Note-Taking Strategy

Using an outline is a good method for taking notes if the instructor is organized and offers information in a logical pattern. Some instructors encourage outlining by writing key words and concepts on the board or an overhead projector. If your instructor organizes lectures or class discussions in that manner, you will be able to write an outline for your notes quite easily. The key to making your outlines effective will be to provide plenty of space between the items so that you can fill in the blank spaces with extra information. An example of an outline for a lecture on effective listening could look like this:

I. Preparing to Listen Effectively

II. Listening Critically

III. Possible Listening Barriers

    A. External

        1. Hunger

        2. Climate discomfort

    B. Internal

        1. Feelings of self-worth

        2. Stress

IV. How Information Is Presented

    A. Chronological

    B. Cause/Effect

    C. Compare/Contrast

    D. Most Important/Least Important

Your Textbook Provides a Great Note-Taking Resource

Writing in the margins of your textbook can be another effective way to take notes, especially if the reading assignment is lengthy. If you don't mind writing directly in your textbook, you can summarize main points that you have read. Writing brief two- or three-word summaries or questions in the margins will help you make sense of and remember what you have read. Brief marginal summaries will also help you review the material before class and after class when you start studying for an exam.

Annotating in your textbook and writing down critical questions are two methods of further reinforcing what you have read that will help you prepare for listening and note taking in class. Critical questions about the reading might include "How do I know this to be true?" and "What else should be considered?"

If you decide to write in the margins of your textbook, be sure that the book you are writing in is not one that you want to sell back to the bookstore. If you do not want to write in your book but still get the benefits of summarizing the material, you can write your summaries on a separate sheet of paper. Make sure that you label each piece of paper with the chapter title and page number of the book.

Highlighting in your textbook is another method that students use for taking notes on reading material. A highlighter pen can be used to mark important concepts for review, but be careful that you do not highlight too much information. Over-highlighting the text can have the opposite effect—instead of making it easier to understand key terms and information, too much highlighting can make everything seem of equal importance. If you do use a highlighter pen, use it sparingly. For example, don't highlight more than two sentences in a row. A better method would be to use highlighting and written summaries together for the greatest effect. (See Chapter 7 for more on reading strategies.)

Tenacity

Asking critical questions intensifies your focus and learning. Showing some GRIT by putting in the effort to annotate your textbook with your own notes will not only help you reinforce main ideas, but will also help you synthesize the information in new ways that will produce connections between concepts, making the material more memorable and more relevant.

The Cornell System Could Work Well for You

Cornell University professor Dr. Walter Pauk developed a system for note taking that has been popular with many students. The Cornell System, also known as the T-System, is ideal for those who benefit from the visual impact of organized notes.

The key to the Cornell System is dividing your notebook paper before you begin writing. To do so, draw a horizontal line across your piece of paper two inches from the bottom of the page and a vertical line from the horizontal line to the top of the page about two inches from the left margin (see Exhibit 8.3).

The largest area, the right column, is used for taking notes during class. The left column is used for asking questions as you take notes, such as material you don't understand during the lecture or possible exam questions that you think about as you are writing. At the bottom, the final section is reserved for summarizing your notes as you review them. The act of summarizing should help you understand and remember the information.

Instinct

Part of being a gritty learner is adjusting your approach or strategy to make sure you get what you need, no matter what.

Design Your Notes to Fit You

The following strategies for note taking in the disciplines are just a sample of what you may encounter in college. Another chapter will discuss specific study strategies within disciplines, but here we give some note-taking strategies, grouped by discipline, that will make reviewing your notes and studying easier.

Your Notes Will Vary in Each Discipline

ART. In an art appreciation class, you will need to identify eras (20th century), movements (Cubism), and artists (Picasso) as well as the characteristics seen in drawings, paintings, and sculpture.

EXHIBIT 8.3	Cornell System
Add questions or important notes here.	Write notes here.
Add summary of notes here after you read through them.	

Review your notes regularly, or they will have little value.

© JOEL NATKIN/GETTY IMAGES

Quickly sketching the works in your notes and listing the characteristic details will help you record the information you are receiving through lectures. You may also notice that in the study of art there are times of intense change (usually coinciding with a world or cultural event) followed by artists who imitate or modify slightly the new style. As you review your notes, apply your grit-infused focus to look for patterns and points of contrast within groups of artwork.

MUSIC. The same suggestions for an art appreciation class will work when you take notes in a music appreciation class. Instead of recreating a painting or sculpture in your notes, you may need to write down descriptions of what you are hearing and what the sounds remind you of. Are the sounds fast or slow? Do you hear one instrument or many? Does it sound like a stampede or a trip down a lazy river? "Translating" music samples into written notes as well as reviewing music clips on your own will strengthen your understanding of the material. As with your art notes, upon review, look for patterns across movements and eras and denote contrasting ideas and elements. Don't be discouraged if the first few attempts are frustrating, or if you have to struggle to get good at this skill. Once you do, it will make learning that much easier.

LITERATURE. Taking notes in a literature class will require that you have completed the assigned readings before class and that you have annotated and highlighted your text. Because literature classes, even survey classes, focus more on discussion than on lecture, you will want to be prepared to take notes on the analysis. As with music and art classes, being familiar with basic terminology before you get to class will help you take better notes. Challenge yourself to learn and even use any new terms as they pop up. As you review your notes, look for ideas that pull the different readings together.

LANGUAGES. Foreign language classes center more on speaking and interacting than on listening to a lecture. Taking notes will not necessarily be advantageous—you will need to focus all your attention on listening actively, processing what is heard, and interacting. Daily preparation is essential to learning foreign languages; take notes as you encounter new material and ask questions in class to get clarification on anything you do not understand. Any notes you do take should be reviewed soon after the class. As you review your notes, categorize material such as "irregular verbs" and include any tips for using or remembering the parts of language.

GRIT GAINER™

GRITTY NOTE TAKING   Note taking requires some real effort and focus, especially at first. It can be frustrating. In school, you cannot control how things are taught or what resources you are provided. But you can dramatically influence how much you *learn*. In the end, only you own the grade you *earn*. It comes down to you and how you respond to the tough stuff.

Try these two gritty note-taking questions to boost both what you learn and earn.

1. What are two or three ways I can use note taking to at least increase the chances that I learn and earn more?

2. What is the one way I can adjust my note taking immediately to gain the biggest benefit?

SCIENCE. Concepts and processes are key in science classes and your notes will reflect that. Prepare for class by reading assigned material, making note of new vocabulary words, and studying diagrams and figures in the text and handouts.

HISTORY. History class lectures are usually presented in chronological order, so using the tips for information that follows a time sequence will help you take notes in this class. However, you will also be required to move beyond specific dates and events by considering overall themes, ideas, and movements. In addition to chronological order, lectures may also use a cause/effect organization. An example of a lecture topic in a history class is "the economic and social effects of the end of the Civil War." As you review your notes, look for major themes and be able to recall actions that have led to important events.

Resilience

As with any class, you can be more resilient and reduce your frustrations when you ask questions, especially if you are having trouble following the steps of a process. Gritty students get the answers they need to proceed. As you review your notes, consider the different ways that you can represent these concepts and processes visually and physically.

MATH. Taking good notes in your math classes will require that you prepare and attend each class meeting. As with foreign languages, studying for math should be an everyday occurrence because the skills you learn in each class build on the ones you learned in the class before. When reviewing your notes, you may want to recopy them and make sure that you understand, line by line, each problem that you are copying. If you have any questions, you can write them in the margins of your notes and ask questions during the next class meeting.

Match Your Note-Taking Strategies with Your Learning Preferences

Instinct

Part of GRIT is asking yourself, "What's a better way to get this done?" Adjust your strategy to fit your preference.

Visual learners benefit from seeing the notes on the page, but they may also benefit from creating images out of the material they have written down. Take, for example, cause/effect information for the increase in electronic communication. An instructor may talk through or write down a few key ideas on the board or in handouts that look like this:

> **In the late 1990s, electronic communication grew at home and in the workplace.
>
> *Effects: closer relationships with those who are far away, increased productivity, long distance costs decrease, decline in stamp sales, need for communication guidelines at work, problems with sharing too much information or sending junk, bombardment of spam and viruses.

A visual learner may take that same information and create a visual representation of the cause/effect relationship. See Laura's notes in Exhibit 8.4.

Reading notes aloud, recording lectures, or recording yourself talking through material are all strategies for recording material. Although "taking notes" implies writing down words and then reading through them, there is no reason that aural learners must suppress their learning style strength during the process. An aural learner, like Laura, can pair up with someone who is a learner with a different style and talk through the material that they heard in a recent class. The read/write learner can then record notes or annotate ones she already has and share them with the aural learner.

The act of taking notes by writing them or typing them provides kinesthetic learners with a physical activity that makes remembering what has been written easier. Kinesthetic learners, like Evan, can benefit from using more physical activity or objects when they review their notes shortly after taking them. For example, if you are using formulas to calculate volume in

EXHIBIT 8.4 Laura's Notes

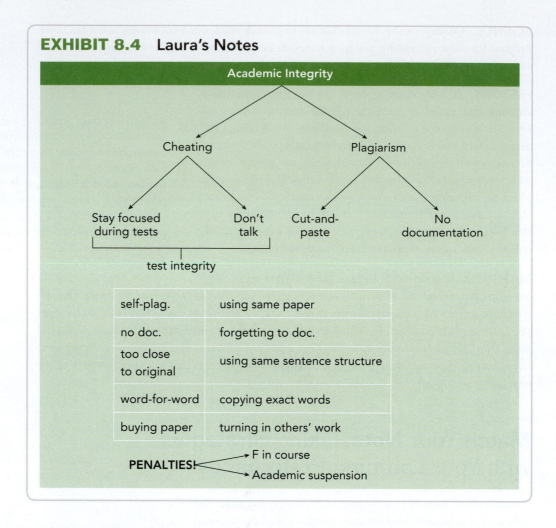

your math class, you may want to create your own volume problems in the kitchen. The act of pouring and measuring water and then calculating your measurements will make it easier to remember the process when you complete homework problems or take a test.

Likewise, a good way for a kinesthetic learner to study for an art history class is to recreate the artwork you are studying. No need to strive for masterpiece quality when recreating works of art; the physical activity of drawing the wavy lines in the background of Edvard Munch's "The Scream" will help you recall the piece on an exam.

It's Helpful to Discover Your Own Note-Taking Style

Laura has developed a special note-taking system for herself because of a learning disability. After taking an introduction to college course, she discovered that the note-taking systems that were discussed in her textbook did not help her take good notes. Through trial and error, she developed a system that works for her.

To begin, Laura writes in pencil on her notebook paper. Before class begins, she dates each page and leaves herself plenty of room to write. When taking notes, she writes on only one side of the page; in fact, most of her pages of notes contain fewer than 50 words. Although she uses more paper, her notes are easier to read.

G R I T
Tenacity

It takes trial and error to figure out the best approach. Don't give up.

Next, she places a star next to words that the instructor says are important. The most important part of her note-taking system is her use of arrows to make connections between ideas. By giving herself plenty of room, she can add connections that are revealed later in the lecture. If her instructor reviews the material before an exam, Laura highlights what she already has and adds notes in the spaces.

One strategy that Laura has developed to help her with her learning disability is that she doesn't worry about spelling. To make connections between ideas, she draws lines between words that relate to each other. She also makes charts for anything that is compared and contrasted (see Laura's notes in Exhibit 8.4). Finally, she keeps all of her notes in a binder that is divided for each class. Staying organized is an important part of her method. Although she uses only one binder during the semester, she keeps her notes easily organized by removing them after an exam. When she takes out notes she no longer needs, she places them in labeled folders at home. Then she carries with her only the notes she needs at that time.

Reviewing and Rewriting Your Notes Leads to Deeper Learning

GRIT
Growth

Reviewing should be done within two days from the time you took them. With this said, it is easy to be lulled into the sense of "studying" by merely reading over your notes again and again. When reviewing your notes, it is best to reorganize the material, make connections between concepts—even across disciplines—and ask questions about what you are learning.

If you use the Cornell System, then you have a built-in area for adding more information, summarizing, and asking yourself questions. However, if you do not use a particular method, you can still benefit from filling in any blanks or holes in your notes

> The purpose of notes is to help you learn. But it takes some GRIT. Notes are only as good as the extent to which you review, rewrite, and reorganize them so they make the most sense. If you never looked at your notes after you took them, they would serve very little purpose. Therefore, to make the most of your notes, you will need to review them.

with information you have since learned. As stated earlier, you should also spell out any abbreviations you have that may cause confusion later. After you fill in any gaps, you should also

integrity matters

Student or professional note takers provide an important service for students with disabilities or unique learners so they can receive the same educational opportunities as other students. There may be a time in which you must rely on a note taker. To maintain integrity, respect your note taker by not missing class or not preparing. The note taker is a supplement when you are absent or cannot take notes on your own. Act with integrity even whether you are borrowing notes from a classmate, relying on a note taker, or taking notes for someone yourself.

YOUR TURN

In 250 words, explain how you feel about taking notes for classmates or relying on others for notes. Discuss the issues you need to consider when relying on a classmate for notes or providing notes for someone.

EXHIBIT 8.5   Tips for Successful Note Taking

Prepare for class by reading all the assigned material before arriving. If you cannot read all of it, then read as much as you can.

Prepare to listen actively by removing distractions and bringing supplies.

Listen actively; concentrate on what you are hearing, seeing, and experiencing.

Listen critically by asking questions, either on paper or directly in class if your professor encourages questions during class.

Use a note-taking strategy that takes into account both your learning style strength and the subject matter.

Go beyond reviewing your notes by just re-reading them; instead, focus on concepts and main ideas, make connections between the large ideas, and ask critical questions of processes and ideas.

Continue the process regularly throughout the semester.

Save your notes! Your chemistry notes from your freshman year may be useful when you take a polymers class during your senior year. It's also helpful to review your notes as you progress through college, because it can build your confidence in how much you're learning.

include questions—either on the same page or a new page—that will help you think about the material on a deeper level. For example, asking "Why is it important to know this?" can help you move beyond demonstrating your comprehension of the material to making it relevant and useful for you.

Reorganizing your notes, especially if you did not initially capture the information in an organized manner, is an effective way to further your understanding of what you have learned. For example, if your professor lectures on a short story or poem and moves from one topic to another about the literature, you may consider organizing your notes, after class, around specific literary elements. Likewise, if your history professor discusses the major effects of the Vietnam War on the economy, you may consider organizing your notes by cause and effect.

Finally, adding to your lecture notes from your reading and sharing with classmates will make the notes richer and more relevant. You may find that the assigned reading provides deeper information about a lecture or information that was not mentioned at all in class. Moreover, a classmate may have captured information that you did not even though you were paying close attention. You can also engage in critical questioning of the material and take turns making connections between major concepts. See Exhibit 8.5 for a review of tips for successful note taking.

GRIT GAINER™

GRITTY LEARNING   For most students, it comes down to one of two things. Either you own your classes or they can own you. Either you take charge of optimizing your time, effort, and learning, or you can get sucked into a whirlpool of frustration, boredom, and missed opportunities. GRIT separates the best from the rest. Here are two GRIT tips:

1. The moment you blame your professor, the textbook, or anything else is the moment you give up control over your own success. It's the moment you lose.

2. The most effective, happy, and successful students use note taking to get what they need *in spite of* whatever distractions, frustrations, or limitations they may face. Let frustration fuel your determination to find a way no matter what.

5 things future professionals need to know about listening and note taking

be ready to take notes,
anytime, anywhere

Your boss, customer, and coworkers will share important information with you while you're riding in an elevator, driving in a car, or eating dinner, so you need to be ready to jot down key ideas at a moment's notice.

technology can be your friend,
but also your enemy

Sometimes a pad of paper and pen is the best tool for taking notes, because the circumstances might prohibit a smartphone, laptop, or other electronic device. You never want to tell your boss, "Can you hold on a moment while my laptop gets started?"

never, ever,
interrupt

The death of a good learning conversation with anyone is when someone interrupts the other person. Let your customer, boss, coworker, or other professional colleague finish his or her thought before you offer your own.

take time to
restate what you think
you heard

The best way to ensure your understanding of what someone just said and to convey to the person that you understood is to simply say, "If I understand you correctly, you said . . . ." Everyone appreciates this, and it gives you a chance to more deeply understand what someone is saying.

try to build time into your
schedule before and after
class, meetings, and other
activities to finish and review
your notes

Immediately after an interaction with someone is the best time to capture your thoughts in writing and take note of any important action items you promised or questions you need to answer. If you don't take these notes immediately after your conversation, you'll forget, no matter how good you think your memory is.

151

THE GRIT ADVANTAGE

Most people are mediocre or poor note takers for one simple reason: They give up. They fall back into old, ineffective ruts, rather than digging deep, enduring the struggle it takes to get good, and experiencing the tremendous benefits real effort provides. Step back, even walk away and take a few breaths, then reengage, retry, and repeat as many times as you need to, until you start seeing some positive traction from your relentless effort. Persistence pays.

Now you are ready to relate this to your own life:

- Practice active listening by focusing on what the speaker is saying and remember what she has said before responding or forming an opinion.

- Start listening critically by considering the speaker's authority, credibility, and accuracy.

- Begin to identify listening barriers that you face in your classes and practice strategies for eliminating them.

- Choose the best note-taking strategy for the type of class you are taking.

- Review your notes within a day or two of taking them.

HOW GRITTY ARE YOU?

Now that you've completed this chapter, how committed are you to:

1. Regularly practicing being a better listener?

   Zero Commitment 0 ———————————————— 10 Fully Committed

2. Not blaming others or other things when you have difficulty listening or remembering what you have heard?

   Zero Commitment 0 ———————————————— 10 Fully Committed

3. Employing the best strategies and going after the most important goals?

   Zero Commitment 0 ———————————————— 10 Fully Committed

4. Not getting distracted while listening or taking down notes?

   Zero Commitment 0 ———————————————— 10 Fully Committed

9 Writing, Presenting, and Information Literacy

Chapter goals to help you *get in, get through, get out, and get paid:*

In order to get in, get through, get out, and get paid, you'll need to write well, deliver effective presentations, and use information effectively to support your arguments. These skills will be very important in your career after college, so your hard work will pay off for a lifetime.

To meet those goals, *this chapter will help you:*

- Anticipate the types of writing assignments you'll be assigned and your professors' expectations for these assignments
- Identify the steps in the writing process
- Recognize all the stages of effective research
- Create and deliver an effective presentation
- Demonstrate the **GRIT** it takes to put the tools from this chapter to use

MyStudentSuccessLab™

Log in to MyStudentSuccessLab.com to deepen your **GRIT** mindset and build the skills you'll need to get through the college experience.

Juanita's Story

© ANDRESR/SHUTTERSTOCK

"A 15-page research paper and five-minute Powerpoint presentation. Due during the last week of class," Juanita repeats to her mother over the phone.

"What do you have to write it on?" her mother asks.

"We get to pick from a list, but I don't even know what some of the topics are, like 'conflict management theory,'" Juanita says as she looks over the list again. "I guess that is the point of research."

"You better get started, Juanita. I know how you are about writing papers—even when you end up doing well." Juanita remembered many nights she stayed up writing papers at the last minute because she didn't know how to get started. She also felt she did better during the excitement of the clock ticking.

"I guess this is my chance to break those bad habits," Juanita says.

"I thought this was sociology, not English," her mother says.

"It is, Mom, but all of my instructors still expect me to write a good paper," Juanita says. "And it is not just a paper. I have to get up and say something about what I learned. You know how nervous I get doing that."

Juanita heads toward the library to start writing her 15-page paper and creating a presentation on a topic that she knows nothing about right now.

Now, what do you think?

- What would you do if you were unsure how to start an assignment?
  - **a.** Not worry; I will find a classmate to help me
  - **b.** Do what I usually do—wait until a few days before to start or get help
  - **c.** Start planning now to understand the assignment and start on it

- What strategies could you use to ensure that you can tackle future writing and researching assignments?
  - **a.** Practice writing and researching repeatedly
  - **b.** Use the feedback I get from my professors to focus on what I can improve
  - **c.** Nothing—I am either a good writer or not and no amount of extra effort will change that

Your Terms for success

when you see . . .	it means . . .
Brainstorming	A prewriting technique that involves writing down everything that comes to mind in a list
Clustering	A prewriting technique that involves visually representing how a subject is related to other subjects
Conclusion	The last paragraph of an essay that presents your overall points and final thoughts
Essay	A type of assignment that has an introduction, a thesis, body paragraphs, and a conclusion
Freewriting	A prewriting technique that involves writing freely and without consideration of punctuation, grammar, or spelling
Organization	How your details for your essay or paper are placed
Outline	The essential parts of a paper or speech; usually presented in a specific outline format using Roman numerals for each major part
Peer review	A process in which a peer or classmate evaluates your paper or project
Physical delivery	The bodily and facial movements that enhance or distract from a speech

Portfolio	A collection of separate assignments or of drafts of an assignment
Research	The act of finding, evaluating, and incorporating sources into an assignment
Rough draft	An unpolished attempt at an assignment
Thesis	An essay's central idea that is supported throughout the writing
Transitions	Words or phrases that signal a change in thought or additional ideas

You Will Write a Lot in College (And in Your Career, Too!)

Homework has a whole new meaning in college. These assignments are more than just a basic review of what you learned in class, and they certainly are not the dreaded "busy work" that you experienced in high school. Instead, the assignments you will be given in college will challenge you to think in ways that you may not be used to, and they will demand much more time to complete than your high-school assignments. For sure, you will encounter familiar assignments such as extra problem solving questions in math classes and research papers in English classes, but you may also be required to complete a class multimedia project that involves using PowerPoint or even a community-based project that entails working with various agencies to develop a solution to a real-world problem and then presenting it to local community leaders. Other types of writing and presentation assignments include those listed in Exhibit 9.1.

EXHIBIT 9.1   College Writing and Presentation Assignments

Journal	Personal reflections an given topics or on your experience during the semester; often considered an informal writing assignment.
Portfolio	A collection of writing that is usually used to showcase development over time.
Project proposal	A written intention of what a project topic, argument, or scope will be; usually a short assignment that is completed early in the process of a larger project.
Essay	Literally defined as an "attempt"; an original composition that presents an argument or viewpoint on a topic.
Research paper	A formal assignment that requires the use of appropriate sources; usually requires an original argument or approach to present the research.
Report	A retelling of a process or experience.
Demonstration	A show of a process or the mastery of a skill.
In-class and out-of-class group assignment	Collaborative work that requires participation by all members.
Formal and informal classroom presentation	A brief expression of an opinion, topic, or experience or an elaborate, lengthy presentation that includes visual aids.

Preparing ahead of time to complete a writing assignment is part of the writing process.

Tenacity

Most students compromise their grades on written assignments because they don't dig deep and show the discipline it takes to hand in their best result. Use your GRIT to give each written assignment your best effort.

© CREATAS IMAGES/GETTY IMAGES

Take the Time to Understand the Assignment First

Before you can bask in the glory of a well-done project or essay, you will have to start with first things first. Understanding the assignment is the first and sometimes most crucial step in succeeding. Too many students start writing right away without fully understanding the directions, the requirements, and the time, equipment, and skills that are necessary to complete the assignment.

Know the Difference Between Due and Do

There are two words you will hear when your professor discusses a writing assignment, and although they sound similar, they have two different meanings: *do* and *due.* You will "do" your paper, meaning research and write it, well before it is "due" to turn in. Waiting to write an essay the night before or even the day it is due can be an undertaking much larger than one originally anticipated. Most assignments in college will require hours of researching, taking notes, constructing outlines, writing drafts, and formatting and printing the final document. In some cases, you may need the entire semester to work on a large project. You may also need to allot enough time to use a computer or other technology. These tasks add to the time it takes to finish an assignment, so say goodbye to quickly jotting down answers or writing an assignment the hour before class. When it is D-U-E, it will need to be D-O-N-E well before.

Read and Follow Directions

Giving yourself the time to complete an assignment will allow you to carefully read and follow the directions. Too often students rush through an assignment sheet only to omit a critical requirement. For example, will you need to submit your assignment via email? Will you need to prepare a list of resources you used to complete it? Does it need to be typed? Does it require a cover page? Will you need to make visual aids? All of these are possible requirements, and if you are unsure of what is expected, despite the assignment details, be sure to ask for clarification. Exhibit 9.2 provides an example of assignment directions. See if you can determine what requirements you will need to consider when you complete it. Underline, circle, or highlight the important information.

Every Assignment Will Have a Length, Audience, and Purpose

Length, audience, and purpose are other key factors in understanding writing assignments. For many assignments, you will be assigned a length, such as a two-page paper or a 1,500-word essay. Instructors often specify the length of an assignment to give you a sense of how detailed and comprehensive your coverage should be. For instance, if your instructor assigns you a one-page review of a website, then a 10-page paper will not be appropriate because too much information will be included. Conversely, if you have a 2,500-word research paper to write, a 750-word paper will not suffice because there will not be enough information and reflection to fulfill the assignment. If you worry that you cannot meet the length requirement of an assignment, talk with your instructor as soon as possible. He or she will be able to help you narrow or expand your topic so that you will have enough material.

EXHIBIT 9.2   Example of Assignment Directions

Topic: Proposal

Due: Wednesday, April 18

Before you begin work on your research paper, you will submit a proposal to me for approval. This process is much like proposals that scholars submit to determine if they will be accepted for a conference. Your proposal must be typed and must contain the following all on one or two pages:

- Your name
- Working title of your research paper
- Working thesis of your research paper
- A 75-word abstract (summary) of your topic
- A 100-word description of how you plan to research your topic

The audience for your assignment describes who will be reading the paper. Is your reader an expert in the topic, or a fellow college student who has never heard of the topic before? You would write the assignment differently for these two audiences, so you need to know what audience your instructor wants you to address before beginning the assignment. Do not assume that the audience is just your professor. If the professor doesn't specify the audience, ask for clarification. If you don't get clarification from your instructor, imagine that you are writing to college students who have been studying the same subject—such as your classmates. How you present your ideas and the words you use should be appropriate for other college students.

There may, however, be times when you will be assigned a particular audience as part of the requirements for a writing project. The reason that instructors do this is to help you focus your ideas, language, and argument. Consider, for example, an assignment that may be part of a health class:

Writing Assignment for Concepts of Health and Wellness

In a three-page paper, discuss the latest information about sexually transmitted diseases.

This is a straightforward assignment that can be completed by anyone who has access to current information. However, how would the assignment change if your audience were 12-year-old students? What information would you add or eliminate? What kind of language would you use? Would you include diagrams and definitions or cartoons? How much detail would you provide? These are all new considerations you will have to make because your audience will have certain limitations. Unfamiliar vocabulary, technical terms, detailed information, and photographs may be inappropriate for these students. Simple terms, diagrams, and personal stories about kids their own age may be a better way to convey the more complicated information.

Now, consider the same topic with an audience of college students. Again, you will have the same questions: What information would you add or eliminate? What kind of language would you use? Would you include diagrams and definitions or cartoons? How much detail would you provide? Obviously, this audience will have different needs than the elementary-school students have. Because your audience is more mature, you will need to think about how to approach a topic that they have definite ideas about. Some may be resistant to hearing about the topic because they believe it is not appropriate to discuss; others may feel they know enough to make their own decisions. Still others will not see the relevance for them. As this example shows, these challenges are unique to your audience—changing *who* you are writing for changes *how* you present the information.

GRIT
Growth

Be gritty. Ask yourself, "Where and how can I get the information or examples I need to do this assignment as effectively and efficiently as possible?"

"Dr. Pennebaker's Basic Writing Assignment" by Dr. James Pennebaker. Copyright © by James Pennebaker. Used by permission of the author.

It's in the
syllabus

- What are the expectations for writing assignments in your class?
- Does the syllabus outline these expectations or provide grading criteria?
- If you are unclear of the expectations for writing in your classes, how can you find out more information?
- What resources are available that can help you determine what to expect?

A final consideration for your assignment is your purpose. Your purpose for writing will be closely connected to your assignment (see the assignment types discussed in the next section), but there are other purposes for writing. For example, in addition to evaluating a website, your purpose could also be to make your audience laugh. As you compare two popular diet plans in a paper, your purpose could be to persuade readers that one of the plans is a healthier choice. The purposes for writing are endless, but it is important to ask yourself why you are writing and what you want to accomplish besides completing an assignment or getting a good grade. The answers to those questions will be your purpose for writing, and knowing that purpose will help you complete your assignment effectively.

Your Instructor's Prompts Determine the Writing Assignment

No two writing assignments in college will look the same, in part because each professor will have a different kind of *prompt,* or verb to describe what kind of response you should provide. Exhibit 9.3 lists and explains many of the types of prompts you will encounter in college. Each one asks for a different type of writing assignment, so be sure to review your instructor's guidelines carefully so that you can make sure you are fulfilling the assignment correctly.

EXHIBIT 9.3 Writing Prompts, Definitions, and Explanations

Writing Prompt	Definition	Explanation
Summary	A brief retelling of a subject	In a summary, you will cover the main points of an event or a text, but summaries do not contain your opinion on the subject.
Evaluation	Asks for your opinion	You will need to consider the subject's strengths and weaknesses, and you will need to provide specific examples to support your ideas.
Discussion or description	Provides specific details about the topic	The more specific details you can provide, the more likely you will adequately describe or define the subject.
Analysis	Breaks a subject apart and looks at its components carefully	Once you have investigated the parts, you must put the subject back together again.
Compare and contrast	Examines two subjects more carefully to make a significant paint about them	Before you describe their similarities and then their differences, you will set up the reason for the comparison and contrast.
Synthesis	Combines two or more sources into an essay	A synthesis uses your perspective or argument as the foundation and provides the reader with ideas and support from other sources.
Persuasive argument	Takes a stand about a topic and encourages readers to agree	A persuasive argument is most effective when specific, accurate evidence is used. Effective persuasion requires that you treat your readers with respect and that you present your argument fairly.

Exams and Portfolios Provide Additional Writing Opportunities

Research papers and essays will not be the only way you will asked to show your professors how well you write and think. You may also be asked to demonstrate your writing ability in other formats and for different occasions. Essay exams and portfolios are the two most popular types of assignments that will require an ability to write well, but you may also need to demonstrate your writing skills in group projects and multimedia presentations. The key to success is to learn what additional writing skills are necessary for these different formats and occasions.

Instinct

GRIT is a huge weapon for research papers, because they are usually pretty difficult and take a lot of work. Ask yourself, "What would be the best way to approach this assignment better and faster than most people would?"

ESSAY EXAMS. Essay exams always cause a little more anxiety than other writing assignments because of the pressure of recalling information and writing with the clock ticking. Because you don't have the luxury of time to write an essay on an exam, you will have to prepare. Students who have trouble writing an essay can improve their performance by practicing for the exam.

If you know the essay topic beforehand, you can practice writing your response by allowing yourself the same amount of time that you will have when you take the test. The key to writing well under pressure is to simulate the same circumstances when you practice. If you don't know what the topic is beforehand, you can still prepare for the essay exam by going back over your notes to see if your professor talked about any major issues that would make a good essay topic. Then practice writing responses to questions you think might be on the exam.

Another helpful strategy is to develop an outline before beginning to write the full answer. List the key points that your essay should include and organize those points in a logical structure. For example, if your instructor asks you to describe how photosynthesis works, your outline should include the terminology and processes in the order in which they occur. Depending on the length of the essay you've been asked to write, you could even use the outline as the headings and sub-headings for your essay. If your answer describes three reasons why Gothic architecture makes use of arches, you could provide three headings in the essay corresponding to the three reasons.

PORTFOLIOS. A writing portfolio is a collection of your writing throughout the semester. This type of project is popular with instructors because it allows students to work on their writing all semester. Instead of getting a grade on the first draft that is turned in, students can revise papers and improve them over time. A benefit of the portfolio method is that students don't have to write perfectly in their first drafts and can polish their writing as the semester progresses.

The best way to handle a writing portfolio is to review the requirements for it, including due dates and policies on completing final drafts, and write and revise your papers early and often. If you have questions about the expectations, especially if you have never completed a portfolio before, ask your instructor and schedule periodic meetings to make sure that you are completing the components successfully. Finally, take advantage of the opportunity to submit multiple drafts and receive feedback on them. Revising essays for a portfolio takes time, but you will receive extensive feedback and help with improving your writing.

Resilience

One way to be more resilient is to proactively minimize potential adversity. Many students fall short on their portfolio assignments because they wait until it's due. Show some GRIT by starting early, sticking with it, and getting it done!

How Your Professor Grades Your Writing Shouldn't Be a Mystery

Your college professors may vary widely in how they evaluate and grade your written assignments. Some professors look for and reward key words and concepts in an essay exam, whereas others count off for grammatical, mechanical, and organizational problems even if the key concepts are easily identifiable. You will soon learn, if you have not already, that each professor has his or her own criteria for grading written assignments, and the sooner you learn what the criteria are, the better able you will be to complete the assignment satisfactorily.

If your professor does not give you a list of grading criteria, respectfully ask for a sample assignment or a list of what the professor will be looking for. You could also bring a sample of your own writing—such as your practice effort to write an exam essay—to your professor's office hours and ask for some feedback. Talking with the professor before and after the assignment is graded is the best way to know what to expect. Asking other students who have taken classes with the professor (and who did well!) is another way to get an idea of how you will be evaluated.

More and more professors are using rubrics for grading assignments, including written work. If your professor provides a rubric, review it carefully because it will provide the criteria that your professor will use in determining a grade. When you practice writing essays, you could even ask a fellow classmate to use the rubric to score your answer. You can also score your own writing using the rubric to check your work before someone else looks at it. If your professor doesn't mention a rubric or provide one before the assignment, respectfully ask the professor if he or she has one available that you could use to prepare for an assignment or exam. The sample rubric in Exhibit 9.4 shows what elements will be scored and what level of success you can earn based on your work. If your professor provides you with a rubric as part of the assignment, use it to make a best guess of what your grade will be.

Remember that professors expect you to write at a college level and that your writing assignments should reflect those characteristics. You may find that although you received good grades on papers in high school, you have to work much harder for those same grades on papers in college. In addition to higher standards, you should be aware that your professors' job is to make you a better thinker and writer, no matter what the subject. They will be correcting errors and making suggestions for improvement. You also need to prepare for the reality that a professor in one class will use very different criteria for evaluating your writing than another professor. Just as you'll have to prepare yourself for different types of managers in your future career, you'll have to adapt to different types of professors each semester.

Having just mentioned future managers and careers, this is a good place to mention that professors and universities require a lot of writing assignments and work hard to help you become a good writer because writing is an absolutely critical skill for your future life and career. Even as the forms of technology that we use to communicate change, our reliance on the written word to communicate with one another and manage our personal and professional relationships endures. Effective writers have influence and success in life because they can communicate their ideas to others. The guidance and direction we offer in this chapter will serve you for a lifetime. See Exhibit 9.5 for a list of the top 10 expectations for college writing.

Tenacity

A wake-up call for many students is that your professors don't grade you for how hard you worked. They grade you for the quality of the result you turn in. Telling them you're tenacious means little; using your GRIT to get it done means a lot!

GRIT GAINER™

GRITTY WRITERS TAKE THEIR TIME   Writing is one of the grittiest requirements and opportunities in your educational career. Most students stop short of giving their best effort on written assignments because they do not put in thet time and hard work to do well. You can build GRIT by:

- Starting earlier, allowing time for at least two drafts of any written assignment
- Asking yourself with each draft, "How can I make this considerably better?"
- Asking yourself before you hand it in, "What is one final improvement I can make?"

EXHIBIT 9.4   Sample Grading Rubric

| Grading Rubric for a Book Analysis and Reflection Paper | | | | | |
Element	Low	Middle	High	Total Possible	Total Earned
MLA format	0–1 does not conform to MLA format rules.	2–3 conforms inconsistently to MLA rules.	4–5 conforms to MLA format rules.	5	
Main Assignment: Development	0–6 does not fully develop per the assignment guidelines.	7–11 develops satisfactorily, but may not develop each element sufficiently.	12–15 fully develops per the assignment guidelines.`	15	
Main Assignment: Originality/ Creativity	0–6 lacks originality or creativity in thought or execution.	7–11 provides some originality and creativity in thought or execution.	12–15 is highly creative, insightful, and original.	15	
Main Assignment: Connection to Themes of the Book	0–6 lacks clear connection to themes in the book or provides very thin connection.	7–11 provides a clear connection to the themes of the book, but may overlook opportunities to strengthen the connection.	12–15 clearly, originally, and thoughtfully makes connections with the themes of the book.	15	
Reflection: Development	0–6 does not fully develop per the assignment guidelines.	7–11 develops satisfactorily, but may not develop each element sufficiently.	12–15 fully develops per the assignment guidelines.	15	
Reflection: Insight/ Original Thought	0–6 lacks originality or creativity in thought or execution.	7–11 provides some originality and creativity in thought or execution.	12–15 is highly creative, insightful, and original.	15	
Reflection: Connection to the Themes of the Book	0–6 lacks clear connection to themes in the book or provides very thin connection.	7–11 provides a clear connection to the themes of the book, but may overlook opportunities to strengthen the connection.	12–15 clearly, originally, and thoughtfully makes connections with the themes of the book.	15	
Reflection: Grammar, Mechanics, and Spelling	0–1 contains many grammatical, mechanical, and spelling errors.	2–3 contains several grammatical, mechanical, and spelling errors.	4–5 contains very few or no grammatical, mechanical, or spelling errors.	5	
Total				100	

EXHIBIT 9.5 Top Ten Expectations for College Writing

Expectation for College Writing	What It Means
Fulfillment of the assignment	Your paper faithfully follows the assignment guideines.
Original thought	Your paper presents your viewpoint of the topic.
Main point or idea	Your paper conveys one major idea.
Organization	Your paragraphs and the details within those paragraphs are presented logically.
Focused paragraphs	Your paragraphs present one minor idea at a time. Each minor idea supports your overall point.
Concrete, specific details	Your concrete details appeal to the reader's senses; your specific details provide a clear picture of your point.
Neat presentation	Your paper is neatly word-processed and printed an clean, quality paper.
Grammatical sentences	Your sentences are complete and error-free.
Correct spelling	All of your words are spelled and capitalized correctly.
Punctuality	Your assignment is turned in on time.

Your Campus Provides Help for Your Writing

There may be times when a writing assignment is confusing or overwhelming. If at any time you don't understand what you are supposed to do or you feel stressed about the assignment, contact your instructor as soon as you can. Stressing out about the assignment will only make it seem impossible to complete. Instructors know you have other responsibilities and classes and are often willing to work with you if you have planned ahead and asked for help early.

When getting help with an assignment, be sure to ask your instructor first—he or she is the one who will best know what needs to be done. If your college has a writing center, you should make an appointment with a tutor as soon as you realize you need some help. Writing center tutors will be able to explain what you need to do to complete the assignment.

Classmates and friends can be other sources of help, but use their help cautiously. Your classmates may not know much more about the expectations than you do. Moreover, your instructor may prohibit any kind of collaboration, even if it is to better understand what you need to do. Getting help from anyone who is not in the class or not taking college courses should be your last resort because they are further removed from your instructor's expectations.

No matter who helps you with the assignment, be sure that you are doing the assignment rather than someone else doing it for you. Some students, out of fear or frustration, have had other people complete part or all of their assignments. The most obvious reason that you should not allow someone else to help too much is that your instructor could penalize you for not doing the assignment yourself. More important, if you do not complete the assignment yourself, you are robbing yourself of an opportunity to learn.

■ Reviewing a peer's work may be a required component of a writing assignment.

© JUPITERIMAGES/GETTY IMAGES

Peer Review Is a Great Opportunity for Feedback

Peer review, in which a classmate evaluates your work, is a process that you may go through in your composition classes or in classes that have an important group project as part of your grade. This may occur in a peer review workshop, common in writing classes, where you and a classmate exchange papers and assess how well each of you has met the assignment requirements. You may also be looking for grammatical and spelling errors, which can be corrected before your final draft or project is submitted. Peer review, especially if assigned as part of your work in a class, can be extremely helpful to you. It can show you what others in the class are writing about and how they are completing assignments, which can in turn help you gauge how well you are doing. It can also help you learn how to correct mistakes, because you may find it easier to see errors in others' papers than in yours. Finally, it can help you get your paper in shape before you complete it for submission.

Sometimes your professor will formally arrange a peer review process in your class or a workshop. However, if the professor doesn't initiate a peer review process, ask your instructor if they are supportive of you organizing your own peer review process with an informal study group in the class. As long as students are not plagiarizing from one another or cheating in some other way (topics we'll discuss later), professors may be supportive of this approach, and you'll benefit from it by getting help and support from your peers to develop a finished and polished paper.

GRIT
Growth

Use your GRIT to reach out—get outside your own brain, your own skin—and seek others' input, feedback, and help to both accelerate and improve your writing.

Tutoring May Also Be Available

Another form of assistance available as you write your papers is tutoring. Most colleges have a learning assistance center or tutoring lab where other students or professional tutors are available to help those who need it. Tutoring is especially valuable if certain skills, such as grammar or spelling, need to be practiced and refined. The tutors at your college are usually trained to help students with the most common problems, and they have the added benefit of having completed the very courses they tutor in, so they know what to expect in terms of assignments and grading. Tutors, just as peer reviewers, cannot assure a good grade on an assignment that is reviewed. They can, however, point out areas that need to be improved and provide you with resources to help you become more aware of your strengths and weaknesses as a writer.

Make Sure You Know When You're Receiving Too Much Help

How do you know when you have received too much help on a writing assignment? If someone else writes whole sentences, paragraphs, and pages for you or supplies you with many main ideas and examples that you use in your paper, then you have probably received too much assistance on your writing assignment. Some professors disapprove of editing and proofreading services as well. When in doubt, check with your professor and explain what kind of help you are getting.

GRIT GAINER™

GRITTY WRITERS LOOK FOR IMPROVEMENTS   Build your GRIT with these two questions:

1. Where can I get the best and most brutally honest feedback on my writing so I can improve faster?

2. Which parts do I simply need to hack away at by myself to improve my skills?

■ Writing is a process that takes time.

Writing Is a Process

Prewriting Techniques Can Help You Get Started

Once you have read and understood the writing assignment, it is time to use one or more prewriting techniques to get your ideas down on paper before you start organizing them and writing your rough draft. You probably have your own way of writing, but it is worth investigating some of these proven methods for generating ideas.

There are three common prewriting techniques that you can use to generate details for your paper. *Freewriting* is a simple way to get ideas down on paper. The only rules in freewriting are to start with an idea and stop only after you have filled a page or after a certain amount of time has passed. When freewriting, you can allow your mind to wander off the subject, but you should write down everything that comes to mind. Later, when you start organizing your details, you can eliminate anything that does not pertain to your subject. If you are a good typist, you can freewrite by typing into a blank document. Don't worry about spelling, grammar, or punctuation when you freewrite—the purpose is to free your mind of that little voice that censors everything you think. (A tip—don't look at the screen when you're freewriting.)

Clustering is another method of prewriting that works well for those who learn better by visualizing concepts. Clusters, or think links, are visual representations of ideas and their relationships to each other. The key to clustering is to start in the middle of a sheet of paper, write down your topic, and circle it. Draw a line from your subject and write down a related topic that is part of the subject. For instance, "types," "prevention," and "treatment" are all parts of the topic "sexually transmitted diseases." In addition, subtopics branch off "prevention": "abstinence" and "condoms." The words and phrases that surround a topic or subtopic must be connected to it, both logically and literally, by drawing a line. If you like using the web or an iPad, there's a great app called Popplet that can help you create these visual clusters.

Another effective method for generating ideas is *brainstorming,* a process that involves writing down ideas as they come to you. The goal in brainstorming is to get as many ideas as possible down on paper, no matter how ridiculous or off-topic they are. The more details you generate, the more you have to work with as you begin organizing your paper. To brainstorm, simply write your topic at the top of a sheet of paper or type it into a new document on your computer, and then start listing any and all ideas that come to mind.

A Topic Sentence or Thesis Will Help You Organize the Details

Once you make a list of details that you would like to use in your paper, give some thought as to what your main point will be—a topic sentence if it is a paragraph or a thesis if it is an essay—before you decide how you would like to organize the details. Your main point will be at least one sentence that tells the reader what the whole writing will present or argue.

Mark Twain once said, "I didn't have time to write a short letter, so I wrote a long one instead." The point he was making is that it's actually more difficult to narrow your topic down to a concise sentence or thesis than to write a long essay that covers every aspect of a topic. Don't be discouraged if it seems difficult to summarize your topic into a single sentence or thesis statement. Give yourself time to write a few versions, review

GR I T
Instinct

> Since part of GRIT is not just how hard you work, but how you approach your goals, use the tools and tips in this chapter to sharpen *how* you approach your writing. Expect the first couple times to be frustrating, then try again.

them, and then try again. Even though the process will yield only a small amount of writing, a thoughtfully developed summary provides a solid foundation on which you can build the details of your assignment.

Once you have your topic sentence or thesis, there are a variety of ways that you can organize them in your paper effectively. You can arrange them from most to least important detail or least to most important detail. Details can also be arranged chronologically, especially if you are writing about an event that needs to follow a specific timeline. Moreover, details can be arranged from general ideas to specific or specific details to general. It is important to organize your details logically; how you arrange the supporting details will depend on your purpose and audience.

For example, suppose you are writing a paper on the greatest challenges to diversity on your campus, and your details include the lack of cultural appreciation activities, a recent racially motivated incident, the fact that there are few minorities in administrative roles, and the lack of African American literature classes offered. The current order of the details provides no logical connections among them, so your reader will have a difficult time understanding the magnitude of the problem. Instead, you could order them according to importance.

Which of the aforementioned details do you think is the most important indication of the challenges to diversity on your campus? Certainly, the most striking is the racially motivated incident. You could use it as the first, most important detail in your paper, something that will grab your readers' attention and keep them interested and sympathetic to your thesis. On the other hand, you could start your essay with a least important detail and use the incident detail as your last, most important point. How you arrange your details, as long as each detail builds on the next and supports your thesis, depends on your purpose for writing.

A Paragraph Should Cover One—and Only One—Topic

Paragraphs are the building blocks of an essay. Well-developed paragraphs can be any length. However, if a paragraph is too short, the reader will think that something is missing; if they are too long, the reader may get lost in what you are trying to say. The key to writing a good paragraph—and you will write many in your college career—is to stay focused on one topic at a time and to let the reader know what that main idea is with a *topic sentence*. A topic sentence can appear at the beginning, middle, or end of the paragraph. As a rule of thumb, paragraphs should not include more than five sentences.

Once you have determined what the paragraph will focus on, you can start putting your details in place. Just as you have considered the overall arrangement of the details in your paper, you will need to give some thought to arranging the details *within* the paragraphs. The same types of organization of details for an entire paper work for paragraphs as well: general to specific, specific to general, order of importance, and chronological. You can use a different method for each paragraph as long as all the paragraphs support your thesis.

Transitions Help You Move from One Thought to Another

To make your sentences flow smoothly and your paragraphs relate clearly to one another, you will need to use transitions. Transitions are words or phrases that signal to the reader that you are moving from one thought to the next. Imagine describing over the phone how to get from the college to your house. If you didn't use transitions, your listener might be confused as to how to get there. Words such as *first, next, then,* and *after* are transitional words that would help the listener see how the sentences of the directions relate to one another.

When you move from paragraph to paragraph in your paper, you will definitely need a strong transitional phrase or sentence to indicate that you are introducing a new idea or that a point is forthcoming. Phrases such as *in addition to, even though,* and *contrary to the point above* are strong enough to slow the reader down to pay attention to your next major point. These words serve as signposts to indicate the beginning of each idea and how each idea connects to the others. A paragraph that begins with the words *the first step* tells you something important: This idea is the first in a series of steps that will follow. The phrase *in other words* indicates that the author is restating the first point in case you missed it. The transition *also* tells you that another point is being made in addition to the one at the beginning of the paragraph. Finally, the phrase *for example* provides an example for achieving the goal in the previous sentence.

In addition to connecting ideas, transitions improve the readability of the paper. When you read your work out loud and it sounds "choppy" or repetitive in rhythm, you may need to add transitions. Adding transitions effectively takes practice. If you need help, see your instructor or someone in the writing center at your college. With a little work, the flow of your writing will improve.

Build Paragraphs into a Complete Essay

The word *essay* has its origins in French and means "an attempt" or "a trial." For college students, writing essays is an attempt, or a trial, in some sense, to meet the assignment without going crazy! In the context of college, an essay is a written composition on a particular subject that offers the author's view. If, for example, you are asked to write an essay on the death penalty or obesity in children, then you will need to present your viewpoint on the subject. Essays do not usually contain research; instead, they are built on your observations, logic, and opinions. They are, in essence, an attempt by you to convey your viewpoint on a subject and perhaps to learn something more about what you think about that subject.

When you are assigned an essay for a class, you need to include some basic components. Without all of them, your essay is simply a piece of writing, just as a few bones do not make up an entire skeleton. At the least, you will need a title, introduction, thesis, body paragraphs, and a conclusion. You have already reviewed the process by which you create the ideas and details that will be part of the paragraphs. To make it a complete essay, you will need to include a thesis, which is a statement of one or two sentences that provides an overall declaration of what your entire essay is about. Your introductory paragraph provides an overview of the topic and your conclusion restates or reflects on the main points you make. Your title connects to your essay's topic or thesis so that your reader has an idea of what your topic is before reading. Exhibit 9.6 provides a sample college essay.

Be Sure to Avoid Plagiarism

Instinct

Being an ethical writer means taking the high road and avoiding sleazy shortcuts, no matter what—even when you're under the gun on a deadline.

Plagiarism is the act of using someone else's words, images, and ideas without properly and accurately acknowledging them. This definition can also cover artwork and computer programming code. Basically, you must properly and accurately acknowledge any material you use within an assignment, besides information that is considered common knowledge. That means you must be familiar with and use the correct documentation format that your professor requires. Common documentation formats include MLA (Modern Language Association), APA (American Psychological Association), and CBE (Council of Biology Editors). Your professors will expect that you learn how to use a documentation format and use it consistently.

Any time that you are creating, writing, or producing an assignment either as an individual or as part of a group, you will need to document the information and sources you use. If your

EXHIBIT 9.6 Sample College Essay

Jasmine Student
Amy Baldwin
ENGL 1312
November 4, 2015
Existential Meaning in "Acquainted with the Night" and "The Road Not Taken"
by Robert Frost

Acclaimed poet Robert Frost is known for his elegant yet simplistic poems that contain a veiled but biting reflection of human nature. Frost was heavily traveled both internationally and across the United States, and thus was no stranger to self-exploration, a concept that he conveys through his poetry (Pritchard). By examining the speaker, structure, word choice, and imagery, one can see that both of Frost's poems "Acquainted with the Night" and "The Road Not Taken" are connected by the themes of the human search for and creation of meaning in an inherently meaningless world.

In "Acquainted with the Night," the speaker is creating meanings for himself and his world by moving outside of society's definitions and values. The repetition of "I have" signifies that the speaker is a single, lonely individual, rather than a group (lines 1, 5, 14). This indicates that the search for significance is a lonely one. It also indicates that the speaker is reflecting on himself and his own quest for meaning. That the "I have" repetition gradually fades from the poem expresses a loss of the self when the speaker reflects on himself (lines 1, 5, 14). Then the last line returns the "I have" to the poem, signifying that you will lose your idea of yourself in your reflection, but you can always create yourself once more (lines 1, 5, 14). Taken in a literal sense, the speaker's actions are intriguing. Most people would not "[outwalk] the furthest city light," but the speaker

Your name, course information, and title go at the top

Introduction provides overview and thesis.

Body paragraphs have one topic that is discussed throughout.

The road itself is a sign of motion in a specified direction, which road a speaker takes is consequential to the direction that his life takes, at least that is what the younger and older selves imagine. That the poem takes place in a wood, rather than the cityscape from "Acquainted with the Night," signifies wildness. There is no need for the speaker to escape from ready-made meanings; he simply has to create his own. The recklessness and freedom of the youthful self's choice is expressed by this setting. The choice was made free from convention and only at the discretion of individual nature, which is to take the seldom used road. However, the older self sighs at the choice with regret for what might have been (line 16). Although the younger and older selves fear that they made a mistake in their choice, the middle aged self acknowledges that he takes the path that makes more sense to him. The speaker's choice of one path, rather than the meanings held in each path, is what truly makes all the difference.

Although these poems were written over a decade apart, Frost carries an existential undertone through both of them. "Acquainted with the Night" suggests the process of breaking down meanings and understanding the void meaninglessness beyond them, only to build up your own meanings. "The Road Not Taken" examines the meanings that we apply to our decisions, understanding them to be innate to the choices. Both poems explore the creation of meaning in an inherently meaningless world. We do not search for understanding; we create it.

Conclusion wraps up all major points.

professor wants the assignment to be completely original—without the use of sources—then you will need to adhere to those guidelines. If you are completing an assignment as part of a group, you may be asked to document which group members completed which parts of the assignment.

The following is a list of specific instances of plagiarism to avoid in all of your assignments:

- Buying or downloading a paper off the Internet and turning it in as your own
- Copying and pasting material from the Internet or print sources without acknowledging or properly documenting the source
- Allowing someone else to write all or part of your paper
- Creating a "patchwork" of unacknowledged material in your paper by copying words, sentences, or paragraphs and changing only a few words
- Including fictitious references

The simplest rule to remember when it comes to plagiarism is that if you had to look up the information or you used part or all of someone else's idea, image, or exact words, you must let your professor or reader know. As in every unclear situation you may encounter, always ask for clarification. Your professor will be able to help you determine what you need to do if you are unsure.

integrity matters

At no time should you copy another student's answers. Just as you would not share answers during a test, it is best not to share your answers on work that is assigned out of class. If you have taken a class in a previous semester, you will also want to keep your assignments from being shared. Instructors may use the same assignments from semester to semester, and you don't want to put a fellow student in an awkward or potentially bad situation.

YOUR TURN

In 250 words, explain how students can compromise academic integrity, perhaps without even knowing it. Then describe what safeguards students can put in place to ensure academic integrity when working with others, whether it be fellow students or tutors.

Research and Information Literacy Are Also Processes

Research papers differ from essays and other written assignments in that they require you to investigate and incorporate sources to support your ideas as you go through the process of becoming an information-literate consumer. You will need to consider length, audience, and purpose, and you will need to pay close attention to the requirements of the assignment. Instructors may require that you research certain journals or databases, or they may ask for survey results or literature reviews. The steps needed to find reliable information and evaluate it before you use it in a paper are included in the definition of information literacy from Chapter 7. As with any writing assignment, you should start early and break it up into manageable parts. For a research paper, you will need to invest a considerable amount of time and energy.

Step 1: Choose a Topic

The assignment information you are given may help you determine what your topic will be. In some cases, your professor will be very specific; for example, an assignment may be "Write a research paper in which you present three methods for teaching preschool children to read." Other professors may be less direct and give you a topic such as "Write a paper on an important

GRIT GAINER™

GRIT TAKES DISCIPLINE   In an era when a lot of device-obsessed people are getting worse at writing, you can use your GRIT to really shine. Writing, like playing music or building anything, involves a series of disciplined steps that, with repetition and effort, can be mastered to create impressive results. Each time you dig deep to deliver your best effort, you prove to yourself how GRIT pays off, which helps you grow even more GRIT for the next assignment or challenge.

historical event." If you are ever unsure as to what your topic should be, always ask well before the assignment is due. Often, you can get ideas for narrowing your topic from your professor or your classmates.

Before you settle on a topic to research, consider the assignment's purpose and length. If you are writing a 10-page paper, your topic will need to be broader than a five-page paper. Also, if you are required to argue a point rather than provide basic information, your topic and subsequent research will be focused differently. Determining your topic first, regardless of what it is, will save you time when you begin to find sources for your paper.

G R I T
Tenacity

> Research sometimes requires tremendous focus and dedication. But when you dig deep and do it right, it can save you a ton of time and help you hand in a top-notch assignment.

Step 2: Find, Evaluate, and Catalog Your Sources

Once you determine your topic, you can then begin to search for sources for your paper. You will definitely want to learn how to use your library's catalog and databases beforehand. The library will often provide an orientation to students or you can get one-on-one assistance from a staff member. Never waste valuable time being confused—ask someone for help if you are not sure how to find information.

Your assignment and topic will influence what kinds of sources you will use for your paper. If your education class requires that you find websites that provide information on cyberbullying in elementary schools, then you will know what kind of sources you will use for your paper. However, if your education class requires that you write a research paper on the latest studies on cyberbullying, you will most likely need to access journals in your library's databases to find scholarly articles on the subject.

Once you find your sources, you will need to spend time deciding if they are reliable, credible, and useable for your paper. Again, look to your assignment or to your professor for guidance if you are unsure whether the source is acceptable for your paper. Most likely, if it was found in the library's catalog or databases, it should be a credible source. Chapter 7 provides specific questions for evaluating sources that can be used in the research process as well.

When you find a source that you plan to use in your paper, you need to catalog information about that source. How you do this will depend on the *documentation style* that your professor requires. Two of the most common are MLA (Modern Language Association) and APA (American Psychological Association), but the Chicago Manual of Style (CMS) and Council of Biology Editors (CBE) are just two additional ones that you may need to be familiar with. A documentation style simply means the format in which you acknowledge your sources within your paper and at the end in the references or works cited page.

Regardless of which style you use, incorporating sources into your paper requires that you provide essential information, usually the author's name and the title of the source, whenever you first use it in your paper. This means that whether you are quoting directly or paraphrasing, which is putting the author's ideas into your own words, you will need to let your reader know from where the information comes. Proper acknowledgement and documentation are essential to incorporating your sources correctly. Your professor will certainly want to hear your thoughts on the topic, but she will also expect that you have found sources and documented them properly to support your ideas.

Step 3: Use Your Sources to Support Your Argument or Thesis

Once you've located sources that provide reliable and relevant information for your paper, you can use these sources to organize, strengthen, and support your argument or thesis. A research paper is different from an essay because an essay relies primarily on your own opinion, whereas a research paper draws on outside sources to support your point.

What types of advertisements or news articles do you believe are the most persuasive? Chances are, you consider ads or articles that use factual data, expert sources, and logical arguments to support their point to be particularly persuasive. The same approach applies to your research paper. If the purpose of your paper is to argue a point, make a recommendation, or critically evaluate a theory or philosophy, your paper will have a stronger argument if you can support it with verifiable facts and outside sources. Once you've written a draft of your research paper, carefully review it and use a highlighter to mark every statement that someone might argue against or any claim that someone might doubt. Then, consider whether you can find an outside source to support your argument or claim. For example, if you're writing a report about the effect of the BP oil spill on the Gulf Coast economy, you could find economic

the unwritten rules
for Information Literacy

- **A majority of your classmates will fall for the Google trap.** Don't be one of them. You can distinguish yourself as an exceptional student by demonstrating an ability and willingness to search for sources of information that aren't retrieved from a Google search.

- **Information literacy is a great skill to emphasize in job interviews.** If you're interviewing for a part-time job, internship, or your full-time career, demonstrating your ability to find, analyze, evaluate, and use information can set you apart. Every job and every career requires some form of information literacy.

- **You may encounter some tricky situations when you critically evaluate information.** In some situations, your professor might present information in a lecture that you later discover is either outdated or factually incorrect. Before you bring such errors to your professor's attention, make sure you have authoritative sources of information to back you up, and then schedule time to meet with the professor during office hours. This is a better option than attempting to correct the professor publicly in class.

- **Quality trumps quantity.** Unless your professor has specific guidelines for the number of sources you should use, you will be better served if you find fewer, high-quality sources of information rather than a trove of unreliable sources.

- **Use direct quotes sparingly.** Direct quotes are your nuclear option, so to speak. Only use them when you don't think you can possibly paraphrase what the person is saying. Otherwise, paraphrase the information and cite the source. Papers that are full of direct quotes give the appearance that the author isn't thinking for himself.

GRIT GAINER™

GET GRITTY WITH RESEARCH   Good research requires plenty of GRIT. With each assignment, ask yourself:

1. Where can I get the best and most credible information on this subject?

2. How can I dig deeper to unearth something new about this topic?

3. Where haven't I looked that might offer some brilliant insights on this subject?

data and quotes from industry experts to support your claims that the oil spill caused negative effects to the region. Your research paper will be better if you can provide research support for most, if not all, of your claims.

Speaking and Presenting Are Life Skills That Will Serve You Well

Learning to effectively speak and present on a topic in college is a skill that will benefit you not only on the job, but also in life. For example, you may need to speak on behalf of the parents at your children's school as president of the Parents and Teachers Association, or you may be asked to make weekly announcements at your church. In your college classes, you will likely get a specific assignment (give a five-minute persuasive speech on a current event) or a specific topic (cloning). However, not all speaking experiences will begin with detailed directions. You may be asked to introduce someone or to "talk for about 10 minutes about whatever you think will interest the audience." Even the moments when you raise your hand in class to answer a question or make a point are opportunities to speak and present. Regardless of how you are assigned a speech, the process will be the same: You will need to plan, prepare, deliver, and assess.

© GOODLUZ/SHUTTERSTOCK

Presenting in front of fellow students will be a part of many of your classes.

Your Speaking Plan Includes Your Topic, Purpose, and Audience

Choosing a topic is the first step to preparing to speak, just as it is in the writing process. At times, you will be provided a topic, but in some of your classes—or for some occasions—you will be allowed to create your own. Topics for speeches can come from your personal experience, current events, or from in-depth research. If you are not sure which personal experience, current event, or research topic you want to explore, it is a good idea to use brainstorming or another method of generating ideas to determine which topic interests you the most. It's also valuable to select a topic for which you have a passionate interest or some personal experience. This kind of relevance will help you convey enthusiasm and confidence, even when you're a bit nervous.

Deciding your purpose will be your next step. You may need to inform, persuade, or entertain your audience. If you will be informing them of your topic, you will likely use details and language that present the information in an unbiased manner. If you will be persuading your audience, you will use examples and language to change their attitudes or beliefs. Entertaining your audience will also determine how you will present your topic because you will include information, details, and language that will get a laugh or amuse. Your speech can have more than one purpose—and sometimes all three—but one will be the most emphasized.

Just as writers need to decide who their audience is before they begin writing, speakers must also consider whom they will be addressing. Audience analysis is the process by which speakers determine who will be the receivers of the message. Audience analysis questions include the following: How many people will be in the audience? What are the characteristics of the audience (gender, ages, race, culture, educational background, learning style, etc.)? What are their attitudes toward your topic? What do they know about the topic?

Occasion analysis questions include the following: When are you speaking? How long will you have to speak? What is the space like (if you can find out in advance)? What else will you need? Visual aids? Handouts? Time for questions or discussion?

Tenacity

Often the things that require the greatest courage or that cause you the most adversity can also provide the greatest opportunities. Presenting is a great exa mple—it scares most people. Doing it well is tough. But it's a skillset that can be mastered with relentless practice, and the benefits are huge!

Your Voice Is the Vehicle That Delivers the Speech

What if you crafted a fantastic speech and no one ever heard it because they couldn't understand what you were saying? Sound impossible? It has, unfortunately, happened before: A great speech is lost because the speaker didn't project his voice or mumbled through the words. Vocal delivery, then, is the most important aspect to getting the words out successfully. Consider the following suggestions when practicing and delivering a speech:

- **Volume.** Speak loudly enough that everyone can hear you clearly. You may feel unnatural speaking at this volume, but you need your voice to carry across the entire room and over any distracting noises.

- **Pace and pronunciation.** Speak slowly and deliberately, making sure that you are properly pronouncing words (check the dictionary) and using correct grammar (consult a writing handbook). Open your mouth and move your lips to ensure that you are enunciating. Speaker credibility is lost when words are not used properly or are poorly pronounced.

- **Variation.** Vary volume, pitch, and speed to create interest and capture attention. Pause between points for effect. Speakers who talk in a constant monotone tend to bore their audience.

Your Body Speaks, Too

Appropriate nonverbal communication while you are speaking can mean the difference between an effective and an ineffective speech. Paying attention to and practicing your body movements will help you develop good physical habits when speaking. Here are just a few to consider:

- Dress appropriately. If you look professional, you appear more credible. Unless you are making a point by dressing down or in a chicken outfit, dress up. A neat and clean appearance also suggests attention to detail and importance.

- Smile at your audience. It demonstrates a positive attitude and puts your audience at ease.

- Plant your feet. Place them firmly on the floor and stand up straight. Slouching or slumping lessens your effectiveness.

- Act naturally. The more you practice, the more comfortable you will be with your body movements and less likely to use unnatural, mechanical hand gestures and head movements.

- Move from the waist up only. Shuffling and pacing are distracting.

- Step out in front. Get in front of the podium when speaking to groups of 30 or fewer; it helps create intimacy and connection.

- Use hand gestures appropriately. Keep arms and hands close to the body and avoid pointing your finger to emphasize an idea; instead, use a closed fist with thumb slightly up. Open hands work well, but avoid banging on the podium or table.

- Maintain eye contact. Use the "figure 8" method of scanning the room so that each area gets your attention throughout the presentation. Think of an 8 lying on its side and trace the curves with your eyes, starting either on the right or the left of your audience.

Instinct

When it comes to presenting, how you do it is as or more important than what you say. The biggest risk is to take no risk at all. Show some GRIT, take some risks, and give it your all.

Visual Aids Can Complement Your Speech

In addition to considering your delivery methods, both physical and vocal, you may also want to keep in mind how you will use any visual aids. Visual aids help capture the audience's attention and, for audience members who are more visually oriented, also help them understand the ideas that you are presenting. A visual aid can be anything from an object, such as a doll or book, to a more elaborately created poster or handout that can emphasize certain points while you are speaking. Slide presentation software can also provide your audience with a visual representation of your topic.

When using visual aids, remember that they are most effective when they help the audience remember your key points, see a point you are making more clearly, and enliven your presentation without distracting them from listening to you. Here are a few tips for handling your visual aids:

- Less is always more with visual aids; make sure they are simple and easy to understand. For example, rarely should a single slide contain more than 25 words, and the font should be at least 24 point.

- To be seen and not heard was once a virtue, but you will want both in a presentation with visual aids. Make sure that your aids can be seen clearly by a person at the back of the room. Clear writing or a large font on a slide presentation will help your audience get your point.

- Be the center of attention even with a visual aid. You don't want it to take away attention from your speech or dominate your presentation. A well-considered prop or visual aid should enhance, not become, your speech.

GRIT GAINER™

PRACTICE MAKES FOR A GRITTY PRESENTATION   Becoming a skilled presenter can really make you shine, build your confidence, and create opportunities throughout your entire life. Build your presentation GRIT by asking:

1. What risk(s) might I not normally take that would have the potential to create the most positive impact?

2. Where can I put more effort into my presentation to at least increase the chances it will be a strong success?

3. Where and when will I practice until I'm ready to shine?

4 things future professionals need to know about writing, presenting, and information literacy

what you write in the workplace will be different, but you'll use the same skills

Most of what you'll write in the workplace will be relatively brief, with clarity and factual accuracy of utmost importance. Email responses to questions from your coworkers or boss will be common, and each one needs to be written well and carefully worded. You might also be responsible for writing that your employer will share with the public, including customers, so knowing your audience will always be an important step in the process.

regardless of your intended career, you will be giving presentations

Some presentations will be very formal, giving you plenty of time in advance to prepare and rehearse. In other cases, you might walk into a meeting and be called on to discuss a topic without advance notice. This, too, is a type of presentation that you should anticipate. As you gain experience, you'll find yourself looking forward to these opportunities, rather than dreading them. Each one is an opportunity to build your reputation among your coworkers and managers.

informality in communication might be OK for friends, but avoid it in your career

If you've established the habit of communicating informally with your friends via email, text, or social media, you'll have the tendency to carry those habits with you into the workplace. Avoid this by any means possible! The use of slang terms, profanity, misspelled words, emoticons, and abbreviations (e.g., "LOL") is, in general, inappropriate in the workplace, even if the other person initiates the communication in this manner.

your ability to critically evaluate information and its source is crucial to your reputation

If you ever catch yourself saying, "I read on the Internet that . . . ," stop yourself. Rely only on reliable sources of information like nationally recognized news media and peer-reviewed publications and stories, and check sites like snopes.com and factcheck.org before passing on information as "the truth." You never, ever, want to be the person to spread misinformation at work.

THE GRIT ADVANTAGE

Apply these tips and all facets of GRIT to write, research, and present better than ever before:

Growth. Seek new, different information and angles—the stuff most students don't find—to inform your writing, research, and presentations.

Resilience. Don't play it too safe. Enter the storm by taking the risks that will help you shine.

Instinct. Before you dig in, think about the best way to approach each assignment and presentation so you save time and come out with a better result.

Tenacity. Practice harder, do more drafts, and dig deeper than everyone else, and you will amaze yourself with your results!

HOW GRITTY ARE YOU?

Now that you've completed this chapter, how committed are you to:

1. Putting extra time and effort into your writing and research to produce even better results?

   Zero Commitment 0 —————————————————————————— 10 Fully Committed

2. Seeking the most qualified and brutally honest feedback you can find to accelerate your improvement?

   Zero Commitment 0 —————————————————————————— 10 Fully Committed

3. Trying over and over until you get skilled at writing and researching?

   Zero Commitment 0 —————————————————————————— 10 Fully Committed

10 Studying and Taking Tests

Chapter goals to help you get in, get through, get out, and get paid:

In order to get in, get through, get out, and get paid, you'll need to perform well on tests. Effective test taking is important not only in college, but even in your career, because many of today's technical fields require testing throughout your career. Even if you battle test-taking anxiety or have struggled with tests in the past, you can overcome those challenges and succeed.

To meet those goals, this chapter will help you:

- Determine the best study strategies
- Anticipate and identify different types of test questions
- Recognize unique features of different types of tests
- Practice effective test-taking strategies
- Demonstrate the **GRIT** it takes to do well on tests

MyStudentSuccessLab™

G R I T

Log in to MyStudentSuccessLab.com to deepen your **GRIT** mindset and build the skills you'll need to get through the college experience.

Four Student Stories:
Studying

TOP RIGHT: © ANDRESR/SHUTTERSTOCK; ALL OTHERS: © MONKEY BUSINESS IMAGES/SHUTTERSTOCK

Studying for their Biology 101 class was becoming an exercise in their own survival. Juanita, Evan, Michael, and Laura formed a study group early in the semester.

"So much work for just one class," Michael said. "It's insane."

Juanita replied, "I'm taking world literature and psychology. The reading alone takes me hours each night."

Michael thought he had studied too much of the wrong things, and Juanita had severe test anxiety.

"Are you starting without me?" Laura asked as she dropped her heavy backpack on the booth seat by Michael.

"Of course not," Juanita said. "Michael was just complaining about how much work this class is."

"My mother finished her degree right before I started school. If she can do it, I think I can," Laura said.

"Does anyone know what the test will cover?" Michael said.

"I have to study everything, even if I don't think it will be on the test," said Juanita. "I suggest we start going over everything that we have done since the first chapter."

Evan offered his advice. "If we just review our notes, we should be fine. When was the last time you failed a test?"

"Because we all seem to have different approaches, it sounds like we would be better off studying by ourselves," said Laura.

Now, what do you think?

- What would you do if your study group had divergent ideas as to how to study best?
  a. Convince them to spend time studying in different ways to accommodate each person's preferences
  b. Study by myself to avoid the distractions of others' needs
  c. Choose the two most effective ways to study and focus on those for the entire group
- How would you prepare for taking a test that will be a challenge for you?
  a. Use my strengths to learn the material in a way that suits me best
  b. Ask the professor what strategies work the best for the material and the type of test
  c. Not change a thing; I already have good study habits

Your Terms for Success

when you see . . .	it means . . .
Academic integrity	Refraining from cheating or using unapproved resources for a test or an assignment; completing a test or an assignment on your own
Cheat sheet	A studying method that includes recording information, outlines, or formulas on a small card or sheet of paper; sometimes allowed by instructors to be used while taking a test
Comprehensive exam	An exam that covers an entire semester's worth of material; usually given as a final exam
Course objective	A goal that the instructor has identified for the student to meet once the course is completed
Essay test question	A test question that requires a student to answer in the form of an essay
Final exam	An exam that is given at the end of a semester
Matching test question	A test question that provides one column of descriptors and another column of words that must be matched with the appropriate descriptor
Multiple-choice test question	A type of test question in which an incomplete sentence or a question is given and the correct response must be chosen from a list of possibilities
Objective test question	A question that presents a limited number of possible answers; includes matching, multiple choice, true/false, and short answer
Online test	A test that is taken through the Internet or through a course management system such as Angel or Blackboard
Open-book test	A test one takes in which one can look up answers in a textbook or in one's notes

A Study Strategy Will Keep You on Track

Although the terms are usually used interchangeably, a *test* is defined as a set of questions that are used to evaluate one's skills, aptitudes, and abilities on certain topics. Usually, tests assess your knowledge and abilities on a part of the course. An *exam,* however, by definition is an assessment of the material of an entire course. Final exams are sometimes called *comprehensive* or *cumulative* exams, which indicate that they will cover what you have studied all semester or term.

Unless your professor tells you directly what will be on the test, assume that anything that was assigned or covered in class may be there. Just about every college student has a story about taking a test that covered reading assignments and not what was discussed in class. These students were surprised to realize that studying the lecture notes was not enough. The following is a list of items that you may be tested on for any class:

- Material from the lecture, discussion, and in-class or out-of-class activity
- Information provided by a guest speaker
- Information from a workshop or field trip
- Multimedia productions such as video or audio
- Assigned readings, including chapters in the textbook
- Handouts, including PowerPoint slides and outlines

You can be assured that you will encounter a variety of test types. Take clues from what you do in class to help determine what kinds of test questions you may encounter. For example, if your professor spends time applying information from a chapter during class or as an assignment, then you will likely have test questions that will ask you to apply the information as well. Listen for clues that the professor gives you, such as "You should write this down" and "This is a really important point." Other cue phrases include "You may see this again on a test" and "If you saw this on a test, how would you answer it?" When you hear these phrases, write them down and review them when studying your other notes. A professor who says these things is begging you to take notice!

The best advice to give college students is plain and simple: Study for all tests. No exceptions. Sometimes you will find that you do not need to study as much for some classes; however, remember that studying effectively is a habit. To form a long-term habit, you must do it even when you don't think you have to, which is fundamental to making an activity part of a routine.

GRIT
Instinct

GRIT is about digging deep and doing what it takes to make it happen, even if you have to sacrifice, struggle, and suffer. Instinct is about going at it the best way. So do yourself a favor: decide now or on the first day of the new term what you are going to give up and do without in order to study and achieve your goals. It will save you time and heartache later.

Space Your Studying Out over Time and Vary Your Study Places

The best time to begin studying is as soon as the semester starts. Be careful of the mindset that because you are not in class every day you don't need to study every day. Some students begin studying the day before an exam, which may be too late to review and remember all the material that has been covered over the past several weeks.

Review your notes within two days of taking them and, if possible, start studying for future exams right now. Research has shown that studying in smaller increments of time, such as 30 minutes to an hour, over a longer period of time, such as a week, is more effective than cramming four hours straight the night before.

If you are a typical college student, then your time will be limited. You may not have the luxury of large blocks of time, so you will need to be creative about studying. Because it is more effective to study for short periods of time, consider studying in between classes, during breaks at work, and on the way to work and school (provided you are not driving). Another way to ensure that you study during the day is to get in the habit of always carrying your notes or books with you—this way you'll be able to take advantage of any unexpected free time. You can also get up earlier or stay up later so you can spend a few minutes studying before starting or ending your day.

If you have the luxury of choosing when to study, rather than sandwiching it in between work and family responsibilities, pay attention to what time of day you are most alert and receptive to learning. The best time for you to study is dependent on your schedule, your responsibilities, your age, and your personal preferences. Some people identify themselves as "night owls," whereas others claim to be "morning people." Whatever your peak performance time, be sure to study your most difficult subjects at that time. If you have a predictable schedule all semester, plan to study at the same time each day.

The environment in which you study is just as important as the time of day and the length of time you spend studying. You will need to find the kind of environment that works well for you. Some people need complete silence with no distractions, whereas others need a little background noise to stay focused. At the least, create a place that is comfortable, has good lighting, and has space for your supplies and books. It is easier to make time to study when you have a place to do it. If you have nowhere at home that is quiet and roomy, then search for a place on campus or a local library that offers study space. Some people find that studying away from home is better because they are not distracted by the television, phone, or family members. Conventional wisdom has advised that the studying in the same familiar place is best, but newer research suggests that varying your environment while studying improves your ability to recall information.

Small children can pose a particular difficulty in finding quiet time. If you have small children, make a concerted effort to find a quiet spot. You may need to hire a babysitter or find a classmate who can trade child care services with you. For example, you could offer to babysit a classmate's kids when he needs to study in exchange for him watching yours when you have a paper to write. Some college students who are also parents find time to study only when their children are asleep. Therefore, their best studying takes place late at night or early in the morning at home. Do whatever works best for you.

Tenacity

Lots of students simply go through the motions, then wonder why they haven't achieved their goals. Setting a time and place to study is one thing. Putting in the effort and digging deep to actually do what it takes to learn what you need is what matters. Sticking to your study regimen, especially when you're tired, it's inconvenient, the weather is bad, or it's simply easier not to, is what the grittiest and the greatest students do.

Effective Studying Is Active and Has a Purpose and Goals

Studying effectively will include studying with a purpose, including setting goals and studying actively, which will most likely entail focusing on what you are studying, reviewing and rewriting notes, and even teaching concepts to classmates. Keeping up with how much you study and *how* you study will also help you study effectively. If you find that you did not do well on a test, you can review the steps you took to study beforehand and make adjustments the next time.

Once you have determined when, where, and how much you need to study, set study and test-taking goals. Your goals could be as simple as the following:

- I will use my time wisely so that I am able to study all my notes.
- I will ask the instructor questions about any notes that I do not understand.
- I will remain calm before, during, and after the exam by practicing breathing techniques and relaxing.

Of course, your goals could also include studying with a group or making a high grade. If you have never written down goals for studying or taking tests, then start small. Once you have achieved your study and test-taking goals, create newer and more challenging ones with each test:

- I will improve my writing skills by practicing the essay questions in a timed environment.
- I will improve my overall retention of the material after the test.

Study Actively

Goal setting is just one way to prepare for exams, but more important is how you approach studying. In order to build a body of knowledge, you will want to study to *learn,* not just to *remember.* In other words, you will want to transfer information from your short-term memory, which holds information for a short period of time, to your long-term memory, which can be retrieved long after it is "deposited" there.

One of the ways to improve your memory of the material you have learned is to actively take it in when you study. The goal of active studying is to make connections between concepts and theories so that you can more easily recall the information and write or speak knowledgeably about it. Rereading texts and notes is actually *not* a good strategy for learning. New research on learning and memory has shown that actively interacting with the material and practicing "retrieving" the information from memory—as opposed to storing it as one would do when reading passively—is best. The following are strategies for improving your ability to access the information for a test:

- Rewriting or summarizing your notes in your own words

- Rearranging the order of the material by importance or in chronological order

- Making connections between what you have learned in one chapter, unit, or class with material you have learned in other places

- Making connections between what you have learned in class and what you have experienced in the real world

- Explaining concepts to someone else who is not familiar with the topic

- Making visual representations of the material

Growth

Most students who do well work harder than they have to. Growth is asking yourself, "How can I do this better?" It's about approaching your studying in fresh ways to get better results. Make it a game. Share or exchange the top five facts you learned that day with someone else, and it will make you more interested and interesting!

A Study Log Can Help You Track Your Progress

After considering your study goals, you may also want to create a study log that will help you keep track of your tests and preparation steps. The study log in Exhibit 10.1 provides space for you to capture important information about the type of class, type of test, and methods for

EXHIBIT 10.1　Study Log

Class	Chemistry
Date	Tuesday, October 12
Material	Chapters 4–7, extra lecture material
Practice/Previous Tests	In library on reserve; answer key for practice test
Question Types	Multiple choice, problem solving
Study Methods	Review notes, work through extra problems, go through practice test, study with group
Time Needed	8 hours total over 4 days
Approved Materials for Test	Paper, pencil, calculator
Number of Points/ Percentage of Grade	150, 15% of overall grade
Notes	Talk to Regina about what to expect. She had this course last semester.

studying. Notice, too, that the study log describes how much the test is worth, an important consideration if the test is worth a significant portion of your grade. Without taking the time to consider the value of a test, you might make the mistake of spending too much time on one test that is worth only a few points and not studying enough for a test that is worth a significant portion of your grade. A study log will help you prioritize your studying strategy.

Course Objectives Are Valuable Clues About the Important Concepts

Another step in studying effectively is to understand the objectives of the course. You will find the course objectives in the syllabus or in other material that has been handed out to you in class. If one of your course objectives is to identify the processes of cell replication, then you can be sure that you will be tested on the processes of cell replication in some manner. Making sure that you study the material that appears in course objectives will help you focus your time and energy on the right course content.

Your Time Is Precious—Use It Wisely

How much time you spend and how many sessions you have will depend on the type of learner you are. You could start with 45 minutes of studying three different times a day over the period of a week to see how well you retain and remember the material. Adjust your schedule as needed. Just remember to be conscious of how effective your study sessions are; if they are not helping you meet your study goals, then make changes. In Evan's case, his biology study group may not be helping him study in the manner that is most effective for him. If that is the case, he may need to find a different group that fits his study goals better or consider studying alone.

No matter how much time you spend studying, it won't be effective if you are unable to concentrate on the subject. Many times you will find yourself distracted by external and internal commotion. Externally, you may have a noisy or messy house, or you may have others who need or want your time and attention. Internally, you may be preoccupied by illness, stress, self-doubt, or fear. Both internal and external distractions make it difficult to study effectively, so you must take care of them or tune them out. If not, you will find that the time you spend studying is not productive.

For some students, planning ahead to study effectively is not an option. Because of poor time management or procrastination, these students often try to study in one long session of cramming. Cramming and marathon sessions should be avoided when studying for an exam because they usually produce more anxiety than learning. If you do find yourself in a situation in which you must cram, try to maximize the effectiveness of the long hours and loads of material. Organize your time into short periods, no more than one hour at a time, and take many breaks. When you return from your break, review the material you had just been studying before you begin on new material. You may want to try a combination of writing down what you know, drawing pictures to represent the material, reciting key concepts aloud, creating songs with the material, or building a model of a key idea. The more learning preferences you use to understand the material, the better your chance of remembering it all for the test.

Resilience

> The reason resilience is a key element of GRIT is because you are going to face unexpected hardships, frustrations, obstacles, setbacks, and challenges along the way. How you respond to them is everything. You won't always have the time, the energy, or the opportunity to do everything we suggest. Weak students make excuses. Strong, gritty students study, in spite of all the ways the world can conspire against them.

Other study tips include making flash cards to quiz yourself or others if you are in a study group. You can also tape-record questions and answers. Instead of playing the tape straight through, stop the tape after each question so you can answer the question aloud. Then play the answer and see how well you have done. If you can push yourself to enjoy studying, you will be more likely to do it often.

Cheat Sheets Aren't Cheating

Creating cheat sheets was once considered an activity only for those who intended to cheat; however, many educators have seen the benefit that creating such sheets can have. You may have a professor who tells you that you can bring a three-by-five-inch index card to the exam with anything you want written on it. Students who may not have studied much beforehand usually jump at the chance to cram as much information as possible on that tiny, white space. The result is that students retain more of the information than they would have if they had not created the cheat sheet. Many times, the cheat sheet is not needed because the student has, in effect, studied adequately in making the sheet.

To create an effective cheat sheet, organization is important. One way to organize the card is to divide it into thirds on both sides so that you have six sections (three on one side, three on the other) to work with. Then, use the top of each section to write a specific category such as "Formulas" or "Krebs Cycle." Underneath each heading, write the information that pertains to the category. If you are listing formulas, for example, be sure to write clearly and double check that all elements of the formula are correct.

Even if you are not allowed to bring a cheat sheet—only bring one if you are given permission—you can still reap the benefits of this technique by closing your books and notes and writing down as much information as you can remember about the subject. For example, if you have a test on genetics, take a blank card and write everything you know about DNA on the front and back. In this case, organization is not important; what is important is to see how much you have learned already. Once you have filled up the card, go back through your notes and books to see what you have missed. Another approach is to anticipate some of the questions you might see on the exam and use the cheat sheet to develop an outline for the answer. For example, if you anticipate a question about the structure of the legislative branch of the federal government, your outline would include the composition and structure of the House of Representatives and the Senate.

Previous Tests and Practice Tests Can Provide Great Study Aids

If allowed by the instructor, study copies of old tests. Your instructor will put them on reserve in the library, post them in an online learning system, or hand them out in class. Previous exams are an excellent source for what kinds of questions you will be asked. If someone offers to give you his old tests from the previous semester, ask your instructor first if you can study from them before taking them.

Equally beneficial to understanding how your professor will test you is to take advantage of practice exams if they are offered. Some instructors may provide opportunities for you to stop by during office hours to take a practice exam or to take an online practice test where you can get instant feedback. If your course materials are available online through a learning management system (LMS) like Blackboard or Moodle, your professor may provide practice tests and quizzes available from the textbook publisher or from prior semesters.

■ Study groups can greatly improve your understanding of material.

© IAN SHAW/ALAMY

Don't Face It Alone! A Study Group Can Help You Succeed

Juanita, Michael, Laura, and Evan took the advice of their orientation leaders early in the semester to create a study group for one of their classes, and they have realized that there are several benefits of studying in groups. First, you have access to

GRIT GAINER™

STUDY WITH GRIT   You can use your GRIT to gain a huge advantage. It will save you time and effort, and produce better results. Slow, sporadic, and sloppy is the way many students study. Dig deep to demonstrate the discipline to sacrifice what you must to study in the best place, in the best ways, at the time that works best for you, especially when there is every excuse not to do it.

more notes and may find that you have missed important information. Second, you experience others' perspectives about the subject, and you may find that your classmates explain major concepts better than your professor. Third, you have a built-in support group while you take classes, because in the process of studying, you establish friendships.

A key to a successful study group is to limit the group to four or five participants or fewer. The more participants there are, the harder it will be to remain on track. It is also best to study with people who are not close friends so that you minimize distractions and off-topic conversations. When choosing members of your group, it is a good idea to discuss expectations for the group. If prospective members think that others will be helping them but they won't be contributing themselves, then they may not be right for your group. You will need members who will take on specific responsibilities that will benefit the whole group.

Once you have chosen your group participants, you should exchange contact information and choose a leader. The leader can change from meeting to meeting, but one person should be in charge of contacting everyone to announce the meeting time and place for the first session. The leader should also be responsible for keeping everyone on task and for assigning roles to each person.

When you meet with your group, be sure that each person contributes to the study session and "teaches" his or her assigned part. Periodically, the group should take breaks to keep people focused. To make studying comfortable, try to meet in a quiet location that allows food and drink; this way there will be fewer breaks and fewer people will be distracted by hunger or thirst. Also consider taking turns bringing snacks and beverages or chipping in for a meal. Better yet, go out for a meal after you study so that everyone has a goal to look forward to.

The difficulty of forming study groups in college is that many students lead full lives and have very little time to schedule extra activities. They also may not have consistent free time if they work different shifts each week or have different family responsibilities from day to day. To make your study group work, you may need to be creative about how you meet and how you organize your time. For example, you may want to join a chat room or use email to create a sample exam and quiz each other.

Test Questions Will Vary, and So Should Your Answers

Learning how to take tests will be just as important as learning the material. Knowing how to answer each type of possible test question will make taking an exam that much easier, and you will have less anxiety because you will know what to expect.

There are two categories of question types: objective and subjective. Objective questions, which require lower-level thinking because they ask you to recall facts and concepts, usually appear in the form of multiple choice, true/false, fill-in-the-blank, and short answer. Subjective questions ask for your opinion about the material or ask you to apply the material in a new way. Essay and problem solving (critical thinking) questions are subjective because there are a variety of ways the questions can be answered correctly.

Sometimes objective questions are easier to answer because they provide a correct answer within the choices. However, objective questions can demand significant brainpower, especially when you must recall an answer with very few clues, which is often the case with fill-in-the-blank questions. Because objective questions usually have only one correct answer, some students believe that there are no "wrong" answers for subjective questions. That may be true, but there *are* better ways to answer them. In the following sections we discuss typical test questions and how to answer them.

Multiple Choice

Multiple-choice questions can test your recall of information or assess your ability to apply information or analyze situations. Despite their reputation for being easier, expect more difficult and time-consuming multiple-choice questions for college exams, and don't be alarmed if the answers are not obvious.

When answering multiple-choice questions, the first step is to read the question or statement carefully. Then mark any special words in the question or statement such as *not, always,* and *only.* Before looking at the choices, see if you can answer the question yourself. For example, consider the following multiple-choice question.

■ Learning to use strategies for different types of test questions can help you eliminate obviously wrong answers.

Notice the word "NOT" and think in terms of what is not an acceptable answer.

What should you NOT do to alleviate anxiety when taking a test?

Should   A. Arrive early for the exam.   *This is something you SHOULD do, so it is not the correct answer.*

Should NOT   B. Skip over the directions.   *This is something you should NOT do, so it may be the right answer. Keep reading the rest of the choices and lightly mark this one.*

Should   C. Pay attention to the time limit.   *This is something you SHOULD do, so it is not the correct answer.*

Should   D. Read all the questions before answering.   *This is something you SHOULD do, so it is not the correct answer.*

After you have read through all the choices, the only correct answer is B.

Consider another multiple-choice question and do the same thing you did before by looking for key words and writing your response to each option next to the assigned letter:

When answering an essay question on a test, be sure to   *This is a positive statement, so you will be looking for things you should do. Also, notice the choice "All of the Above" before you start reading all the choices.*

Should   A. Answer each part of the question thoroughly.

Should   B. Organize your essay before writing it by sketching out a quick outline.

Should   C. Read the directions carefully.

Yes, all of them   D. All of the above.

The correct answer is "D. All of the above."

When you are ready to answer a multiple-choice question, read each choice carefully and eliminate any answer that is obviously wrong. If you have to guess, eliminate any answer that is misspelled (usually a sign that the instructor has hurriedly added false answers) or any answer that is shorter than the others. Also, pay attention to choices labeled "All of the above" and "None of the above." If you can determine that at least two of the choices are correct, then "All of the above" is probably the correct answer.

When studying for a test that will include multiple-choice questions, be sure you know all the material well. Practice answering multiple-choice questions by using those in your text

Tenacity

(or on a companion textbook website, if one is available) or create your own multiple-choice questions based on the material you are studying. You can work through them yourself as part of your studying or you may share with a classmate who has also created multiple-choice questions and take turns answering them.

> It's GRIT that will help you get better at all kinds of tests. One of the best ways to study is to practice. Get or make up sample test questions. Use a classmate. Test each other. Train your brain by saying after each question, "Again!" Do it over, and over, and over. You will master different formats until you are undaunted by the test.

Matching

A matching section on an exam presents you with two columns: a list of words or phrases that are to be matched with a list of descriptors. Matching sections usually require basic recall of information, but you will need to read the directions carefully. There may be more than one match for an item in the list or there may be extra descriptors that are not matched to anything. All of these distracters are there to make sure you know the content well enough to make the right decisions.

To complete matching questions, first read through the entire list and choices to match before beginning. Then determine if there could be multiple matches to a word in the list. Make sure that you have chosen the correct letter to match with each word in the list. If there are a few terms that you don't know for sure, try to narrow the possible choices down by matching the terms you do know for sure. Also, because not all terms will be the same type, you may be able to eliminate some descriptors because they do not logically "go with" them. For example, a matching term may be "Emancipation Proclamation" and a descriptor may be "Person responsible for passing Prohibition legislation." Because the Emancipation Proclamation is not a person, you can easily eliminate that descriptor as a potential choice.

To study for matching, you will need to know major terms, people, and events from the material. Because professors often use similar definitions and descriptions, rather than those directly from the text or glossary, it may be helpful to rewrite your definitions and descriptions in your own words. If you have a study partner or group, ask them to do the same and share the answers they record.

Example of Matching Questions

Notice that the directions say that some terms may be used more than once and others may not be used. Chances are good that you will do both.

Match the following descriptions of interests and strengths with the appropriate multiple intelligences category. The categories may be used more than once; some may not be used at all.

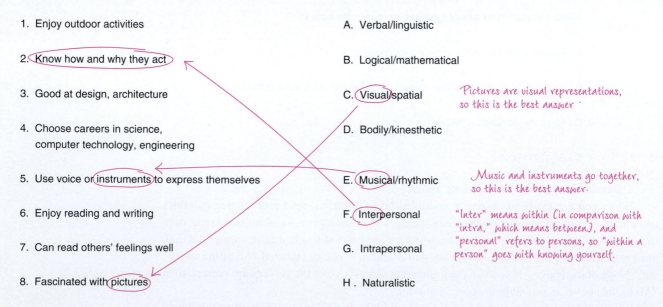

1. Enjoy outdoor activities

2. Know how and why they act

3. Good at design, architecture

4. Choose careers in science, computer technology, engineering

5. Use voice or instruments to express themselves

6. Enjoy reading and writing

7. Can read others' feelings well

8. Fascinated with pictures

A. Verbal/linguistic

B. Logical/mathematical

C. Visual/spatial

D. Bodily/kinesthetic

E. Musical/rhythmic

F. Interpersonal

G. Intrapersonal

H. Naturalistic

Pictures are visual representations, so this is the best answer

Music and instruments go together, so this is the best answer.

"Inter" means within (in comparison with "intra," which means between), and "personal" refers to persons, so "within a person" goes with knowing yourself.

Answers: 1. H. 2. F. 3. C. 4. B. 5. E. 6. A. 7. G. 8. C.

True/False

True/false questions can be tough even though there are only two possible answers. Guessing or randomly answering true/false questions should be done as a last resort. It is better to read the statements carefully, noting key words that could point to the correct answer such as *frequently, sometimes,* and *a few.* These words usually indicate a true statement. Words such as *never, only,* and *always* usually indicate a false statement. If you're struggling with a particular true/false statement, take a moment to "flip" the statement and see if your answer would change. This helps you work through any double negatives and other somewhat confusing phrases.

Studying for true/false test questions is similar to the study tips for multiple-choice and matching questions: know the material or course content well enough that when presented with questions about it, you can recognize major concepts and questions. Also, write out sample true/false questions that you think would make good additions to the test. Share with a study partner or group and take turns answering each other's sample questions.

Example of True/False Questions

Determine if the statements are true or false. Circle the appropriate choice.

1. Howard Gardner's theory of Multiple Intelligences includes the category Nutritional/Health.

A. True

To answer this correctly, you need to know Gardner's categories and not get this made-up category confused with "Naturalistic."

B. False

2. OK5R is a test-taking strategy.

A. True

The key word here is "test-taking." OK5R is a reading strategy. One of the five Rs is "reading."

B. False

3. Priorities are what are important and they never change.

A. True

The word "never" should be a clue that this is false. A review of the definition will note that priorities change depending on what is going on in your life at any given moment.

B. False

The answers for the True/False are as follows: 1. B. 2. B. 3. B.

Fill-in-the-Blank/Short Answer

Fill-in-the-blank and short answer questions require that you recall definitions of key terms or items in a series. To complete these types of questions, first read the sentence or question carefully. Often, points will be lost if you don't answer exactly or misspell the correct term. These can be particularly difficult if you are not familiar enough with the material. One way to study for these question types is to create flash cards in which you place terms or major concepts on one side and a definition or description of the term or concept on the other.

Example of Fill-in-the-Blank/Short Answer Questions

1. The (T-System) for taking notes is also known as the _____.

The T-System is another name for Cornell Method. There is little other information in this sentence to provide you with hints, so you will need to know alternative names for terms.

2. (Abbreviating) words and phrases is called _____.

If you have studied your definitions with flash cards, then recalling that the abbreviations goes with "shorthand" should be easy.

3. An instructor who is (difficult to understand) because she has an unfamiliar accent is an example of a listening _____.

This phrase should clue you into the barriers that one can encounter when trying to listen.

Answers for the fill-in-the-blank/short answer are 1. Cornell Method. 2. Shorthand. 3. Barrier.

Instinct

Problem Solving

Problem solving or critical thinking questions are used by instructors so that students can demonstrate or apply the concepts or ideas they have learned. When you answer problem solving questions, read the question carefully, marking multiple steps or parts to the directions. Next, determine what information you will need to solve the problem. Then, break the problem into parts and write down what process or operation you will need to perform. Work through the problem, and once you arrive at an answer, check the question again to make sure you have adequately answered it.

> Problem solving is largely a matter of instinct, the kind you can grow. Be a gritty problem solver by asking, "How would the smartest person in the world solve this problem?" or "What would be a different, potentially better way to go at this?" Try at least two angles and see how well you do!

Here is an example of a problem solving question; an explanation for solving the problem follows:

> Rosa has a scholarship that requires she maintain a 3.2 GPA while she is in college. During her first semester, she had four three-hour credit courses and made two A's and two B's. Now, she is taking one four-hour course and four three-hour courses. Can she make an A in her four-hour course and B's in her three-hour courses and keep her scholarship?

In order to answer this question correctly, you will need to know how to calculate GPA. If we break the steps down further, you will need to know the definition of grade points and quality points and how GPA is calculated when a student has taken classes for more than one semester. Then, you will need to know how to multiply, add, and divide. These sound like common sense, but writing down every operation that you will need to perform will enable you to prepare to answer the question correctly and help you check the process by which you arrived at the answer.

Studying for problem solving tests, such as math and science tests, most likely will involve practicing similar problems. Look to the additional problems in your textbook, homework assignments, and notes for extra practice. Also, you may find sample problems online with answers so that you can check your responses.

Example of a Problem Solving Question

1. Lenise is taking a history class in which her grade is made up of four exams, all of which are worth 100 points with a total of (400) points that are available to earn during the semester. So far, she has made a (65% and a 74%.) What are the lowest grades she can make to get a (C) in the course? Is it mathematically possible for her to earn a (B?)

Total number of points possible.

Convert these to 65/100 and 74/100 because you know that each test is worth 100 points. She has a total of 139 points so far.

You will need to know the minimum percentage for a C and a B in this context. Many universities designate a 70% as a C and 80% as a B. If this is the case, then, the student needs to earn 280 points (70% of 400) to earn a C and 320 points (80% of 400) to earn a B.

The answer to the problem solving question is a 70.5 (or 71%) on the remaining two tests and, yes, she has the opportunity to earn a B if she makes at least a 90.5 (or 91%) on the last two tests.

Essay Questions

Instructors use essay questions to help them measure students' ability to analyze, synthesize, and evaluate the concepts they have learned. This type of question gauges more than students' recall of facts or terms. You can be assured that you will encounter more essay questions in college because they allow students to demonstrate a deeper understanding of the material. In an earlier chapter we defined an essay as a statement of one's own opinions on a topic. In an exam context, the term *essay* can also refer to questions that require detailed, well-developed answers that use material from the course to support a particular thesis or describe a particular concept. Your answers to essay questions in an exam should not be based on your own opinion (unless the professor specifically asks for your opinion). Instead, your answer should demonstrate your understanding and recall of important information from the class (e.g., textbook readings, lecture notes) to address a particular challenge or to explain an idea.

One thing to remember about essay questions is that, although you won't have an enormous amount of time to complete an essay, your professor will still expect that you answer the question thoroughly and clearly. Always read the directions carefully. If the essay question has more than one part, be sure to mark each part and answer it in the body of the essay. If the directions specify a length, be sure to meet or exceed it. Before you begin writing, create a brief outline of what you will cover during the essay. Make a short list of transitions and details so that you can refer to the list if you get stuck during the exam.

Finally, because your professor will be reading and grading many essays, a clearly organized essay will stand out and make it easy for her that you have discussed the key points. Just be sure to give yourself plenty of time to write the essay and use any remaining time you have to proofread and edit your work.

Study for essay questions just as you would problem solving questions by practicing with possible topics. If your professor has provided a list of topics or sample topics, use those to create outlines and memorize those outlines—they will serve as the basis for your essay. If you do not receive any sample topics, create your own by reviewing the course material and your notes to find emphasized topics or material that you spent the most time on. These may be good indications of essay topics.

Example of Essay Questions

These words indicate an argument should be written. Think about what kinds of evidence you will use to prove your point. Don't worry about whether or not you agree with the premise. The quality of your argument will be assessed.

These words should appear in your essay to tie back to the prompt. You may want to take some time first to brainstorm a list of ways colleges can be diverse and the costs (financial or otherwise) involved with each idea.

1. Justify this statement: Colleges should strive, at whatever cost, to ensure that their campuses are diverse.

2. Compare the costs versus the benefits of investing time and money in a college degree.

These words indicate that you will be looking at two elements side by side.

These words indicate that you will present the drawbacks and the advantages of both of the subjects.

These words or synonyms will be used in your answer — they are part of the topic you are exploring.

Answers for essay questions will vary.

GRIT GAINER™

STUDYING TAKES PRACTICE   There is nothing that can accelerate and strengthen your mastery of tests faster than relentless practice. GRIT matters most on the kinds of tests that are most scary and difficult for you. Spar with others, make it a game. Start simple, and build up the intensity, difficulty, and speed.

Tests Also Come in Different Forms

Just as important as what types of questions you will encounter is what kind of test you can expect in different classes. For example, a math test will look quite different from a music test, and the strategies for studying for them and taking them will be different. Here we discuss a few different types of tests you may encounter in college. You may be able to apply the same tips to exams in other disciplines.

■ Different courses will require different types of tests.

Math and Science Tests

For taking math and science tests, it is best to work through the problems you know first, then complete the problems that you do not know as well. If you complete your test early, consider reworking the test questions on another sheet of paper and comparing your answers. If you discover two different answers for the same problem, figure out which answer contains the error. Always show your work and complete as many parts of a multiple-part problem as possible. You may receive partial credit for completing the process correctly even if you have not arrived at the right answer.

When answering questions on science tests that involve processes or major concepts, draw a picture to create a visual of the process and to help you answer questions about the steps. Regardless of what question types you will encounter, you will need to recall terms and definitions.

Fine Arts and Literature Tests

When taking exams in fine arts and literature classes, it is as important to explain the significance of the selected work as well as identify key passages, authors, terms, and eras. When taking exams in both disciplines, work through the easier questions first and save plenty of time for the writing portions. Think about the major themes and the historical importance of the works and look for those themes to be part of the questions on the test. Although recall of facts about eras, dates, and creators of works will be part of the exam, there should be a significant emphasis on synthesizing the material.

G R I T
Resilience

One serious adversity many students face is a lack of structure or deadlines. When you have take-home, open-book, or online tests where no one is standing over you, pressuring you, you need to pressure yourself. Set yourself up to win. Think prime time, prime spot, prime focus, prime energy, prime effort.

Open-Book and Take-Home Tests

There will be occasions when you are given an open-book or take-home test. Although they sound as if they are the easiest kind of test to take, professors who hand out open-book tests well make sure that you must work hard to answer the questions correctly. In other words, these may be harder than in-class, closed-book exams. If you know ahead of time that you will be given an open-book exam, you will still need to study for it. Instead of spending too much time looking through your book and notes for the answers to the questions, you should be able to find the answers quickly. Chances are good that there will be many questions on an open-book exam. Likewise, take-home exams are often more difficult and time consuming than a regular test. At the least, your instructor will expect more from you if he allows you to take the test home to complete it. Because expectations are higher, you will need to give yourself plenty of time to formulate your answers and to check your work. Even though you will be unsupervised when writing the exam and probably expected to use a variety of resources for help, you will still need to maintain integrity. In other words, unless you receive permission from your instructor, do not accept help from or give help to other classmates.

It's in the
syllabus

- What types of test questions do you anticipate from your classes?
- What evidence in the syllabus leads you to believe you will have certain types of test questions? (Hint: Look at the course description, if included.)
- How often will you have tests?
- How will the tests be organized—around units, chapters, concepts?
- Will they be online, on-campus, take-home?

Online Tests

Whether you take an online class or not, you may be required to take a quiz or test through an online learning system or through a website, such as a publisher's site that supports your textbook. Instructors often place a time limit for online exams to discourage students from reviewing notes, going through the text, or surfing the Internet for answers, which means you will need to keep an eye on how much time you have left after you answer each question. If your professor provides a practice test, consider taking it so that you can get a good feel for how much time you will have and what types of questions you will answer. Additional considerations include revisiting questions, if possible, to make sure you have not chosen the wrong answer for multiple-choice questions; ensuring that you have saved your answers before submitting your exam; and not sharing information about the exam with other students who have not taken it yet. If the online test gives you a results page or a completion page, it's generally a good idea to print this page and keep it with your course materials. Occasionally, glitches occur with online tests, and having some form of documentation as evidence of your completion can be a lifesaver. It's similar to having a receipt if you ever need to return some merchandise.

Comprehensive Exams

Comprehensive or cumulative exams are usually given during a week dedicated for finals. Not all final tests are comprehensive—some professors choose to give their students shorter tests instead. However, most of the finals you will take in college will reflect the culmination of what you have learned all semester. Taking comprehensive exams at the end of the semester will seem like a daunting task if you have several classes, but there are some tips that will help you manage the task. First, it is important that you study for all your classes regularly. Reviewing notes daily will help you keep the information fresh. Second, make sure that you keep your notes and course materials organized so that you can easily find what you have covered throughout the semester.

When you get closer to the date of your final exam, begin studying more intensely by reviewing the most current material and working backwards toward the material that was covered at the beginning of the semester. You'll discover that if you've been reviewing and rewriting your notes and course materials on a daily or weekly basis throughout the semester, the challenge of studying for a comprehensive exam will be far less daunting, and even somewhat enjoyable. Studying for comprehensive exams can be a rewarding time when you reflect on everything you've learned in the semester and you see how various concepts that didn't seem related before now fit together.

GRIT GAINER™

GRIT TAKES LESS, RESULTS IN MORE Gritty students quickly learn that less is more. It takes less time if you dig deep and put forth the consistent, regular, disciplined, focused, intense effort into your studying and test preparations to produce more results than it does if you save it for later. Later requires more stress, more frustration, more time, for less or inferior results.

Test-Taking Strategies Provide a Game Plan for Success

Get Your Body Ready

Before you begin to think about what is on a test and how you should study, you must make sure that you are taking care of yourself. Eating and sleeping are fundamental to doing well on tests. If you are not healthy, then you cannot perform at your highest level. Just as athletes prepare for performance days by eating carbohydrates and resting, you should focus on getting regular sleep and eating well days before the exam. At the least, get a good night's rest the night before the test and avoid refined sugar (candy, cakes, and cookies) and caffeine.

Maintaining a good attitude as you prepare for the exam is another effective strategy. Monitor and eliminate any negative self-talk about your ability to do well on exams. Instead, visualize yourself taking the test successfully and earning a good grade.

© PIXEL 4 IMAGES/SHUTTERSTOCK

■ Get yourself physically ready for your test as well as mentally.

Set the Stage for a Good Testing Environment

Once you have prepared for the test both physically and mentally, you should be ready to take it. Before you leave for class, be sure that you have the appropriate supplies: Will you need a watch, paper, pen, pencil, calculator, or dictionary and thesaurus? Are there any approved test-taking aids that you need to bring as well? Will you be able to use your textbook or a cheat sheet? Once you arrive in class, take a seat away from distractions and where you feel comfortable to spread out and get to work. If you are not wearing a watch, sit somewhere you will be able to see a clock. Cell phone access, which many students use to keep track of time, may be restricted during tests, so be sure to keep track of time some other way. When taking tests that use a Scantron or bubble form, be sure to bring at least two sharpened pencils.

When the Test Begins, Take Time to Read It All First

When you first get the test, read through all the questions, noting which ones will take longer to answer than the others. Taking that time to read all the questions is actually a time saver, because you will know what to expect and how to pace yourself. Turn the paper over to see if there are questions printed on the back.

As you read through the test, make note of the types of questions and use the tips in this chapter to answer them. Read the directions for each section carefully and mark any special instructions. For example, in a matching section, there may be more than one match for an item in one of the columns; in an essay writing section, there may be a choice of topics. Also, be aware of how many points each section is worth. If one section is worth half the points for the entire exam, you will need to spend a majority of your time working that part.

Pacing yourself during the exam is very important. Before you begin the test, you should determine how much time you need to spend on each section based on the types of questions, your comfort level with the questions, and the number of points the question is worth. As a general rule, you should spend less than a minute per multiple-choice and true/false question and 15 minutes or more to answer essay questions. For the other types of questions, you will need to spend somewhere between one and five minutes. If you get off track and spend too much time on one section, don't panic. You will just need to work quickly and carefully on the rest of the exam.

Working the easiest questions first, mark questions that you don't know the answer to or that you find confusing. Don't come back to them until you have completed all the questions that you can easily answer. If you are unsure of an answer, mark that question as well and plan to review it before turning in your exam. If the question or problem has multiple parts, work through as many of the parts as you can. Do not leave questions unanswered. Partial answers may receive partial credit unless you have been instructed otherwise.

Finally, leave yourself five to 10 minutes to check your work. If you finish an exam early, always go back through the questions to ensure that all questions are answered and that all parts are completed. If you have written an essay, read through your response and check for grammatical, spelling, and punctuation errors. Initial each page and number the pages of your essay, if appropriate. Also, make sure that you write your name on every page of the exam (unless instructed otherwise). Turn in your exam and any paper on which you worked problems or drafted an essay.

the unwritten rules
for Studying and Taking Tests

- **Cramming for an exam or pulling an all-nighter is rarely useful.** If you try to study for an exam only a day or a few hours in advance, you won't remember much of what you study, and the stress caused by your procrastination will probably deplete your creative thinking.

- **Credit is credit, even if it's partial credit.** Let's say you have an essay question on an exam that's worth 20 points, and you're confident that you know part of the answer but not all of it. Take the time to provide the part you do know so you can get some points for the answer.

- **Prepare yourself for the testing conditions as much as the test itself.** Depending on your university's exam schedule, your final exams may take as long as three hours to complete. When's the last time you actually sat in one place for three hours working on a test or exam? You can't prepare for a marathon by running 100-yard sprints. The only way to perform well during a three-hour exam is to

prepare yourself for thinking and writing for that block of time.

- **If you don't understand a question when the professor hands out the exam, privately ask her for clarification.** It will be up to the professor to decide how much help and clarification to provide, but it never hurts to ask. Don't start writing your answer until you completely understand the question.

- **Really long answers are rarely really good answers.** When faced with an essay question about a broad topic, students are tempted to write everything they know about that topic in the hope that something they write will satisfy the professor. We call this the "everything but the kitchen sink" essay answer. This rarely works. Pay attention to the verbs that the professor uses in the question—*compare* is different from *evaluate*—and write an answer that directly answers the question in a complete but concise manner.

Exams Will Test Your Integrity

You may have recently read about the new lengths that students go to in order to cheat on exams or to plagiarize. Advances in technology have made cheating easier and have made it seem more widespread. Although there is no clear evidence that more students are cheating now than they were 30 years ago, there does seem to be more confusion about what constitutes cheating. For example, some professors require group presentations and collaboration on projects; however, very few offer guidelines on who should do what and how to document the part that each student does. In addition, collaboration on homework assignments, which was encouraged in high school, may now be prohibited in college. When in doubt about how you should complete homework or group projects, ask your instructor for specific guidelines.

Integrity and GRIT go hand in hand. One fuels the other. Use your gut instinct to do what's right, especially when it matters most, or when it's tested, or when you have to sacrifice something. Don't let short-term temptations compromise your long-term goals.

The integrity rules are a little clearer when taking a test. Unless otherwise stated, do not use notes, books, or classmates as references for the exam. Most instructors will ask you to clear your desk of any material except paper and a pen or will ask you to move away from the nearest person. All of these actions are to ensure that there are no questions about the originality of the work. Other instructors are more trusting of students and may leave the classroom or give the class a take-home test. An instructor who allows such freedom is sending you a message about integrity: He trusts that his students will act maturely, responsibly, and honestly. Violating that trust can have grave consequences, because not only does the cheating student create problems for herself, but she has also damaged the relationship of trust for the entire class.

To ensure that you act with integrity when taking an exam, whether supervised or not, do your own work and keep your work surface clear of books, papers, folders, cell phones, and even drink bottles. If possible, distance yourself from other students so that they are less likely to cheat off you. If you are ever in doubt, however, about your actions or the requirements for an exam, be sure to ask your professor.

Keep Your Test Anxiety in Moderation

The test-taking strategies and suggestions for preparing for exams can help reduce some of your anxiety, but it's not unusual to still experience some nervousness. Some degree of nervousness is normal and can actually give you an adrenaline boost. If you find yourself experiencing extreme anxiety accompanied by excessive sweating, nausea, and crying, schedule time to see an academic or health center advisor.

integrity matters

Numerous recent studies have reported that nearly 75 percent of college students admit to cheating at least once. The reasons, say, for cheating are many: Some don't believe that their professors notice or care about their work; some believe that they can justify their cheating because the class or test is unfair; others believe that getting the good grade is the most important goal if scholarships and program admissions (such as nursing school) demand high standards.

No matter what the reason, cheating can ruin your college experience. Colleges do take cheating seriously and often have no tolerance for those who cheat. Penalties can range from an F in the course to expulsion from the college.

YOUR TURN

In 250 words, discuss why you think such a high percentage of college students have reported that they have cheated. Describe what colleges can do to help maintain an environment of academic integrity.

In order to cope with mild anxiety, there are a variety of activities you can do to relieve tension. Basic relaxation techniques such as deep breathing and visualizations can take the edge off the tension of taking a test. Taking the time to breathe deeply whenever you feel overwhelmed will help you stay in control. Also, visualizing yourself relaxing or succeeding at a test can help you get beyond self-defeating doubt and stress.

GRIT GAINER™

TAKE GRIT SLOWLY   Slow down to speed up. Take the time to breathe, read the questions, strategize, *then* engage. GRIT is not a sprint. It's a lifelong ascent to amazing views through some pretty rough and exciting terrain. Take it on one question, one test, one class at a time.

3 things future professionals need to know about studying and test taking

test taking doesn't end when you graduate

Depending on your career choice, you may have to pass proficiency tests or certification exams at least once or even once a year. Failing an exam in college may not mean the end of your academic career, but failing a licensing exam or a certification test could very well be the end of your job. Thus, the stakes—and the stress—will be much higher on the job. Although the pressure to pass will be greater, chances are good that since you have been to college and passed many tests, your test-taking skills will get you through exams on the job.

those who can study really stand out from the crowd

When employers post advertisements for good jobs, they typically receive hundreds if not thousands of resumes. This means that job candidates need to do everything they can to differentiate themselves from the others. A candidate who can provide evidence that he or she has the self-discipline to invest the time and effort to deeply study a topic is on the right track to stand out. That's because most students have developed a tendency of only skimming content and taking little time to really understand and contemplate what they're reading or studying. But not you! By developing good habits of studying well and practicing effective test-taking techniques, you'll prove your value to a prospective employer.

taking advantage of test prep services is a sign of wisdom, not weakness

In addition to reviewing the test-taking strategies that are outlined in this chapter, you should also take advantage of any test preparation seminars that your employer offers. Also, now is the time to demonstrate your ability to study with others. There is no better study group than your coworkers because they all have the same investment as you: They want to pass the exam in order to keep their jobs or advance to a higher position.

THE G R I T ADVANTAGE

Growth. Getting good at studying and exams is about effort more than intelligence. Ask yourself, "How can I put in smarter, better effort to learn what I need to learn?"

Resilience. Most students fail to study or prepare for exams because something got in the way. Whenever an obstacle arises, ask yourself, "How can I get past this as quickly as possible so I can get on with my studies?"

Instinct. Ask yourself before every test, "What would be the best, most effective and efficient way for me to prepare for this challenge?"

Tenacity. As you practice different test questions, by yourself and with others, keep repeating, "Again! Again!" until you've got it down cold and you're ready for prime time.

HOW GRITTY ARE YOU?

Now that you've completed this chapter, how committed are you to:

1. Changing how you study so you can enjoy better results?

   Zero Commitment **0** ———————————————————————————— **10** Fully Committed

2. Practicing before tests and exams to improve your ability and confidence?

   Zero Commitment **0** ———————————————————————————— **10** Fully Committed

3. Applying these tools to enhance your memory and performance in school?

   Zero Commitment **0** ———————————————————————————— **10** Fully Committed

4. Sacrificing, even struggling, to do what it takes to study and do well?

   Zero Commitment **0** ———————————————————————————— **10** Fully Committed

11 Planning for Your Degree

Chapter goals to help you *get in, get through, get out, and get paid:*

Throughout this book, we've repeated the mantra "get in, get through, get out, get paid." Developing a plan to complete your degree is the most essential element to accomplishing the "get out" component of this strategy. In this chapter, we'll give you all the tools you need to plan and complete your degree.

To meet those goals, *this chapter will help you:*

- Identify the required steps to complete your degree
- Anticipate what to expect at the end of the term or quarter
- Evaluate alternative methods for paying for college
- List the benefits of both staying in college and returning after a break
- Remind you of the role your **GRIT** plays in making it all happen

Log in to MyStudentSuccessLab.com to deepen your **GRIT** mindset and build the skills you'll need to get through the college experience.

Juanita and Laura's Story

LEFT: © MONKEY BUSINESS IMAGES/SHUTTERSTOCK; RIGHT: © ANDRESR/SHUTTERSTOCK

"Hey, Laura, who are you taking for world history?" asks Juanita.

"I have Dr. Franks," she says. "I interviewed him and Professor Martinsen last week to see which one would be a good fit for me."

"Really? I just checked out that website where you can write about your instructors. I think I am going to get Dr. Bernstein," Juanita says.

"It's hard to get a good idea of what they are like just from a website, don't you think?" asks Laura. Because of Laura's dyslexia, she spends lots of time rewriting her notes and working on assignments. Getting professors that she feels comfortable with is important to her.

"Maybe I need to find someone who can also help me with my degree plan," Juanita says.

"Are you still worried that your parents are going to be upset if you choose something other than engineering or nursing?" Laura asks.

"Probably, but now that I am 18, I guess I don't have to worry about my mom calling my advisor to tell him what I should major in," Juanita says.

"Pick up your things and come with me. I need to go to counseling anyway to talk about my scholarship," says Laura.

Laura gathers her books and stuffs them in her backpack. Juanita follows Laura to the campus center, hoping to get some answers to her questions about how she should plan her next term.

Now, what do you think?

- How would you choose which professor's class to take?
  a. I would find someone who teaches to my learning style preference
  b. Ask advisors and other professors who would be the best for my career choice
  c. Ask other students who gives the least amount of work

- If you are not sure what you want to earn a degree in, how would you proceed?
  a. Ask my parents and friends what the best options are for me
  b. Spend time discovering my interests, skills, and work values first
  c. Choose a degree that will enable me to finish quickly without too much work

Your Terms for success

when you see . . .	it means . . .
Accelerated classes	Classes that are faster paced than a regular term; may require more time per week to complete the classes, but may also allow you to complete sequences of classes more quickly
Cooperative learning	Classes that require you to work in small groups or teams to complete class assignments
FAFSA	Free Application for Federal Student Aid
Hybrid classes	Classes that are held on campus for part of the term and online for the other part; will require access to a computer and the Internet
Intersession classes	Classes held in between regular terms; sometimes offered in January or May before or after a spring term; usually faster-paced and limited to only one or two available classes
Learning communities	Classes with a "cohort" or the same group of students for two or more classes that often share similar assignments and course content
Perkins Loan	Low-interest loan that helps students pay for undergraduate education
PLUS loan	Parent Loan for Undergraduate Students
Self-paced classes	Classes that allow you to complete the course requirements at your own pace; if you need more time than a traditional term, you are allowed to continue in the classes until you have successfully mastered the course content

Service learning	Classes that require students to participate in a community project as part of the course; the project will reinforce the concepts and content of the course
Work-study	A financial aid program that allows students to earn money while working on campus; depending on the position's duties, you may be able to study when you are not engaged in a task

Completing Your Degree Is a Goal, and You Need a Plan

It is never too early to begin thinking about your educational future, especially if it involves completing a certificate or degree. Understanding what you need to do—in addition to passing your courses—may mean the difference between graduating on time and staying another term to finish just one class. Visiting your advisor regularly can help you stay on track, as can reviewing the college catalog and reading the college's website and other information for updates.

This Is Your Degree

In most cases, your goal for enrolling in a four-year university is to complete a bachelor's degree. Even if it's facing tough budget times, your university invests a lot of resources to help you succeed in this goal. Professors, advisors, tutors, classrooms, computer labs, websites, dorms, university unions, and dining halls are just a few of the resources that a university establishes to help you succeed. These are all here for you, and every member of the staff and faculty who work at your university are committed to your success. But these resources and services will only be helpful if you take personal responsibility for completing your degree. In college, the responsibility shifts to you, and it's up to you to take the initiative to schedule appointments, complete the appropriate forms and applications for scholarships and entry to a major, and make sure that the courses you take fulfill the requirements for the degree you are pursuing.

© JACK HOLLINGSWORTH/GETTY IMAGES

■ Use the resources and people on your campus to help you choose a major or degree plan.

If all of this sounds a bit intimidating, don't worry. The faculty and staff at your university are very willing to help. You just need to ask for that help. But before you schedule an appointment with an academic or financial aid advisor or a professor, make sure that you've studied the issue yourself. Although they are supportive and kind, you'll find that faculty and staff at a university have very high expectations for students and they will expect you to take the lead on solving a problem or suggesting an appropriate course of action. They can advise you, but you will be asked to ultimately make the final decision. To help you develop a plan of study for your degree, then, we'll break a bachelor's degree into individual parts and show you how it all comes together, putting you on the stage to receive your diploma. Exhibit 11.1 provides an overview of different degree plans at both community colleges and universities.

GRIT
Tenacity

This is where GRIT kicks in. Owning your degree, taking charge of it, shaping it, and driving it to completion is entirely up to you.

EXHIBIT 11.1   Program Types

Program Type	Length/Requirements	Purpose
Certificate	One semester or two; 15–30 credit hours	To obtain skills necessary for a job-related or personal goal or for direct entry into the workforce; not intended to fit into a higher degree
Associate of Applied Science Degree	Four semesters: about 60 credit hours	To obtain knowledge and skills for direct entry into the workforce; usually not intended to fit into a higher degree
Associate of Arts/ Science Degree	Four semesters: about 60 credit hours	To obtain knowledge and skills for transfer to a higher degree program or for direct entry into the workforce
Bachelor of Arts/ Science Degree	Eight semesters; about 120 credit hours	To obtain knowledge and skills for transfer to a graduate degree program or for direct entry into the workforce
Master's Degree	Number of semesters depends; about 30 credit hours beyond bachelor's degree	To obtain knowledge, skills, and mastery of a field or discipline for further graduate study or entry into the workforce
Doctoral Degree	Number of semesters depends; about 60 credit hours beyond bachelor's degree	To obtain knowledge, skills, and mastery of a field for research in that field and/or entry into the workforce

Defining Your Major Is a First Step

When you applied to your university, you were probably either admitted to the university at large, or to a specific major within a school or college. If you were admitted to the university, you may need to go through a second competitive application process to get accepted into the major that you want to pursue. For example, some university students are classified as "pre-business" students because they intend to pursue a business major, but haven't been formally accepted into that major yet. If you've been accepted into a university, but not a major, you need to learn about the application process for majors and be sure to meet all the requirements and deadlines. If you've been accepted directly into a major within a school or college, you won't have to go through this additional application process. Take a moment to identify your particular situation.

Your Plan of Study Will Include Three Parts

When you first get started in college, take some time to locate the list of degree requirements that you will have to fulfill. If the list looks long and complicated, don't get intimidated. Advisors provide this detailed information to help you along your entire four-year path. For now, let's just focus on the three big pieces that comprise a bachelor's degree: general education courses (also called *core curriculum* or *basics*), courses in your major, and courses in your concentration or specialization. The first set of courses that you have to complete towards the completion of a degree are your general education or GE courses. These courses might include English composition, math, science, history, and social sciences, just to name a few. Although these courses may not seem to be related to your chosen major or career, they are an important part of your academic preparation, and they help you become a well-rounded student and citizen of society. You'll also be surprised to learn that some of the most significant and important advances in business, medicine, engineering, and psychology were inspired by the classical disciplines you cover in your GEs. You'll also learn that employers place tremendous value on your overall writing, communication, critical thinking, and scientific reasoning skills, and your

EXHIBIT 11.2 **Three Parts to the Major**

Courses	Definition	What to Do
General education (GE) courses	These are sometimes called the "basics" or "core curriculum." Courses such as psychology, composition, algebra, and speech communication often make up the first two years of a four-year degree.	Check your degree plan to determine what GE courses are required for your degree. Make note of the courses that are prerequisites to other courses. Try to complete these courses in the first four semesters.
Major courses	These courses are required for you to complete a specific degree. Often, some GE courses are prerequisites to major courses.	Check your degree plan to determine which courses must be completed as prerequisites. Keep your advisor informed as to your progress.
Concentration or specialized courses	These courses provide in-depth exposure to material related to your major field. They may have prerequisites that must be completed first.	Check your degree plan to determine if specialized courses are suggested or listed. Talk to your advisor about any special permissions needed to take these classes and about your progress in them.

GE courses help you develop those skills. They build a foundation of knowledge and values for your career and life. See Exhibit 11.2 for an overview of these three parts.

If you have transferred into a four-year university from a community college, you may have completed most of your GEs already, which were part of your associate's degree. If you're an entering freshman, you may have earned some advanced placement (AP) credits towards your GEs. Be sure to take the initiative to check on these. It's important that the first component of your plan of study include the completion of your GEs. They may also serve as prerequisites (classes you need to complete before you can take other classes) for the courses in your major.

Once you have a plan for completing your GEs, the second major part of your plan of study is the required courses and electives in your major. The difference between required courses and electives is how much choice you have in selecting the courses. If a course is required for your major, you have to take that specific course in order to fulfill the requirements of the major. You'll want to note any prerequisites for that course (classes you need to take first) and build both the prerequisite and required course into your plan of study. If a course is an elective, it's one of several options from which you can choose. For example, the requirements of your major might include three term units of a statistics or other quantitative applications elective. That means you have to take a three-term unit course in statistics or quantitative applications, but you have the option of picking which course from a list of possible courses you want to take. Just be sure that the course you've chosen is on the approved list.

In additon to your general education courses and the required and elective courses in your major, some majors also give you the opportunity to pursue a specialization or concentration. A specialization is a specific area of expertise within a major. For example, you may choose to pursue a major in mathematics with a specialization in statistics. Because today's careers often require highly specialized skills and knowledge, your choice of a specialization or concentration within your major is an important component of your plan of study.

Your plan of study is a living document, and you are its primary author. Your advisors and professors can help you develop it, but the final decision about the courses you'll take and when you'll take them is up to you. When you first get started in college, take time to develop your plan of study and review it with others. Then, as your interests take shape and conditions change, you can update your plan of study accordingly. With the help of the faculty and staff at your university, your plan of study is a map that will guide you through the successful completion of your major. See Exhibit 11.3 for an example of a degree plan.

EXHIBIT 11.3   Degree Plan
Major: Business Administration - Accounting - BS

FIRST YEAR

Description Fall Semester	Course	Units
GE Composition		3
GE Math/Major Prep	STAT 119 or ECON 201	3
GE Social and Behavioral Science/Major Prep	ECON 101	3
GE Humanities American Institutions		3
Total Units:		**15**
Cumulative Total:		**15**

Spring Semester		
GE Intermediate Composition		3
GE Oral Communication		3
GE Physical or Life Science		3
GE Humanities		3
Major Prep	MIS 180	3
Total Units:		**15**
Cumulative Total:		**30**

SECOND YEAR*

Description Fall Semester	Course	Units
GE Humanities		3
GE Social and Behavioral Science		3
Major Prep	ACCTG 201	3
Major Prep	ECON 102	3
Major Prep	MATH 120	3
Total Units:		**15**
Cumulative Total:		**45**

*Best time to prepare to study abroad.

Spring Semester		
Take the Writing Placement Assessment exam (WPA)		
GE Physical or Life Science*		3
GE Lab		1
GE Humanities		3
American Institutions		3
Major Prep	ACCTG 202	3
Major Prep	PIN 240	3
Total Units:		**16**
Cumulative Total:		**61**

THIRD YEAR*

Description Fall Semester	Course	Units
Your WPA score could require you to take either RWS 280 or 281		
GE Explorations		3
Major	ACCTG 321	6
Major	B A 300	1
Major	FIN 323	3
Major	MGT 350	3
Total Units:		**16**
Cumulative Total:		**77**

*Best time to study abroad.

Spring Semester		
Major	ACCTG 322	6
Major	MKTG 370	3
Major	MIS 301	3
Major	MIS 390W	4
Total Units:		**16**
Cumulative Total:		**93**

FOURTH YEAR

Description Fall Semester	Course	Units
GE Explorations		3
Major	ACCTG 421	6
Major	MIS 302	3
Elective		3
Total Units:		**15**
Cumulative Total:		**108**

Spring Semester		
GE Explorations		3
Major	MGT 405 or BA 404 or BA 458	3
Major: Accounting Elective		3
Major: Accounting Elective		3
Total Units:		**12**
Cumulative Total:		**120**

GRIT GAINER™

SHAPE UP YOUR DEGREE PLAN Students with GRIT get through, get out, and get paid. Build your GRIT by asking yourself these two questions:

1. What can I do to hone my degree plan?

2. Whom can I talk to to get help with my plan within the next week?

A Successful Term Requires a Strong Finish

The end of the term is a good time to start assessing how you have done and where you want to go. Before you can begin planning for next term, there will be some loose ends to tie up for your current term. You should know what to expect at the beginning of next term, and with that additional information, you should be able to make better choices and prepare yourself for what lies ahead.

Course Evaluations Provide Important Feedback

Course evaluations (sometimes called *student evaluations* because students evaluate the course and the instructor) are an integral part of taking a college class. Each term, you may be asked to complete an evaluation form for your instructor. The evaluations are anonymous and are not given to the instructor until grades have been posted; thus, you should feel comfortable being open and honest about the course when answering the form's questions.

The purpose of course evaluations is to provide the instructor and administrators a description of how students feel about the instruction they received in the course. Some colleges look very closely at course evaluations and determine raises and promotions based in part on the scores that instructors receive. Other colleges merely use it as a discussion tool to improve the instructors' teaching. No matter how your college uses the information, providing candid and constructive criticism, rather than general comments, is most helpful to the instructor.

Phrases such as "Professor Banks is not a good instructor" or "Dr. Wright is perfect" do not provide specific information that will help your instructor improve or help him or her to continue doing what you think works very well. Instead, you may want to offer suggestions such as "The instructor graded fairly and handed back exams in a timely manner" or "The professor rarely explained the assignments." These statements allow your instructors to pinpoint exactly what worked for you and what didn't.

Most student evaluation forms contain questions that you answer by checking a box or filling in a bubble as well as questions that you answer by writing a narrative response. Here are examples of two types of questions that you may see on a course evaluation form:

1. My instructor uses class time effectively.

   A. Strongly Agree

   B. Agree

   C. Disagree

   D. Strongly Disagree

2. My instructor grades fairly.

 A. Strongly Agree

 B. Agree

 C. Disagree

 D. Strongly Disagree

3. What can your instructor do to improve the course? _____

4. What does your instructor do well? _____

When answering questions such as these, take time to reflect on the instructor's performance during the term. Create a list of activities that you did in class during the term and think about them. Then consider the overall performance of your instructor. Did he come to class on time? Was she easy to contact when you needed her? Did he act professionally? Did she seem to have a good knowledge of the subject matter? Remember that the objective of student evaluations is to provide feedback that will help instructors improve, so the more information you provide, the better.

You Can Survive Finals!

Another traditional ending to the term is final exams. Surviving "finals week" is often considered a well-earned badge of honor for a college student. The reason that finals are so stressful for some college students is that they often carry more weight than any other tests during the term, they contain questions about material from the entire term, and they are all scheduled around the same time.

To help you survive finals, go back to Chapter 10 and review the material about taking tests. There are additional steps you can follow to get ready for them quickly in these final weeks of the term. First, be sure to note the day, place, and time of each final and write it down on your calendar. Double-check this information a week before the exam. Be aware that where and when you take your finals may differ from where and when you took your classes during the term. Whenever possible, confirm the exam time and location with your professor.

A few weeks before the final, ask questions about the exam. What will you be allowed to use? What do you need to bring? What should you study? Is photo identification required? Get plenty of rest during the days that lead up to the exam. When you take the exam, use your time wisely. Final exams usually take longer to complete than regular tests, so be sure you use the entire time that you are allotted (one to three hours). Be prepared by bringing ample writing supplies and any approved items such as a calculator or dictionary.

Consider Your Options for Next Term

Even if you have not completed your classes this term, you can start planning for next term. By now, you should be familiar with the college catalog and can identify the courses that you may want to take. Both the description and your plan will help you determine which classes you need to take in order. Exhibit 11.4 is a typical catalog description for a developmental math course.

In addition to reviewing the catalog descriptions for a course, you will also want to determine if the course has a prerequisite you must take beforehand. In the example of Elementary Algebra, a student will need to either provide a test score that meets the minimum requirement or successfully complete the *prerequisite. Corequisites* are other courses that must be taken before or at the same time as the course. For instance, a Chemistry I course may have a corequisite

It's in the
syllabus

Look to your syllabus for information regarding the final exam. You should find out if it will it be comprehensive and what percentage of your overall grade it will be.

- Start asking questions about the final exams in your classes.
- Consider the following questions to ask your instructors: How long do we have to take it? Are there previous exams we can use for studying?

EXHIBIT 11.4 Catalog Description

DEVE 0336. Elementary Algebra

This course includes, but is not limited to, the following concepts: operations on integers and rational numbers; solving linear equations and inequalities in one variable; graphing linear equations and inequalities in two variables; operations on exponents and polynomials; and problem-solving techniques. Prerequisite: DEVE 0334 with a grade of C or better, or a COMPASS Algebra placement test score from 23 to 32, or a score of 16 or 17 on the mathematics section of the ACT. Final grade will be A, B, C, or NC (no credit) (3 credit hours)

This information shows that you must complete a course successfully before enrolling in this one.

---

of Intermediate Algebra, which means a student can complete the course before enrolling in Chemistry I or can take the course during the same term.

Classes Come in Different Formats

In addition to which courses to take, you may also want to research your options for the design of courses. Many colleges are now offering classes in a variety of formats. You may have the opportunity to take classes in a *learning community,* which means that two or more classes are linked together by a certain topic. The students in the learning community classes stay together for each course. For example, a class of 25 students may take a morning speech communication class and then the same students take an afternoon college writing class. Even though each class is taught by a different professor, they may study a similar topic or the students in the learning community may be required to work on a project that links both courses together.

Blended or *hybrid* classes are another format that you may want to consider when registering for next term. The term *blended* or *hybrid* usually means that some part of the class will be online and that you will be required to complete work online. In these courses you may only meet on campus once a week, instead of two or three times in a traditional face-to-face format, and then do the rest of your course work online. Good computer skills, access to a computer, and a reliable Internet connection will be requirements for this type of class.

Some courses may be offered entirely online. There are no face-to-face class meetings, and you have to complete all of the requirements for the course by reading and reviewing content from the course website and uploading your assignments electronically within specified deadlines. In these classes, you communicate with your instructor primarily through email, chat, and live web video, although you may have an opportunity to meet with him during office hours, if offered.

Another course format is *alternative pacing.* These courses can also be called *accelerated classes,* where you are able to complete your work in a class at a faster pace than a regular 16-week term. They can also be self-paced classes spread over one or more terms. Usually, accelerated and self-paced classes require online work and testing to ensure you are mastering the material.

Finally, *intersession* classes are those offered between terms and function much like accelerated classes. Intersession classes may give you an opportunity to catch up or get ahead with a particular course, but you need to be prepared to invest all your effort and energy in these classes because they cover a large amount of material in a short period of time.

With all of these different formats—traditional face-to-face, learning communities, hybrid, online, self-paced, intersession—how do you know which option is best for you? As with any decision in college, it's a good idea to consult with your advisors and professors and with any upperclassmen who have been successful in college so far. Learning communities are great if you want to get to know other students really well and be part of a cohort of students who are all taking the same classes. If you're a freshman just getting acclimated to the college environment or a transfer student who wants to join others in the transition to a four-year university, the learning community format may work well for you.

Traditional face-to-face classes are a good choice if you learn best in the typical classroom setting. Your classes meet regularly, you see your classmates and professor often, and you complete your homework and reading outside of class. You could consider hybrid or online classes if you have scheduling complications that would make it difficult for you to attend the live face-to-face classes, and if you want more flexibility when you review the course materials and complete the assignments. If you have work or family responsibilities during the day, hybrid and online courses give you more flexibility to do your classwork early in the morning or at night.

Alternative pacing classes may also be an ideal option if you have certain scheduling preferences or restrictions. For example, if you don't have plans during your term break and you want to get ahead on some of your general education requirements, you could take a GE course during the winter intersession. Or, if you were away for a term as part of a study abroad program, intersession classes give you a great chance to catch up on any classes you missed while you were gone. See Exhibit 11.5 for an overview of course formats.

Instinct

There is a difference between making choices and optimizing your choices. Optimizing means making it the best it can possibly be, and it takes GRIT. Rather than asking, "How do I get through?" or "What do I have to do now?" ask yourself, "What can I do to optimize my next term and my overall path to my degree?" That may lead to much better and more rewarding choices.

EXHIBIT 11.5 Course Formats

Format	Definition	What to Do
Traditional/ face-to-face	This format requires you to attend class on campus.	Determine which courses would be better for you to attend in a traditional format, and make sure the courses fit in your weekly schedule.
Learning community	This format requires you to take more than one course with the same group of students, sometimes called a "cohort."	Make sure that the learning community classes are part of your degree plan. Check the schedule to determine if the courses are back to back or close together and that you have time to take both.
Blended/hybrid	This format requires some face-to-face interaction, as well as online work.	Be sure you have reliable access to a computer and the Internet. Pay attention to how the course is scheduled. You may be required to meet all semester or only for a portion of the semester.
Online	This format requires online work and may have required on-campus components, such as tests.	Be sure you have reliable access to a computer and the Internet. Note any on-campus requirements, and be sure to log in regularly to complete your work.
Intersession	This format is provided in between regular terms.	Make note of the length of time and how many days each class will be held. Be prepared for an intense, fast-paced learning experience.
Self-paced	This format allows you to complete work at your own pace.	Be sure you have the self-discipline to complete this type of course, and make note of any specific requirements of final completion.
Study abroad	This format allows you to experience another country and culture while studying courses.	Be sure to review the requirements and costs before embarking on a study-abroad course or program. Determine what the expectations are and how you will meet them.

Learning Also Has Different Formats

After considering the format of your classes, you may also want to think about how classes may require you to learn. *Service learning,* which involves community service as part of the learning process, is gaining popularity at many colleges. A course that includes a service learning project may require that students work at a homeless shelter, design a neighborhood playground, or test area drinking water. The project and the hours needed to complete it will depend on the course and the instructor's assignments, but such a course offers a unique opportunity for students to apply the concepts they learn in class to help solve a community issue.

Cooperative learning is another type of format that requires students to work in small teams to learn the material in a course. Cooperative learning groups work all term to help their teammates learn concepts and complete projects. Different from small group work that you may participate in for other classes, cooperative learning is sustained and deliberate—the teams work together for the entire term.

Internships and *co-ops* provide learning experiences in the context of a job. If your university offers credit for either of these types of courses, you could earn college credit while working and earning money. The types of jobs that qualify for internships and co-ops need to be approved by a professor or advisor beforehand, so be sure to meet with them to discuss this opportunity.

Your Choice of Professors Is an Important Decision

Just as important as what classes and in which formats you take them next term is with whom you take those classes. By now, you should realize that choosing the right professor could make the difference in how much you enjoy and learn in a class. If you have the option of choosing a professor, then you should start talking with other students about them. Ask specific questions and ask a variety of people. Remember that each student has his or her own view of what makes a good professor, a view that might not match your own. Questions you should ask need to move beyond "Is she a good teacher?" Instead, you should ask about her teaching style, the types of assignments she gives, and how available she is during office hours. Be wary of Internet sites that rate professors. They are not reliable because anyone can post just about anything he or she wants without regard to accuracy (or sometimes decency). There is no mechanism to keep the same people from posting multiple positive or negative comments, which can present only part of the picture. Online rating sites also tend to capture only the most extreme student opinions—both positive and negative—so you may not be getting information from the majority of the students who were somewhere in between.

An even better way to determine which instructors are the best for you is to talk with them before you enroll in their classes and review their course syllabi. Make an appointment with a potential instructor and ask pertinent questions: How much reading is involved? How do you teach the course? What led you to become a professor? Do you require a research paper? What do you expect students to know when they complete the course? The benefits of interviewing your instructor before you sign up for the class are that you get to determine whether the instructor is a good fit with your learning style and you get to make a good impression by demonstrating your maturity and interest in your education.

G R I T
Growth

Because employers place a strong premium on how well you navigate difficulties, rather than asking yourself, "How hard is this class schedule going to be?" ask yourself, "Is it tough enough?" And within reason: "What, if anything, should I do to make it a little more challenging?"

■ When planning for next semester, consider the obligations that you have and how you will balance college with them.

© JENNY ACHESON/GETTY IMAGES

Build Your Schedule to Fit You

What worked this term and what didn't? Why? What will change for you next term? Did you have enough time in between classes? Did you waste time that could have been spent more productively? All of these questions will need to be answered before you set your schedule for next term.

When planning your next term (and beyond), consider four factors: how many hours you need to take, how many hours you need to work, what other obligations (planned trips for work or with family, for example) you have, and how much stress the first three factors will cause.

- **Number of credit hours.** To determine how many credit hours you need to take, be sure to review your financial aid, scholarship, and plan of study. If you are receiving financial aid, you may be required to take a full load, which often means at least 12 hours.

- **Number of study hours.** As a general rule, for every hour that you are in a face-to-face class, you will need two to three hours outside of class to study and learn the material and complete homework assignments and projects. For example, if your class meets four hours every week, you should set aside another eight hours during the week to study for that class. When you apply this guideline to your schedule, you'll quickly realize why 12 term units typically makes you a "full-time" student. Classes alone are a full-time job, which is why the responsibility of having work obligations on top of a full-time academic schedule can be such a challenge.

- **Number of work hours.** If you will not be working next term, you can skip this section. However, even if you are only working a few hours a week, you will need to schedule your work hours so that they do not overlap with the times you are in class. You also need to allow plenty of time to get to and from work and school and, if necessary, to eat a nutritious meal before class. Be realistic when calculating this time and plan for delays. Building enough margin into your schedule will help keep your stress levels at a minimum.

- **Amount of learning support and learning opportunities.** If you know or anticipate a need for learning assistance or tutoring, be sure to build that time into your schedule. You may also need to see each of your professors on a regular basis, some more than others, which should also be a consideration when creating a schedule. If you leave little time for meeting with your instructors, it will be difficult to get the help and advice you need. Good time management and a flexible schedule will allow plenty of time for visits to the computer lab to get help with sending an attachment to an email, to the library for assistance in using the databases, and to the tutoring lab at the hours and locations that are most convenient to you.

- **Other obligations.** Working, going to school, exercising, taking care of a family, and participating in social and community activities all require your time and energy. To balance all your activities, you will need to keep an eye on upcoming events and make sure you plan accordingly. For example, if you are thinking about registering for the fall term and you know that you must take a weeklong trip for work in October, you should contact potential instructors to see what their policies are for missing class. Likewise, if you like to participate in your child's school activities, you will need to consider how much time you can give if you are also studying for classes. You may find that you need to cut back on social and volunteer commitments or at least postpone them until after the term.

G R I T
Growth

A big part of the college experience is stretching yourself and expanding your capacity to do more, in less time, more effectively. Be gritty. Use your schedule to challenge yourself to grow in new ways.

- **Stress levels.** Your work schedule, course load, and other responsibilities can lead to high levels of stress. For example, if you have to take 15 hours of courses to maintain your financial aid and you have to work 40 hours to pay your bills, but you feel overwhelmed and anxious about balancing it all, then you are not likely to handle both well. If you find yourself in this situation, you will need

GRIT GAINER™

> **ADDING GRIT CAN CREATE GRATIFICATION**   There is a difference between something being fun or easy and being gratifying. Feeling gratified is that deep, complete satisfaction that only comes from successfully taking on a meaningful challenge. *Gritified* might be a better word! Ask yourself, "What new challenge can I add to my life, or swap for another challenge, to grow myself in the ways I want and need to grow?"

to reconsider your plans before you get in over your head. Getting locked into a rigid schedule that doesn't allow you to drop a course that is too difficult or to decrease your hours at work will lead to frustration and high levels of negative stress. On the other hand, you may thrive on such a schedule because you work better when you have to manage your time carefully. You may be the type of person who cannot study well if you have unlimited amounts of time to do it. If this is the case, you may feel excited about having so much activity in your schedule. Still, you could encounter a problem in which having flexibility will help you cope. If you don't have this flexibility, then you need to pay extra attention to staying on top of your work. For example, if you find on the first day of the term that one of your classes will be much more demanding than you had anticipated, you will need to be more careful about keeping up with assignments and managing your stress effectively. Planning ahead and managing your time will help you cope with a stressful schedule.

What should you do if you cannot work your schedule out despite your efforts to make it all fit together? There may be a term that a course you need is not offered or the class is filled before you can register. Take advantage of the relationships you have cultivated at college to develop alternative solutions. Now is the time to talk with fellow students, professors, and advisors. They may be able to offer solutions that you have not considered. If there is an academic need for you to get into a class or rearrange your schedule, schedule time with the professor who teaches the class or a school official such as a department chair or associate dean to discuss your situation and make your case for a seat in the class. Professors and school officials sometimes have flexibility to add a few more students to a class, but only for compelling academic reasons.

You Have Options for Paying for College

When thinking about your financial future, paying for college will most likely be at the top of your list. Even if you have a solid plan for paying tuition, fees, and books, it will be worth your time to investigate other methods in case your current plan falls through. Regardless of where you choose to go to school, you'll need to identify your different options and select the alternatives that work best for you, both in the short and long run.

Scholarships

Winning a scholarship is by far the most financially and psychologically rewarding way to pay for college because it is literally free money—you don't have to pay it back. There are thousands of scholarships available for needy and accomplished students, but you often have to work hard to find them. To find the ones that match your profile, you will need to get the word out that you are looking. Talking with friends, family, employers, and college officials is a great way to start the process. They may know of obscure scholarships that will fit your needs perfectly.

Another way to get information about scholarships is to talk with the financial aid officers and counselors at your college. They have access to and knowledge of scholarships that may fit your profile, such as single-parent scholarships. Other effective methods for finding scholarships are to investigate sources at your library and online. Searching print and web-based databases will provide you with more than enough information, but you'll need to narrow your focus so you can locate the options that best fit your qualities and circumstances.

Whatever information about scholarships you find—whether it's in books, in counselors' offices, or on the Internet—don't pay for it. There are services that claim to match your qualifications with scholarship qualifications but charge a fee to do so. You can get free help from high school and college counselors as well as libraries and Internet searches. No reputable scholarship will require that you pay a fee to apply, and very few scholarship services will require payment. There are legitimate scholarship searching services out there, but be careful. The website FinAid! (www.finaid.org) provides information about different types of financial aid for college students as well as tips for avoiding scholarship services scams. According to this site, any service that guarantees to match you with a scholarship or that offers you an award that you did not apply for is likely to be a scam. Many colleges recommend www.fastweb.com as a great starting point for finding scholarships that match your accomplishments.

Grants

By definition, grants are a form of financial assistance that does not need to be paid back. A common federal grant is the Pell Grant, which can be awarded for full-time or part-time enrollment. To determine your eligibility, talk with your financial aid counselor or visit any of the various websites that provide governmental information about financial aid. When you research Pell Grants, you will find that there is a maximum to the amount of the award ($5,500 for 2014–2015) and that your college will receive the money and then disburse it to you once classes start. Because of recent federal requirements about grants and student loans, colleges may wait several weeks before paying students. If you are expecting to receive your grant the first day or week of classes, you should make alternative arrangements to pay bills (including your bookstore bill).

Another type of grant that a student can receive is the Federal Supplemental Educational Opportunity Grant (FSEOG), which is available to those who demonstrate an exceptional need. The difference between a Pell Grant and FSEOG is that colleges and universities are guaranteed to receive enough funding to award Pell Grants to all eligible students, but FSEOG funding is not guaranteed. This means that FSEOG funding is more uncertain. The procedure for receiving an FSEOG is similar to that for receiving a Pell

G R I T
Tenacity

The tighter your budget, the more GRIT it takes to complete your degree. But the more difficult it is, the more you learn, and the prouder you will feel when you get there. You can tell the story of how you navigated adversity to get your degree for the rest of your life.

integrity matters

Student loans, because they are low interest and have a long-term payment plan, are often a good way to pay for college. However, there are serious consequences if you do not pay them back whenever you are required to do so. Defaulting on student loans can make you ineligible for future federal aid and can have negative consequences on your credit rating.

If you find yourself unable to make a payment after your loan payments become due, notify your lender immediately. The lender may work out a repayment plan for you.

YOUR TURN

In 250 words, discuss your concerns about paying for college. Describe what would be your plan for repaying a loan, should you take out a loan.

Grant; your eligibility will determine the amount that you receive, and your college will disburse the money to you after the term begins.

You will need to maintain good academic standing at your college to remain eligible for a grant, so be sure to make note of the minimum GPA that you must maintain to receive future grant money. One last tip for continuing to receive grant funding: Make sure that you adhere to the college's attendance policy. You may be penalized (and lose your grant funding or have to pay it back) for missing too many classes or for dropping a class. As always, check with your financial aid officer to make sure that you clearly understand the expectations for receiving grants.

Student Loans

In the event that you are not eligible for grants, or if they aren't enough to cover all your costs, you should investigate student loans. The idea of taking out a loan to attend college makes many students shudder with fear because they don't want the added pressure that they must pay back what they borrow. If you can avoid a student loan, then by all means do so. However, receiving a student loan sometimes makes more financial sense in the long run, if the alternative is to forgo college.

Federal student loans are typically low interest and can be paid back over 10 years. For families that would otherwise have to deplete their savings or borrow against retirement or their mortgages to pay for college, a low-interest student loan is a good option. Most loan programs allow you to defer (which means to delay) payment until after you graduate; you can sometimes continue to defer payment if you remain unemployed after you graduate. However, these loans may accumulate interest during this deferral period, so be sure to know the specific terms of your loan before making decisions.

One type of loan is the Stafford Loan, which comes in subsidized and unsubsidized versions. A subsidized loan is one in which the government pays the interest for you while you are in college. Once you graduate and start making payments on your loan, you will accrue interest as well. The government does not make interest payments for an unsubsidized loan, so you would need to decide whether to pay the interest while you are in college (usually a small amount), or allow the interest to be added (or capitalized) to the overall loan amount and wait until after you graduate to make any payments. This is a classic "pay now or pay more later" type of decision that you need to carefully evaluate.

A federal Perkins Loan is a loan between you and your college. One benefit of a Perkins Loan is that you may be able to cancel up to 100 percent of the debt if you meet certain criteria. For example, upon graduation, if you choose to teach in a teacher shortage area or if you serve as a full-time nurse, you may be eligible for cancellation of your loan. As you would for any type of federal financial aid, check out their website (https://studentaid.ed.gov) for the most current information.

EXHIBIT 11.6   Loan Payment Recalculation

	Stafford Loan Subsidized	Stafford Loan Unsubsidized
Loan Amount	$5,000.00	$5,000.00
Interest Rate	4.500%	6.800%
Fees	1.500%	1.500%
Payment Term	10 years	10 years
Estimated Monthly Payment	$51.82	$74.17
Total Amount of Repayment	$6,128.30	$8,900.31

PLUS, which stands for Parent Loan for Undergraduate Students, is another method for receiving money to help pay for college. If you are fortunate enough to have parents willing to take out a loan to help you pay for college, a PLUS is a possible option. To qualify, you must be a dependent student, which means your parents support you financially. A PLUS can be provided by the government or by private lenders. Parents who take out a PLUS are usually trying to make up the difference between the cost of tuition and the financial aid package that their children receive. Nonetheless, it is the parents who are ultimately responsible for repaying the loan, which can be as early as 60 days after they receive it. See Exhibit 11.6 for repayment calculations for both a subsidized and unsubsidized loan.

Military and Veterans Financial Aid

Being a member of the military can be especially helpful when you are paying for college. There are numerous benefits for active members and veterans as well as their dependents, one of which is the Montgomery G.I. Bill. To find out about military benefits, talk with a financial aid officer or a special counselor at your college or at a Veterans Affairs office for specific information. According to the United States Department of Veterans Affairs website, the Post-9/11 G.I. Bill, which went into effect on August 1, 2009, provides benefits for qualified applicants to help pay for tuition and some expenses related to attending an accredited and approved institution of higher education. There are differences between the Montgomery G.I. Bill and the Post-9/11 G.I. Bill; you can find a benefits comparison as well as a form to complete on the website www.gibill.va.gov.

As you evaluate your different options for financing college (grants, loans, work), be sure to include potential military support as an option. The Army, Navy, and Air Force offer ROTC programs (reserve officer training corps) at thousands of campuses nationwide. These programs provide additional scholarship support for students who are interested in and willing to commit to a specified period of military service during college and after graduation (www.rotc.com).

Work-Study

Work-study is a program that allows students to earn money while they work on campus. The job may allow for you to study when you work, but most work-study positions are similar to office assistants and will keep you busy the majority of the time. To work in such a program, you must be eligible for federal work-study money, and you will be limited to a certain number of hours you can work per week. Not everyone who is eligible for work-study will be able to find a position on campus, however. Each department and area of the college advertises, hires, and manages work-study positions; sometimes, hiring can be competitive. There may be specific requirements (such as computer skills) that a candidate must meet before being hired. Because some positions require working with students' personal information, work-study students must also abide by the college's privacy standards.

Tenacity

Many of the most successful students have stories about how many times they got turned down, how hard they had to fight, and the different options they had to piece together to somehow find a way to fund and complete their education. GRIT gets you through.

The benefits of participating in work-study are that you can earn some money that will help pay your expenses and you will be able to work closely with college employees. By getting to know professors and administrators better—and by working for them—you may have access to valuable advice and information. To investigate whether work-study is available for you, talk with your financial aid officer. He or she will review your eligibility and help you apply for on-campus employment.

Internships and Part- and Full-Time Jobs

For many college students, working during college will be an important and necessary part of their plan for paying for college. Having a job while attending college can be demanding, particularly because of the heavier schedule that it requires, so if you plan to work during college

Planning for next semester includes taking into account how you will pay for both college and living expenses.

you'll need to be especially mindful of how you manage your time. However, students who work also have an opportunity to develop an exceptional degree of discipline and time management skills that will serve them well when they are pursuing full-time careers after college. Like student athletes, students who work their way through college are a special group of individuals who have a demonstrated capability to endure challenges and succeed.

If you're working during college, you may need to reduce the number of credit units you enroll in during each term. With experience, you'll get a better sense of your capacity for classes and work hours. The trade-off of working while in college is that it can provide the financial support you need, but it may also cause you to take longer to finish college and transition to a full-time career, which can lead to higher educational costs. Take time to compare your options for financing college and seek input from advisors, professors, and family members to help you make this important decision.

If you do decide to work while you're in college—either during the regular academic year or the summer—look for internship opportunities. Internships are jobs that provide experience that is directly related to your academic interests and, in some cases, can earn you academic credit. For example, a student majoring in recreation, parks, and tourism might work for the city parks department during the year or the summer, organizing youth programs and other community activities, and earn credit towards his or her major for doing so. Internships can sometimes offer the dual benefit of helping you earn money for college while earning academic credit. However, some internships may be unpaid, which means that you may only earn credit or experience for completing them. Talk to your professors and advisors to find out about the options available at your school.

Tuition Waivers for Employees

Another source of financial help is your employer. Large corporations sometimes offer financial assistance for employees, although there may be stipulations that you work for a certain amount of time after graduation. If your employer doesn't offer scholarships to employees, you should still ask if he or she is interested in doing so; employers will benefit from employees who further their education. Finally, your college may offer tuition waivers for its full-time employees. Some students take jobs offered at colleges so that they can take classes for free or at a reduced cost. If you need a part-time or full-time job while you are in school, you may want to check out the openings at your college.

Applying for Financial Aid

Each college is different in how it handles the application process, but it is worth talking generally about what to expect when applying for financial aid. Even if you have applied for and received financial aid for this academic year, there may be some information that you need to know before applying again. The first step in the process is obtaining a Free Application for Federal Student Aid (FAFSA), which can be picked up from the financial aid office of your college or accessed online (www.fafsa.ed.gov). The website provides particularly helpful information broken down into steps, which can make the process less intimidating.

Be sure to remember that financial aid applications must be renewed each academic year; the timeline for receiving aid for a year starts in August and ends in July. Thus, if you applied for financial aid in November and received it for classes that started in January, you will have until July to use that aid; then you will need to reapply for aid for the fall term.

As part of the FAFSA application process, you will need to determine whether you are considered "independent" or "dependent." The federal government defines a student's independence by certain criteria, such as being married, being born before 1986, or having both parents deceased. Students who fit the definition for dependent status but have extenuating circumstances may be able to request their status be changed to independent. In addition to determining your ability to pay for college, you will also be asked to provide an Estimated Family Contribution (EFC) amount; for example, if you receive child support or Social Security payments, you will have to report that income as part of your EFC. One other consideration when applying for financial aid is that each year a certain percentage of loan applications get identified for verification. This means that certain student financial aid applications may take longer to process because of the requirements of verification.

G R I T
Instinct

Unfortunately, many promising students give up on school because they get too frustrated with the complexity, delays, and confusion involved in getting the right kind and amount of aid. It takes significant GRIT to navigate the system and develop the instincts to find the best way to get what you need.

Renewing Financial Aid and Paying It Back

In order to continue to receive financial aid, you will need to make sure that you understand and follow the requirements of your college. Many colleges maintain a satisfactory academic policy that states you will need to stay enrolled in a certain number of credit hours and maintain a certain grade point average to continue to receive grants and loans. Sometimes, the required GPA is higher than the GPA to remain in college. For example, you may have to maintain a 2.7 GPA to continue to receive financial aid whereas you only have to maintain a 2.0 GPA to stay in college. If you do not meet the requirements for a term, your college may place you on financial aid probation, which means you must meet the college's requirements for the next term to be removed from probation. The next step after probation can be suspension from financial aid. This means that you may not be able to receive financial aid, but you may still be able to enroll in classes as long as you pay for them yourself. Just in case your suspension is the result of extenuating circumstances, some colleges have an appeals process for financial aid suspension. This means you may file an appeal and meet before a group of people who will determine if you can reapply for financial aid.

Whenever you apply for loans, you will need to consider how you will pay them back after you complete your degree or when you stop attending college. Student loan default is a common problem nationwide and there are stiff penalties for failing to pay back the federal government. On the other hand, loan forgiveness programs are often available for students who major in fields that are in high demand in their community. To find out more about these types of programs, be sure to talk to someone in the financial aid office at your college. There are also some useful resources that you can consult for guidance about financial aid and borrowing.

- The Free Application for Federal Student Aid (FAFSA) site (www.fafsa.ed.gov) provides extensive information about the FAFSA itself and the various forms of federal student aid.

- The Pay Scale Score website (www.payscale.com/college-roi) provides information about your ROI, or return on investment, for different institutions of higher education. You can research a career to find out if the earning potential outweighs your investment in the degree.

- The College Board (https://bigfuture.collegeboard.org/pay-for-college) provides a number of resources, including a scholarship search tool and a net price calculator for estimating the total cost of attending college.

GRIT GAINER™

FIND THE FUNDS Use your gritty mindset to help fund your education so you can complete your degree. Ask yourself the following questions:

1. What potential sources of funding have I not yet pursued that might provide some real help?

2. What am I willing to sacrifice to do what it takes to fund my education?

3. Whom can I ask and what resources can I explore to come up with even smarter answers?

The Decision to Stay in College Is Yours to Make

Achieving your degree will be a proud moment for you and your family.

There is tremendous pressure on those who do not have higher degrees to get them. Frequently high school students hear this pitch from parents, counselors, and teachers: Success in life is dependent on obtaining a college degree. People who have been in the workforce know as well that a college degree can be the difference between doing the same job until retirement and being promoted.

But does everyone need to go to college? College is a great place to continue your education and to make your career dreams a reality. There are also indirect benefits to pursuing higher education, such as improving your health and financial well-being. Nonetheless, going to college is not the only key to success. There are many vibrant, intelligent, successful people who have not completed a college degree.

College Should Be Right for You

How will you know if college is not right for you? It may be difficult to tell, but you shouldn't quit going if you are unsure. The best way to discover how you feel about being in college is to ask yourself a series of questions. Then, talk about your responses with a college counselor, advisor, or trusted friend who can give you good advice.

- Who wants me to be in college?
- Do *I* want to be in college?
- How do I feel when I am in class?
- How do I feel when I am studying?
- How do I feel after I take an exam?
- What do I want to major in? Why?
- What do I want to do with my life? Do I need a college degree to do it?
- What do I value about higher education? What can it do for me?
- What is my passion?
- Am I doing everything I can to be successful in college?

Take your time answering these questions. You may find that your discomfort about being in college is really fear about a new beginning and the unknown. Being apprehensive about a new program or a new environment is perfectly normal and does not necessarily indicate that you are not right for college. Also, if you find yourself struggling in your classes or with your schedule, there may be some specific strategies you could implement, such as joining a study group, to get you back on track for success. On the other hand, you may know very clearly that you do not want to be in college at this point in your life. College may not be right for you *right now*, which means that you should consider returning when you are certain it will be your top priority.

> **GRIT**
> **Tenacity**
>
> It's pretty clear that it's not always the students with the biggest brains that graduate. It's the ones with the most GRIT. Getting through takes tenacity. You have to dig deep, stick with it, and see it through, especially when you are most downhearted about the experience.

Benefits of Continuing Your Education

If you are considering whether to continue your education next term, it may be helpful to think about the benefits of going on. First, you will be that much closer to finishing a degree. More completed classes mean more degree requirements checked off the list. Second, if you have to take courses in a sequence (e.g., Writing I and Writing II), then you are more likely to remember what you learned in the first course. Staying out too long between courses that need to be taken close together may mean you will forget important concepts, which could make the second course more difficult for you. Finally, staying in college now will mean you are more likely to stay friends with classmates. Even taking a term break may mean that you lose touch with people you know and rely on now.

Benefits of Taking a Break

If you decide you need a break before you complete your degree, be sure to make the most of your time away from college. Some students use that time to earn extra money, take care of personal issues, or work on their academic skills outside of college. A much-needed break can help you stay focused; instead of burning out, you may find yourself reenergized so that you can return with more focus and enthusiasm. A break can help you clarify your goals, and it can also help you recommit to the degree path you started on. Of course, during your break, if you decide to change degrees or career directions, you can return with a renewed sense of purpose.

If you do decide to take a break, be sure to meet with an academic advisor and make a plan that you can follow. Colleges have specific requirements for students who don't enroll every term, and if your admission to the university was through a competitive process, they may not hold your spot unless you have a specific reentry plan in place. Remember that your advisors and professors and other staff at the university are there for your success, so talk with them about your plans and stay in touch with them even while you're gone.

Consider Your Life Without College Before Choosing That Path

If you're uncertain at this point whether you can or want to continue with your college degree, and you're giving some consideration to dropping out, take some time to consider what your life will be like—both in the short and long term—without a college degree. Consider these facts:

- Among adults who were born after 1980, those who had graduated from college earned, on average, $17,500 more annually than adults of the same age with only a high school diploma (Pew Research Center, 2014).

GRIT GAINER™

GIVE YOURSELF A BREAK   If you decide to take a break, make sure you are doing it for the right reasons and that you will use that time to expand and improve yourself along the way. Optimize your break by asking yourself, "How can I use my break to enhance my performance in school and to enhance my job prospects when I graduate?"

- In 2013, the average hourly wage of Americans with a four-year college degree was 98 percent higher than those without a degree (Leonhardt, 2014).

- College grads generally show higher rates of civic participation, engaging in volunteer work and donating blood at more than twice the rate of high-school graduates (Shellenbarger, 2009).

- College-educated adults are less likely than others to be obese, and children living in households with more educated parents are less likely than other children to be obese (Baum, Ma, and Payea, 2013).

There are many very successful and happy people who do not have a college degree, and you, too, can have a successful life if you choose not to complete your degree. However, you should weigh this decision carefully, knowing that the odds for success will be more in your favor if you stick with it and finish your degree. It's not easy, especially if you're the first person in your family to go to college or if you face significant financial challenges or have a lot of work or family responsibilities. But, there are many who have gone before you who faced similar challenges and who succeeded in college and in life, and you have what it takes to follow in their footsteps. Depending on your circumstances, taking a break from college may be a good choice, but don't write yourself off as a future college graduate. A college degree can still be in your future.

the unwritten rules
about Degree Planning

- **Take advantage of fast-track options.** If your college provides accelerated terms during the summer and winter breaks, use them to take a class or two to get ahead. The course often moves quickly, but you can knock out a semester by taking advantage of just a few of these types of terms.

- **Do your homework before signing up for classes.** You should know what the syllabus looks like, what kinds of assignments are given, and how the professor teaches the class. You can find this out by asking other students, advisors, and the professors themselves. Don't rely on anonymous online ratings for all your information.

- **Be proactive about paying for college.** You will have to hunt for alternative opportunities for paying for college. Let everyone know you are looking for ways to earn more money or reduce your college expenses. You may be surprised to find out millions of dollars in scholarship money goes unclaimed every year.

- **Know what you owe.** Although it may seem better to worry about student loan repayment after you graduate and get into college, it is better for you to know what you owe each term and calculate what the final bill will be when you graduate. This may motivate you to stick with a class rather than drop it, get tutoring for a class you may fail, and take advantage of options to accelerate course completion.

3 things future professionals need to know about degree planning

you may need to interrupt your college career to return to your full-time job

Balancing financial and educational goals may be too difficult to handle at the moment, which may mean that your financial needs take precedence. If this happens to you, there are some ways of dealing with the transition back to the world of work while still keeping your eye on returning to college. First, realize that going back to work doesn't have to be forever. Just because you are unable to return for more than one term doesn't mean you never will. Second, talk with your employer about your desire to get a degree. There may even be financial assistance for employees who take college classes.

the mindset and skillset of degree planning will serve you well in your career

Successfully developing and implementing a degree plan provides an outstanding demonstration of project management skills, which employers highly value. When you interview for internships or full-time careers, be sure to use this experience to demonstrate your ability to make and implement a plan, even with obstacles and setbacks.

there's no avoiding the fact that student loan debt will affect your career

You'll face decisions in your career about which job offer to accept, whether to take a risk and start your own business, when to get married and raise a family, or whether you need to take on extra responsibilities at work for extra pay. Each of these decisions will be influenced by how much student debt you're paying off after you graduate. Decisions today will affect your decisions in the future. Do yourself a favor and keep your student loan debt to a minimum so that you aren't burdened by the debt payments after graduation.

THE GRIT ADVANTAGE

Completion is all about GRIT. More than smarts, talents, privileges, money, or any other asset, GRIT rules the day. Use yours to get through and get out so you can get paid by asking the following questions:

Growth. In what ways do I need to expand, grow, and improve? And how can I use my degree plan to help me?

Resilience. What can I do to make my schedule tougher to stretch me to become more than I am today?

Instinct. What would be the best way to at least increase the chances I fund and complete my schooling? Who can I ask to enhance my approach?

Tenacity. Where have I given up or stopped short, that if I worked/tried harder, might lead to some real benefits on my path to graduation?

HOW GRITTY ARE YOU?

Now that you've completed this chapter, how committed are you to:

1. Owning your degree, making and sticking to a plan so you graduate strong?

Zero Commitment 0 —————————————————————————— 10 Fully Committed

2. Researching and pursuing whatever options are necessary to fund your education?

Zero Commitment 0 —————————————————————————— 10 Fully Committed

3. Create a plan not to survive, but to optimize your time in college?

Zero Commitment 0 —————————————————————————— 10 Fully Committed

12 Preparing Your Career

Chapter goals to help you
get in,
get through,
get out,
and get paid:

We've used the phrase "get in, get through, get out, get paid," and in this chapter, we cover the last, most rewarding step in the process—getting paid!

To meet those goals, this chapter will help you:

- Identify the tools and methods available for career exploration
- Develop an effective resume and cover letter
- Engage in networking activities that help you build important relationships
- Develop a plan for your life beyond college
- Appreciate and employ the **GRIT** edge for your career-related efforts

MyStudentSuccessLab™

GRIT

Log in to MyStudentSuccessLab.com to deepen your **GRIT** mindset and build the skills you'll need to get through the college experience.

Evan and Michael's Story

© MONKEY BUSINESS IMAGES/SHUTTERSTOCK

The big red arrow pointed to the ballroom. There were dozens of booths inviting students to leave their resumes and to learn more about a variety of businesses and industries.

In jeans and his university sweatshirt, Evan stopped to pick up a company brochure. "I'm planning on going to all the booths. Are you?" Evan asked.

Michael, wearing khakis and a white shirt, had done a little research and had already decided on the two booths he wanted to visit.

"No," he said. "I plan on finding the two companies I checked out on the Internet and leaving my resume."

"Aren't you afraid you will be cutting yourself short? Shouldn't you hit every one of the booths, just in case?" Evan asked.

"I think it is better to focus on one or two companies rather than all of them. Besides, I don't want just any job," Michael said.

Evan pulled out 30 copies of his resume from his backpack, walked to the first table, and introduced himself.

"I'm Evan. It is a pleasure to meet you," he said to the woman representing an aeronautics firm. "So, tell me what your company does and what I would do if I worked for you."

Michael walked straight to one of the two health care companies at the fair with his resume.

Now, what do you think?

- If you were unsure of what company you wanted to work for, how would you approach a career fair?
  - **a.** Focus more on how companies are trying to recruit me rather than how I can impress them
  - **b.** Be selective and do my research before I attend
  - **c.** Be open to all the possibilities by going to every employer—you never know what you may like or who may like you

- How would you introduce yourself to a potential employer?
  - **a.** Provide a general resume that would fit any job and say that I am interested in all jobs
  - **b.** Tell the employer that I want to be the CEO in two years so that I impress them with my ambition
  - **c.** Explain what I know about the company, the open position, and how I am qualified for the job

Your Terms for Success

when you see . . .	it means . . .
Career fair	An event that brings various employers together into one place
Cover letter	A letter that covers a resume and provides a more detailed description of a job applicant's qualifications
Internship	A supervised position that allows a student to receive on-the-job training
Networking	Creating connections among people for the purpose of helping them or having them help you
Objective	A statement in a resume that explains your career goals
Recommendation letter	A letter written to provide a recommendation of your abilities and skills
References	People listed on a resume who can provide a recommendation of your abilities and skills
Resume	A document that provides information about you, your education, and your work experience
Resume padding	The act of exaggerating or lying about educational or work experience on a resume
Social networking	Creating connections through websites for the purpose of communicating with others

Your Career Starts Here

Whether you know exactly what career you want or you are still exploring the possibilities, your college experience can help you focus on what you want out of your professional life. After reading the following section about getting ready for a career, remember that the people you meet at your college can help you in many ways: they can help you decide what career is a best fit for you as well as help you prepare to find and secure that job.

Although it may seem like your career won't start until you're done with college, the exciting reality is that the decisions you are making today are already starting to form your career. College is the time for exploring and preparing for a career, and the first step is to know your goals and values.

G R I T
Growth

> Smart isn't enough. New research shows employers put a premium on GRIT. The tougher the challenges and obstacles you face, and the more difficult path you take, the more attractive you will be. The choices you make now will show up in your resume and job interviews later.

Career Values and Goals Set the Course for Your Journey

Before you begin delving into the resources and services available at your college, take some time to reflect on what your career values and goals are. Values are personal and professional qualities and principles that are deeply important to you. For example, you may have a passionate interest in working for a company that has a positive social and environmental impact. Or, it may be critically important to you to work for an organization that is honest and ethical. A sample list of values is provided in Exhibit 12.1, just to give you a starting point for identifying your own.

In addition to considering your values as they relate to your career, you may also want to consider what your goals are. Goals are tangible outcomes that you want to achieve in your personal and professional life. For example, is your goal to move up quickly in a company or to find a business that will allow you to travel and meet a diverse group of people? When you get to the point that you will be creating clear, realistic, and reachable career goals, they will be influenced by your values. Your values and goals will also help you with talking with a career counselor, searching for a job, and interviewing. You may have a goal of earning a salary that will allow you to pay off your student loan debt within three years of graduating or providing enough income to support your parents. Your goals

---

EXHIBIT 12.1   Career Values

Advancement	Excitement	Learning	Security
Authority	Family	Money	Social status
Beauty	Fast pace	People	Solitude
Challenge	Financial stability	Physical challenge	Spirituality
Community	Helping others	Pressure	Teamwork
Competence	Independence	Recognition	Tranquility
Creativity	Friendship	Power	Structure
Decision making	Influence	Relationships	Travel
Education	Knowledge	Safety	Variety

Tenacity

may also relate to a specific job title or position, such as becoming a partner in a law firm or accounting firm. Or you may have goals about your contributions to society, such as having a career that allows you to contribute at least 10 percent of your time and money to charitable causes.

> A Gallup poll of 25 million people shows 70 percent of working people are disengaged, meaning they are not excited about what they are doing and not giving their best. Those who have jobs with the most alignment with their values and goals and those with the greatest GRIT are the most engaged. They *enjoy* their work.

Besides your personal values and goals, it is worth considering what you value in a career and what kinds of experiences you want to have. For example, do you value working with others in projects with strict deadlines or would you prefer to work alone with little supervision? Your answer to that question and others can help you determine what you value and what careers work best for you. If, for instance, you have a strong interest in writing, but you prefer working with others, you may decide to choose a career that has many opportunities for collaboration when writing. Look at Exhibit 12.2 for other ways to consider what kind of career culture or environment you most likely will enjoy.

If you are not sure where to start when considering your career values and goals, then you may want to check out the various career assessment programs, such as DISCOVER or Kuder, at your career counseling center. There are also a number of websites and books, such as Richard N. Bolles's *What Color Is Your Parachute?* (2011), that offer helpful guidance for identifying your career interests, even at the early stages of your college career.

The career landscape can seem daunting and complex, especially because technology seems to cause careers to change so quickly. Careers that existed 10 years ago may not exist four years from now, and careers that didn't exist a few years ago are now emerging. For that reason, don't put pressure on yourself to identify a specific company and job title for your career goal. Instead, keep your focus on the kind of career you want to have in terms of its general characteristics—work environment, industry, technical requirements, individual versus team environment, highly structured versus unstructured organizational structure and job functions, and the like. Take time to browse career listings on websites such as careerbuilder.com

---

EXHIBIT 12.2   Career Interest Questions

Do you like working in a team?	Yes	No
Do you like working on your own?	Yes	No
Do you want to work in a predictable, structured environment?	Yes	No
Do you prefer more spontaneity and ambiguity?	Yes	No
Do you prefer a steady, predictable paycheck?	Yes	No
Do you prefer the opportunity and risk of getting paid in proportion to your success and effort?	Yes	No
Do you want to work primarily in an office environment?	Yes	No
Do you want to travel and/or live internationally?	Yes	No
Do you prefer to work on quantitative and analytical projects?	Yes	No
Do you prefer to work on social and creative activities?	Yes	No
Do you want to work for an established firm with a well-defined organizational structure?	Yes	No
Do you want to run or own your own business someday?	Yes	No

and save a copy of the posts that capture your interest. These will help you paint a picture that captures your values and goals as they emerge and develop over time.

It's OK if your interests change over time; that will happen as you take more classes and gain new perspective from your college experience. In fact, in today's work environment, the average individual will have several careers over their lifetime. What you're developing in college is the ability to identify your interests and abilities and match them with the career opportunities in the marketplace. You may not want to face this reality now, but you may very well find yourself back in college later to pursue an advanced degree or certificate or a second bachelor's degree as you recreate yourself throughout your lifetime. As you learn to use the tools and resources we'll discuss in this next section, you'll be encouraged to know that they can serve you well throughout your career journey.

Career Counselors Can Be Your Best Supporters

Long before you think about graduating and finding a career, you should visit the career counselors at your college. Preparing for a career takes longer than a few weeks, and the more planning you do, the smoother the process will be. Even though you won't pursue a full-time career until you graduate, commit yourself to meeting with a counselor your freshman year so you can put an effective plan in place for both internships and your career. Each college offers different services in its career center, but most provide access to interest inventories, which can help you pinpoint which careers you are best suited for. Most career services also provide "career libraries" that include information about different types of careers, their responsibilities, and their pay potential. In addition, career centers may offer help with writing a cover letter and resume and tips for interviewing for a job. Evan could spend some time in his college's career library to learn more about careers before he hits all of the employers at the career fair.

GRIT
Growth

The job world is changing so fast that many of the most exciting jobs you might want to consider when you graduate don't even exist today. They aren't on the standard menu. Show some GRIT by asking anyone who looks like he or she enjoys his or her work or whose life you admire about what the person does and what he or she would suggest you consider.

Don't forget that your professors can also be great career counselors because they often have connections with people in the field (or have friends or relatives working in different industries). You never know when your sociology professor may have a contact at an accounting firm or a biology professor may have a connection with the human resources department at an advertising firm. Tell professors what you want to do as a career whenever you have a chance. They may remember you and your goals when they meet someone in your field of study.

Career Fairs Offer an Ideal Forum for Personal Contacts

Career fairs are another way to get information about jobs and employers in your area. If your college sponsors a fair off campus or provides one to students on campus, be sure to take advantage of it. Whether you are graduating next month or next year, it will pay to approach a career fair with the goal of making contacts and learning more about area businesses.

Use career fairs or on-campus events to network and put your best face forward to potential employers.

When you attend a career fair, there are several steps you can follow to make the most of your visits with potential employers. This list is just a start; you can get even more tips from your college counselors:

- Dress professionally. Also, carry a professional-looking bag (no backpacks!) and a folder with copies of your resume. Neatness counts.

- Do your homework. Find out what companies will be present at the fair and research the ones that interest you. You can find out more about them through their websites or by visiting retailers or other locations where their products or services are sold.

- Avoid asking, "And what does your company do?" Your research should tell you what the company does. Asking that question gives an immediate clue to the recruiter that you haven't taken the initiative to learn about them first.

- Choose a few booths to attend. Instead of blanketing the fair and hitting every representative, be selective and limit yourself only to companies that you would like to work for.

- Write a standard introduction, practice it, and then use it when you meet someone at the fair. Make sure the introduction is brief (state your name, your interests, and any relevant experience you may have) so that you maximize your time at the fair. A 30- to 60-second "elevator pitch" (the average length of a ride in an elevator) is a good standard to meet.

- Be energetic and positive. Recruiters and employers want to meet eager, exciting potential employees.

- Be clear and unapologetic about what you want. If you're an underclassman, you are probably trying to get an interview for an internship or an informational interview (more on this concept later). If you're a senior, you want an interview for a full-time position. In either case, try to learn as much as you can beforehand about the positions they have available so you can clearly specify your interest. Company representatives who come to career fairs are expecting this from students, so you don't have to hesitate or apologize for asking for an interview.

G R I T
Resilience

Be prepared to share your story about whatever struggles, sacrifices, and hardships you faced to get to where you are today. Employers value resilience and GRIT.

If you cannot make your college's career fair, you may be able to participate in a virtual career fair, which allows job seekers to "meet" participating companies and send resumes. Virtual career fairs are usually linked to a college's website and coincide with the actual fair. For example, the virtual career fair link may only be available while the on-campus fair is open. Some colleges and organizations, however, provide a perpetual virtual career fair so that students can investigate potential careers and companies at any time. One such website is www.michiganvirtualcareerfair.com, which offers job seekers access to a variety of employers. Other sites, such as www.collegegrad.com/careers, offer more general information about careers as well as advice and preparation for job seekers. Other sites, such as www.collegegrad.com/careers, offer more general information about careers as well as advice and preparation for job seekers.

Internships Give You and Your Employer a Chance for a Test Drive

Another work option for college students is an internship. This is a supervised position that allows students to work for an organization before they graduate. Some internships are unpaid, which makes them less attractive to students who need to work. However, you may be able

GRIT GAINER™

GRITTY GO-GETTERS   GRIT is the most powerful weapon you have in winning the job wars. Many people who have the most exciting and fulfilling careers were turned down, often multiple times. They were told "no," but they used their GRIT to help achieve a "yes" on the things that count.

Without a lot of self-editing, briefly describe the kind of career you want to pursue when you graduate. Then, identify two or three tangible action items you could commit to now to put you on a path toward that career.

to earn academic credit for a paid or unpaid internship, so check with your advisor well in advance about this possibility. Internships are a great way to make progress toward your degree and explore careers. Another idea is to volunteer once or twice a week at a place of business. If you have a few extra hours a week or can trade college credit for an internship, then you should investigate the benefits of interning.

Why are internships such a good opportunity for college students? One reason is that they allow you to work closely in a field that you may be interested in pursuing. In addition, internships can help you explore different ways that a major can be used in the workforce. For example, an English or journalism major may want to participate in an internship at a newspaper or as a technical editor at a company. A computer science major may want to intern at a small business to get practical experience with computer networking issues. These opportunities can give you firsthand experience with using what you're learning in your degree.

Internships also allow you to network with others who can help you find a job once you graduate. Even if you decide that you don't want to work in the same area as your internship, you will have contacts who may help you find a job in other fields. If you decide to intern, you should treat it as a career. Some employers rely on interns to complete certain projects each year, and they will expect that you be serious about the position, even if you don't get paid. Keeping a good attitude and being self-motivated are excellent ways to shine during your internship. In addition, you should meet regularly with your supervisor to ask questions and get guidance on projects. Most of all, make the best of your unique opportunity, and add that experience to your resume.

Your Resume and Cover Letter Establish Your Personal Brand

In addition to educating or training you for a career, your college may also offer services that help you land the job you want. Many specialized programs, such as nursing, business, engineering, and journalism, provide job placement services as well as a degree or minor. Other degree programs, such as psychology or health sciences, may provide fewer career services, but the professors and advisors in those programs can still be valuable resources as you prepare for the workforce. At the very least, you will need to know the basics for finding a job after you graduate. Writing resumes and cover letters, as well as polishing your interviewing skills, will be necessary for you to move into your career of choice. As you progress through your degree, your resume and cover letter will serve as a tangible representation of your personal brand—who you are, what you know, what you can do, and how you're different from your peers and other individuals competing for the same jobs as you are. Just as McDonald's, Buick, Lenova, and Siemens invest significant effort and resources in defining themselves through a distinctive brand, you also need to establish a distinctive personal brand that makes you recognizable and relevant to organizations who need a talented workforce. If you'd like to learn more about developing your personal brand, Tim O'Brien's book *The Power of Personal Branding* is a great resource (www.thepersonalbrandinggroup.com).

Your Resume Puts Your Life on Paper

Learning to write a resume is an essential skill for new graduates, and there is no time like the present to begin honing that skill. A resume is no place to be modest, but neither is it a place to embellish or misrepresent your skills or experience. Prospective employers and recruiters will be looking for action verbs that describe your experience and abilities, and they're looking for evidence that you have something unique and valuable to contribute to their organization. Everyone has something—whether it's the classes they've taken, the projects they've completed, or the hardships they've overcome in their personal life—that makes the person special and gives him or her experience and personal qualities that are important to an employer. The challenge is to describe these qualities in a resume.

When writing a resume, the first thing you will include is your name and contact information, including your address, phone number, and email address. Make sure your voicemail has an appropriate message on it and that your email is professional as well: ejcantu@abcmail.com is preferred over bananafreak72@chunkymonkey.com. Double-check that there are no errors in your contact information—one mistake can cost you an interview because a recruiter won't be able to contact you. Michael's resume contains a new email address to replace the more personal one that he uses for friends and family because he wants to separate career email from more casual correspondence.

A successful resume will also contain a clear objective, or a statement that tells others what your career goals are. Think of it as a mini-mission statement for your career! Objectives are not always written in a complete sentence. For example, your objective may be "To join an aircraft maintenance team at a highly rewarding company" or "To use my knowledge and skills to manage employees in the retail industry effectively." Writing a good objective takes time and consideration, and you may need to develop more than one if you plan to apply for different jobs or jobs in different industries. Be sure that your objective matches the job for which you are applying. If, for example, your objective says that you want "To have a fulfilling career working with infants and toddlers in an accredited daycare" and you are applying to teach classes at a nursing home, then you may not get a second glance, much less an interview. Counselors and professors can help you craft an appropriate objective as you build your resume. You may also want to develop more than one version of your resume with different purpose statements so that you can personalize what you send to different companies in different industries.

Once you include an appropriate objective, you will need to include information about your educational accomplishments and job history. If you have not completed your degree at this point, you can write down the anticipated date: "Bachelor of Arts, May 2016." Be sure to include any other certificates or degrees that you have earned. The most recently earned certificate or degree should be listed first, and the rest of your academic accomplishments should be listed in reverse chronological order. Information about your work history may be placed either before or after the information about your education. Again, list your most recent job first and include the date you worked, your position title, the name of the company and location, and a list of bulleted items of job responsibilities, written with action verbs such as *organized, developed, implemented,* and *managed.* Exhibit 12.3 shows a very basic format for reporting your work experience on a resume. Depending on what kind of format you use, the order of the information may vary.

EXHIBIT 12.3   **Sample Part of Resume**

| 2008–2012 | Dental Assistant | No Worry Dental Group | Tacoma, WA |

- Cleaned clients' teeth and identified problem areas
- Took x-rays of clients' teeth and updated their charts
- Provided guidance for preventing tooth decay and improving gum health

Depending on how much experience you have had, the first few parts of a resume may be easy to complete. Many students have previous or current work experience and know what educational experiences they have. However, a part of the resume that is sometimes more difficult is the section that contains extracurricular activities, organizations, or awards. If you are early in your college career, you may not feel as though you have been able to participate in extracurricular activities to add to your list of accomplishments. Nonetheless, with just a little creative thinking, you may be able to create a list of activities and endeavors. For instance, if you received a college scholarship, you can list it as an award. If you volunteer regularly with your child's school, you can list it. If you have participated in a fundraising event, organized a community meeting, coached a sport, or sat on a committee at your church or synagogue, you can list it. You may not realize all the ways you have been involved with others that can show that you have other interests than college and work.

Instinct

A ground-breaking study looked at 30,000 resumes to figure out what, if any, factors made the difference on who gets the job and who doesn't. The resumes that had a statement that communicated GRIT—a tough goal they took on and achieved against daunting odds—had *triple* the chance of getting the job.

Your college will also provide you with future opportunities to add to a resume, so be sure to keep your eyes and ears open for chances to participate in a one-day event or a semester-long program. The key is to get involved at any level and record your involvement so that you can remember it when you need to develop your resume. Here are just a few opportunities for students to get involved that colleges often provide:

- Dean's List or President's List for specified grade point averages
- Student Ambassadors' Organization for promoting the college in the community
- Student Government Association for representing the voice of students
- Honor societies such as Phi Beta Kappa, as well as honor societies for specific disciplines, such as Sigma Kappa Delta, an English honor society
- Special events such as fundraisers, cultural events, political or community rallies, and celebrations

One last part of the resume is a list of references or a statement that says references are available upon request. As you meet people in college, you may want to create a list of potential references. A professor whom you got to know well, your advisor whom you see each semester as you plan your degree, or a campus official with whom you have worked closely on a project are good candidates for letters of recommendation or references. People you have worked with—either on the job or through a community project—are other excellent possibilities for references. Make sure these people know you well enough to speak of your strengths and potential in the workplace. Getting their permission before you list them is essential to getting a good reference.

Exhibit 12.4 is an example of one type of resume. There are many ways to grab an employer's attention; books will provide you with examples of the various formats. However, a format that is concise, easy to read, and professional is usually best.

As you consider what content to include in your resume, think of it as a body of evidence to support every claim you would want to make about yourself in an interview. If you believe that you are a hardworking person, then your resume might illustrate how you've managed to work during college. If you're an effective communicator, the resume itself should be well written, and you could reference the high grades you've received in your composition and technical writing classes or that you've participated on a high school debate team. If you want to support your claim that you have strong computer skills, your resume can list the types of software programs that you use regularly and some of the technical features of these programs, such as mail merge in Microsoft Word or animated graphics with Java. Picture yourself in an interview, making each claim and then pointing to a particular line in your resume as the evidence. A resume that can serve this purpose in an interview is in good shape to be sent to prospective employers.

EXHIBIT 12.4 Sample Resume

Juanita Cook

1234 Broadway Street

Anyplace, US 01234

555-555-1234

jrcook@anyplace.edu

Objective: To use my experience and education to work as an accounting manager.

Education

Bachelor's of Science in Accounting. Juno University, May 2013

Experience

Bookkeeper, Mays and Associates, August 2010–present

- Send invoices to clients
- Pay invoices from clients
- Maintain general ledger
- Supervise one staff member

Work Study, Financial Aid Office, Juno University. January 2009–July 2010

- Filed financial aid applications
- Maintained communication with students through newsletter

Honors and Awards

- Accounting Award for Outstanding Student, May 2013
- President's Scholarship, August 2010–May 2013
- Volunteer of the Year, Humane Society, October 2009

References Available Upon Request

Your Cover Letter Is Your Personal Introduction to Each Employer

A cover letter accompanies a resume and explains in detail how your qualifications match what the employer is looking for. As with a resume, keep a cover letter brief and to the point, usually no more than a page unless you have enough work experience that you believe it needs to be detailed in the letter. The reason that cover letters should be short is that many employers simply scan these documents to see if candidates meet the minimum qualifications and then quickly decide whether to interview them. The more concise your resume and cover letter, the easier it will be for potential employers to determine whether you are right for the job.

When writing a cover letter, be sure to address a specific person. Avoid starting your letter with "Dear Sir or Madam" or "To Whom It May Concern." If you do not know to whom to address the letter, call the company and ask for the appropriate person's name, along with the correct spelling. If you are responding to several different job advertisements, double-check that you have correctly matched each letter with its corresponding addressed envelope. Also be sure that you have not made any references to people or companies other than to whom you are sending the cover letter.

The basic format of a cover letter is simple—once you type in your address, the date, and the potential employer's name, company name, and address, you can follow this format:

1. Introduction Paragraph
   a. Introduce yourself
   b. Describe the specific job title or position you are seeking within their organization
   c. Tell where you learned about the job (Internet, newspaper, person at the company)

2. Background Paragraph
   a. Tell more about yourself and how you are qualified
   b. Relate your education and skills to the ones that the company is looking for

3. Closing Paragraph
   a. Tell potential employer how to contact you
   b. Thank the person for her time and say you are looking forward to hearing from her

Exhibit 12.5 is an example of an effective cover letter that could accompany the resume in Exhibit 12.4.

EXHIBIT 12.5   Sample Cover Letter

1234 Broadway Street

Anyplace, US 01234

June 1, 2015

Dr. Judy Pile

Ingram Enterprises

6789 Levi Lane

Anyplace, US 09876

Dear Dr. Pile,

I am responding to your advertisement in the Tonitown Times for an accounting specialist at your company, Ingram Enterprises. As you will see from my resume, I have earned a Bachelor of Science degree in accounting from Juno University, and I have experience working as a bookkeeper for a local company.

My additional work-study experience in the financial aid office at Juno has allowed me to improve my people skills as well as understand how an organized and efficient office works. I have also learned to use the following computer programs effectively: Microsoft Word, Microsoft Excel, and QuickBooks.

I am sure that you will find both my education and experience fit the position that was advertised. If you would like to interview me, I can be reached during the day at 555-555-1234. I look forward to hearing from you.

Sincerely,

Juanita Cook

The Interview Is Your Chance to Shine

■ Practice interviewing with a fellow student or a career counselor before going there for real.

© RUBBERBALL/GETTY IMAGES

Another important component to a successful career search, if not the most important, is interviewing for a job. If your winning resume gets you an interview, you are about halfway to getting a job. Consider the following tips to maximize your performance at the interview. Do a little research by checking out the company's website or search for other company information that may have appeared with the job advertisement. The goal is to find out what the company does and where it is going. Exhibit 12.6 provides five top tips for preparing you to interview with a company.

Don't forget to practice interview questions with your friends or family. Try to simulate the interview process by sitting across from the person who is practicing with you. Ask that person to make note of any fidgety habits and unclear answers. When you interview, dress professionally and pay attention to the details. Keep your fingernails clean and short. Check out hems and cuffs for tears. Make sure your clothes are clean and pressed and your shoes are polished. For women, be sure that there are no runs in your hose and that your heels are not scuffed.

When you score an interview, be sure to arrive early. Introduce yourself to the receptionist and prepare to wait. During the interview, listen carefully to the interviewer's questions, pause before answering, and speak slowly and carefully. Be sure to look all of the interviewers in the eye when speaking, sit up, and lean forward slightly. Show by your body language that you are interested and relaxed, even if you are nervous. It is normal to be nervous, but be sure to avoid fidgeting with a pencil

EXHIBIT 12.6   Top Five Tips to Prepare for an Interview

1. Know the company: what it does or sells, how big it is, how successful it is. If it's a company whose shares are publicly traded (i.e., you can buy its stock as investor), find the most recent annual report and read it, especially the CEO's introductory comments. If it's a privately held company, check with your reference librarian to get help in obtaining more information beyond the company website.

2. Know the industry: who are the competitors and who is winning and losing in the industry, what major trends or environmental forces are affecting the industry. Your reference librarian can help you find resources to do this research.

3. Know the job: you may have a job description from the job posting to help you, or you can poke around on the company website to see if it lists an employee directory or organizational chart.

4. Rehearse your 30– to 60–second "elevator speech" about yourself and practice using your resume to cite evidence for every claim you mate about yourself.

5. Prepare for the famous behavioral questions. Employers who are looking for employees with specific qualities will often ask you to "Give me an example of a time when you demonstrated perseverance" (or any other personal quality or experience). Prepare for these questions by generating a list of the qualities and experiences that the recruiter might want for the position. Then, identify specific life events you've experienced that demonstrate that quality. These events don't all have to be from college. In fact, some of the most powerful testaments to your creativity, work ethic, problem solving ability, and communication skills might involve experiences from your earlier life and the challenges and failures you've overcome.

integrity matters

Although you may be excited to include your accomplishments on your resume, you will need to be sure that you do not go overboard. A good rule to follow is to always provide accurate, truthful information in your resume and cover letter. Highlight your accomplishments without exaggerating them.

Lying on a resume is called *resume padding*, and it can get you in serious trouble. At the very least, you may not get the job; at the very worst, you could be fired after you are hired if the company finds out that your resume contains false information.

YOUR TURN

In 250 words, describe where you think the line exists between making your accomplishments noteworthy and exaggerating them. Discuss what steps will you take to ensure that all of your information for a resume or a cover letter is accurate.

or paper and tapping your fingers or feet. Some degree of nervousness is a good thing, because it demonstrates to the recruiter that this interview is really important to you.

Be sure to highlight your strengths. Even if you don't meet all of the job's qualifications, you may be able to persuade the employer that you can do the job. It's generally a good idea to avoid asking about the salary at the beginning of the interview. Instead, ask about the job responsibilities and benefits—the interviewer may provide a salary range as part of the information. As a last question, you may want to ask what the next step is in the interviewing process and what the timeline is for filling the position. Knowing when the company will be making the final decision will help you prepare for the next step.

As you leave, thank everyone you meet, shake his or her hand, and follow up with a thank you letter to each interviewer (see Exhibit 12.7). If you do not know how to spell their names, call the receptionist the next day to get the correct spellings. Although email is widely used for thank you letters and provides timely communication, also consider the possibility of accompanying the email with a handwritten personalized thank you letter to each interviewer. Such a practice may seem unusual, but it's the kind of effort and courtesy that will differentiate you from the other prospects who either don't send a thank you note at all, or who choose to write a brief, informal email that reads more like a text message than a carefully written letter. Every opportunity you have to make contact with a prospective employer is another chance to build and reinforce your personal brand and distinctive qualities.

If a question was raised in an interview that you weren't able to answer, or a topic came up that you know or read something about, use the follow-up correspondence as an opportunity to share that information. For example, if one of the interviewers seemed to be particularly interested in one of your class projects in which you developed an idea for helping senior citizens navigate the Internet, follow up by sending a copy of the project to them or providing a more detailed description. This is an example of an opportunity to move yourself from a recruiter's short-term memory to long-term memory. You'll remember that concept from Chapter 6, and you can apply it to your career search in powerful ways.

Interviewers want to hire people who are energetic, polite, professional, and appreciative. Put your best face forward and try to relax and enjoy the process.

Tenacity

Interviews are the perfect opportunity to help employers discover your GRIT. Think about the one situation in your life where you had to try the hardest, persist the most, and keep trying when others might have quit. Try to find a way to share that part of yourself with the employer. GRIT matters.

Instinct

Remember, part of GRIT is not just how hard you work, but using the best approach to achieve your goals. Turn any weakness, the one that concerns you most, into a strength. "I may not have the best grades of anyone you might interview, I might not look the best on paper, but I'll tell you what I do have. I have tremendous GRIT. Let me tell you what it took just to be here today . . . "

EXHIBIT 12.7   Sample Thank You Letter

Juanita Cook

1234 Broadway Street

Anyplace, US 01234

555-555-1234

jrcook@anyplace.edu

July 12, 2015

Dr. Judy Pile

Ingram Enterprises

6789 Levi Lane

Anyplace, US 09876

Dear Dr. Pile,

Thank you for interviewing me yesterday. I enjoyed meeting you and your colleagues and learning more about how your company works.

After speaking with you, I am more firmly convinced that I would be a good person for the job. My education and experience would be a great match for what the position demands. I enjoy professional challenges, and I think your company provides the type of opportunities I am looking for.

Please feel free to contact me at 555-555-1234 or jrcook@anyplace.edu. I look forward to hearing from you.

Sincerely,

Juanita Cook

Informational Interviews Get Your Foot in the Door

Traditional job interviews are arranged when employers have specific job openings and are evaluating potential candidates for hire. Sometimes, however, you may have a strong interest in working for a particular company, even if there aren't job openings available at the time. For example, you may discover during your junior year that you really want to be an architect at a regional architectural firm in your area, but the company doesn't have any openings at the time. An option to consider is an informational interview. In an informational interview, you arrange to meet with one or more employees in the organization who have positions that are similar to the career you want to pursue. Your purpose is to learn more about their day-to-day responsibilities and what it's like to work at the company.

Because you aren't directly seeking a job like in a traditional interview, you can often convince someone in an organization to schedule an informational interview with you, even when it isn't hiring. An informational interview gives you a chance to really learn about a particular position, what it takes to be successful in that position, and where that position might lead in the future of a long-term career path. You can also gain insights how the person presently in that position secured the job in the first place. All of this information can help you develop your own career strategy. A side benefit of an informational interview is that it helps you create a relational network within that organization so that when you are in job search mode, you have a specific person to contact who knows about you and your interests.

The Internet Offers Great Opportunities (and Potential Pitfalls) for Your Career Search

The Internet has made it so much easier to find and apply for jobs, communicate with potential employers, and network to improve your contacts and connections. However, it can also be a potential hazard if it is not used appropriately and professionally. Most people are aware that posting messages, information, and photos can be risky—even dangerous—to your professional health, but they may not be aware how much potential employers look for—and find—before they interview candidates. Many employers and company recruiters search for potential candidates online to see what kinds of information and images are out there. In some career fields, the more a candidate exposes himself (literally and figuratively), the less likely it is he will get the job.

What can you do to protect yourself? Deleting your accounts can be your best defense, but you may also change your account settings to private. Be aware, though, that if you have a large network of "friends," people who want to find out about you may still be able to do so. It is best not to post anything that you think may be questionable to a potential employer. If you have posted anything that may jeopardize your ability to get the job you want, delete it. Also, keep in mind that your friends may have posted photos on their Facebook or other sites and tagged you in them. As you consider the digital footprint that you've created to date, carefully consider the reality that this content could very well emerge in the public arena and stay there for a long time. Chances are, you're reading this book at an early stage in your college career. That gives you a great opportunity to establish online habits that can establish a positive personal brand.

the unwritten rules
about Career Planning

- **The early bird gets the worm.** Those who are the first to pursue an opportunity have a better chance of seizing it. This holds true for your career pursuits. If you're proactive and earlier than your peers in developing a resume, building a network, and applying for internships, you're giving yourself a better chance of securing a good job while you're in college and after graduating.

- **The best careers come from where you least expect them.** While serving as a restaurant waiter or hostess, you might serve a client who turns out to be a major employer, recruiter, or entrepreneur. By demonstrating some interest in that person and listening well, you could pick up clues that open the door for you to introduce yourself and express interest in their company. Be ready to give your 30-second elevator pitch at any time, even in the bathroom!

- **Students can have business cards, too.** If you have access to a computer, you have what you need to design and print a professional-looking business card. Include your name, the university you attend, your major, and your contact information, and have some of these cards available at all times.

- **Eportfolios are coming.** An eportfolio is a website where students compile a carefully selected sample of their academic work and accomplishments to show to prospective employers or graduate schools. Increasingly, employers want to see more than just a resume—they want to see samples of your actual work, including papers you've written, computer programs you've developed, projects you've completed, and problems you've solved. If you start collecting and organizing your work immediately during your first term, you'll have a lot more content to use for an eportfolio when you're ready to build it.

Resilience

Having a back-up plan keeps you moving forward, rather than being knocked down. Ask yourself, "If my plan doesn't work, then what will I do?" Having a strong Plan A and Plan B makes you more resilient.

Your Career Plan Should Include a Contingency Plan

All college career counselors want students to walk into high-paying jobs the day after graduation, but the reality is much different. Students who major in sought-after fields, such as information technology and health services, sometimes do not find the jobs that they thought were plentiful. Fluctuations in the economy are usually the cause for changes in the job market. Being prepared in case the job market has changed is your best defense.

To keep yourself grounded, formulate a plan for what you will do if you don't waltz into a dream job immediately. When writing your plan, be sure to answer the following questions:

Are you willing to take less money if the opportunity is good?

- Are you willing to relocate for a better job?
- Are you willing to take a job in a different field from what you expected?
- Are you willing to repackage your skills and knowledge to be considered for different types of work?

These are all questions that both Evan and Michael would do well to ask themselves. Even though Michael is very sure of the kind of job he wants, he may want to have an alternate plan in case those jobs are not readily available when he graduates. Evan can ask himself these questions to help him focus on what is most important to him in a job.

In addition, start building up your network of friends, family, coworkers, classmates, and acquaintances, if you have not already been working on it. Let them know that you are about to graduate and will be looking for a job.

Finally, consider the process that you must go through if you are to be successful in finding the right job for you. Getting a job requires that you:

- Consider what field best suits your skills, personality, and dreams
- Attend workshops and information sessions that provide assistance with resume writing, interviewing, and networking
- Prepare a solid resume
- Network with friends, family, and acquaintances
- Actively look for work
- Respond to job advertisements by sending out your resume and cover letter
- Follow up job interviews with a thank you letter
- Remain positive and flexible but stick to your goals

GRIT GAINER™

GET STARTED EARLY WITH GRIT It's a shock to many students that a college degree doesn't promise you a job, and no one else (parents, professors, career center) is responsible for finding you employment. You, and only you, own your career. It's yours to craft. If you had to build a house, you wouldn't start hammering nails when winter hits. You'd start early, so it's built and ready when the weather turns and you're not left out in the cold.

Networking Opens Doors for Your Career

Networking is developing relationships and contacts with people now who may, sometime in the future, prove to be helpful to you in pursuing your goals. Now, more than ever, networking is an essential part of an effective career search. If you ask 10 recent college graduates who have full-time careers how they landed their jobs, chances are that at least six of them will tell a story about how someone they knew helped them meet someone in the organization to get a first interview. If you establish good relationships with a variety of individuals across multiple companies and industries throughout your college experience—including your freshman year—these individuals will be your primary gateway to those initial interviews.

It's important to establish what networking can and cannot do for your career search. Effective networking throughout your four years of college can help you get your foot in the door at various organizations, and may help you land that first interview. At that point, however, it's all up to you. Someone else's referral on your behalf is often enough for a recruiter to take time to give you an interview, but it's not enough for the recruiter to hire you. You have to prove yourself in the interview process and, once you're hired, you have to prove yourself on the job. In a competitive job market in which hundreds of people are applying for a single position, landing that first interview is a crucial step, and networking can help you get there.

Networking Is More Than Exchanging Business Cards

When you see the word *networking,* what scene or activities do you picture in your mind? The stereotypical perception of networking is a bunch of people introducing themselves to each other and chatting at a social or business function. Some people think they've done a good job of networking if they came home from an event with a lot of business cards in their pockets. However, networking is a lot more than that. It certainly begins with an initial point of contact, and for that you need to make a professional first impression. How you dress, what you say, and how you act during the initial social exchange will be important. But once you've made that initial contact with someone, how you follow up and maintain contact really determines the value of your network.

Let's say that you're at a relative's wedding and you meet someone who has a highly successsful career at an accounting firm. At the time, you have no interest in accounting, nor do you know much about the company he works for, but you take time to ask questions about his career and organization, and you politely ask him for his business card or contact information. Was that networking? Yes, but you're just getting started. It's what happens after the introduction that matters most. When you get home, you need to add that person's contact information to a database, then compose a follow-up email or personal letter expressing your sentiments that you enjoyed meeting him and learning about his career, and that you'd like to stay in touch as your college career progresses. If you have a current resume prepared, you could send that to his, even if you don't have a present interest in a career at his organization.

In the months and years to follow, you can use a calendar system to remind yourself to touch base with that person. You can update him on your own accomplishments in college, ask him about his career accomplishments, ask him questions about how they chose his career, arrange an informational interview at his firm, and share any news articles that you read that have something to do with his industry or company. As you invest in this relationship over time, you're building a connection. Then, when you really need the individuals in your network to help you secure that first interview, they know you well

■ Networking with your professors can yield important leads.

© HERO IMAGES/GETTY IMAGES

People love to be asked for advice. A gritty way to get what you want is to sincerely ask people for their advice on who or what you should pursue and how best to go at it.

enough to trust in your personal qualities and professionalism. When someone takes the risk of recommending you to one of his friends or associates for a job interview, that person is putting his own reputation at risk on your behalf. This is a significant request! Successful networking—over time—establishes a range of personal and professional relationships that can help you make the right connection at the right time when your career search gets into full swing. If you wait until your junior or senior year to start networking, it will be far more difficult for you to prove your sincerity and professionalism through the test of time. Start early and build a broad network, because you never know where your interests may take you in the future.

Networking Face to Face

The most effective method of networking is by building relationships through face-to-face interactions. There are a number of specific activities you can pursue that will help you form broad, long-term connections:

- Look to clubs on campus that share your interests. Even if they are not career-related, such as a drama club, you will meet people who may be future contacts for jobs.

- Scan your school newspaper and announcements for events such as guest speaker events and discussion panels. Universities often host influential experts or industry leaders for speaking engagements. Attend these events when you can, not only to learn new perspectives, but also in an effort to meet these individuals and introduce yourself.

- Join a university ambassador club or other host-related student organization. Many universities have a student ambassador group that plays a lead role in hosting distinguished university guests, provides campus tours for visitors, and represents the university at community events such as Chamber of Commerce meetings and special task forces and committees.

- Consider a student leadership position on your campus. Student leaders, such as the members of the student council, often have special access to university administrators and community leaders.

- Get involved in community service and philanthropic activities. Industry and community leaders—the kind of people who are ideal to have in your personal network—are often actively engaged in nonprofit organizations, community service activities, and philanthropy. By committing your own time to these types of activities you are not only giving back to your community and society, you might also have a chance to network with individuals who have a relatively exclusive and high-profile network of their own. You probably wouldn't bump into the CEO of a large organization in your daily life as a college student, but if you invest yourself in community service and philanthropy, you might find yourself working next to someone who could eventually become a valuable member of your network.

Gritty students don't just sign up, they show up. And they contribute. They do the hard part, which is investing their time, effort, and energy into helping others, in whatever organizations they sign up for. Employers can spot the difference between "resume padders" and real contributors.

As you pursue these networking opportunities, it's important that you carry them out with a genuine interest in making a contribution to these organizations and that you aren't simply participating just to meet people. Before you commit to any club, organization, community event, or philanthropic cause, be sure that it's something you really believe in and are willing to support. Otherwise, your lack of sincerity and commitment will hurt your reputation, and you'll do more harm than good. However, if you get involved in something you really support, the personal network of relationships you establish will open doors for you in your career that you could have never imagined.

Networking Online

One of the largest trends in networking is using online websites such as LinkedIn and Facebook to create networks of friends, family, and special interest groups. The possibilities seem endless as to how you can use the Internet to connect with others. With this said, if you decide to join a network that focuses on an interest of yours, such as computer programming, be sure to investigate who runs the group, what kinds of information are shared, and how active the group is. Some networks will be more active than others, which will make it easier to connect with others and get involved; other networks or groups may be less active, which won't help you if you are using it to get to know others as potential contacts in the future. Because creating networks of your own is so easy, you may want to consider creating a group if you cannot find one relating to your career of interest. Networking sites such as Facebook allow you to set up groups that can be used for professional, educational, or social purposes.

If you decide to set up a profile on a social network site like LinkedIn, take time to establish a profile that is well written, professional, and informative. These sites often allow you to post a photo, so provide one that shows you dressed professionally, as you would appear for a job interview. Upload your resume and make sure that all of your contact information is current, accurate, and professional. These types of sites often have a mechanism for you to connect with others, and in most cases this requires the other person to accept your invitation. Be sure to initiate these invitations with a courteous, respectful approach, recognizing that if you choose to connect with you, it's comparable to the risk they face when recommending you to others. This is not a trivial decision on someone's part, so be sure that your profile and your request are presented in a manner that gives the person confidence that you will represent yourself—and his or her reputation—well.

Recommendation Letters

Recommendation letters and letters of reference are an important part of the career search process. Some individuals prefer to write letters of recommendation that you can send to prospective employers (some employers require these); in other circumstances, your references will simply want you to share their contact information so that the employer can contact them to discuss their recommendation in person.

Employers will often call or contact references as one of the final steps in the hiring process, and if an employer detects any type of concern or unfamiliarity from the reference during that call, it could bring the hiring process to an end. Conversely, if the employer receives a lot of positive feedback from your references and your references know you well, those recommendations could propel you to the next step in the hiring process. If you have taken the time to build an extensive network, you will have an easier time asking for and receiving a recommendation letter or reference that is full of specific information about the quality of your work and your character.

When considering someone to ask, choose a person who has had the chance to see you at your best. If you worked closely with a professor or spent many hours talking with a counselor, ask him or her to write a recommendation letter for you. The better the person knows you, the better the recommendation letter will be. In addition, give this person plenty of time to think about the quality of your work, recall specific examples, and write a polished letter. If you are on a tight deadline, such as a week, be honest with the person and give him or her a chance to decline the opportunity. If the person does agree to write a recommendation letter on such short notice, be sure to provide him or her with all the necessary materials to complete it properly, including an addressed, stamped envelope and the correct forms. You may also provide the person with your resume so that he or she can speak specifically about your accomplishments.

Once your recommendation letter has been written, write a thank you note and show your appreciation for the favor. Consider a handwritten note that expresses your gratitude rather than a verbal or email message of thanks. Finally, when requesting a

G R I T
Resilience

Ideally, your recommendation letter will say something about the challenges you took on, overcame, or used to do great things and/ or achieve your goals. If you have faced and successfully worked through real adversity, you might consider making sure that gets known.

GRIT GAINER™

recommendation, you should take the necessary steps to ensure that you do not read the recommendation letter. If you must hand-deliver the letter, ask that it be sealed in an envelope first. The reason that you should not request a copy or attempt to read it is that doing so jeopardizes the honesty of the individual who is writing it. Committees that evaluate recommendation letters want truthful descriptions of your abilities and strengths; if they know that you have seen the recommendation letter, they may doubt how accurate the description is.

Life After College Is Something to Anticipate

It is now a cliché to say that commencement—the ceremony you participate in when you graduate—means "a beginning" rather than "an ending." Many graduation speakers address that point each year: when you graduate from college, you are not just ending your academic career; you are beginning the rest of your life.

What will be left for you once you graduate? You may be on track to pursue a full-time career, or the career you've chosen may require you to pursue an advanced degree or professional education in law or medicine. Other students have the opportunity to explore the world through travel or volunteer work before they step into the full-time career world. Or, because of challenging economic conditions, perhaps you're not able to find a full-time career in your chosen field, and you have to pursue your contingency plan of finding other employment that can serve as a stepping stone to a future career. Whichever options are available to you, don't overlook the importance of celebrating your accomplishment. Also, seek the advice and support of your family, friends, and networking contacts to help you choose the alternative that is best for you.

The competencies that you have developed in college, such as information literacy, critical thinking skills, and cultural competency, will serve you well in your pursuit of lifelong learning. To be a lifelong learner acknowledges the reality that even when you've completed your degree, you will have an opportunity to continue to learn throughout your lifetime. You may find yourself in several different careers throughout your life, each one requiring you to reinvent yourself and develop new skills. The changing cultural, social, economic, and technological environment of our society will also challenge you to be a lifelong learner and adapt to changing conditions.

Growth

GRIT is not like a textbook, something you pick up and use only while in college. It is something you work at, grow, and use your entire life. Make it a personal goal to look back five years after graduation and be able to say, "I have so much more GRIT now than I even had back then."

Even though you may be graduating from your university, you now enjoy all the benefits of being an alumnus, which gives you such privileges as access to the library resources and career services, invitations to university events and programs, and lifetime connections with your professors, advisors, fellow alumni, and other individuals in your network of relationships. Your relationship with your university is a permanent bond, and it provides tremendous value for your lifelong success.

Your Mission, Values, and Goals Are Your "True North"

In Chapter 2, you wrote down your values, goals, and mission statement. Do you still have that information in a convenient location? If so, get it out and reflect on how well you have met your original short-term goals and how far you have come to reaching your long-term goals.

EXHIBIT 12.8   **Goal Achievement and Goal Setting**

Goals I Have Met:

1. Completed my courses with above average grades

2. Created a study group with classmates

3. Kept up with my commitments on the job

4. Paid my tuition

New Short-Term Goals:

1. Get registered for next semester

2. Speak with a counselor about career possibilities

3. Make at least two A's in my classes

4. Take more time to relax

Have your values changed? Or have they been strengthened by your achievements? Have you followed your mission statement? Is there anything that you would change about your mission statement?

To answer these questions, you will need to reflect on your achievements over the past semester. Your mission and values should not have changed much in the past weeks, but if they have, you can make a new list of values and rewrite your mission statement. Some of your short-term goals should be met, and you have no doubt moved on to a new list of them as you make your way to your long-term goals. Now is the time, then, to revisit your long-range plans and make adjustments if you need to. Also, you should keep a record of the short-term goals you have reached and create a new list. Keeping up with what you have accomplished will serve as a reminder of your success if you ever feel unsure about your progress. Exhibit 12.8 is an example of a new list you can make.

Once you revise your short-term goals, you may notice that your time line for reaching your long-term goals needs adjusting as well. Keeping your list in a convenient location and looking at it every day or week will help you stay on track.

GRIT
Tenacity

Having a personal mission statement, goals, and values is one thing. Living them, staying true to them day in and day out, is something else entirely. Doing this takes a lot of GRIT. It's tough. But those who do have the most fulfilling lives.

You Serve an Important Role in Your Community

Although most of your focus during college will be on yourself and moving on either to another degree or to a new job, consider looking for opportunities to improve your community. One of the purposes of higher education is to improve the lives of individuals so that the community benefits as well, and it is essential that educated community members give back and make improvements.

Professional clubs, social and civic groups, churches, and volunteer organizations offer opportunities for you to get involved in the community after college, if you have not done so already. The people you meet in these groups and the connections you make, both professional and personal, can enrich your life and your career. If you are not part of a community group, seek out one whose interests are similar to yours; also, look for ways to participate in events in your community, whether it is a 5K run or a recycling drive. Participating in strengthening your community will allow you to give back to those in need, improve your community, and gain friendships and business connections that may last a long time.

■ Giving back to the community is one way you can serve as a role model for others.

Now may not be the time to encourage you to help your university financially, but think about how you can continue to support your school after you have left. In order for a university—or any educational institution—to be successful in improving the lives of the people in its community, it must depend in part on its graduates to make a good name for themselves and to give back with their time, talent, and financial resources. There are a variety of ways that you can contribute to the education of those who will surely follow in your footsteps. If you ever have a chance to talk with someone who has made a significant gift to his or her university, you'll realize that the person received as much satisfaction and reward from the experience as the university did from the gift.

By being a productive, educated member of society, you are already giving back to your university. Because higher education's mission is to improve a community by increasing the knowledge and enhancing the values of its population, we all benefit from students who graduate and continue to lead productive, happy lives. The skills and knowledge you have obtained in college are a good advertisement for the school. Alumni who make a difference in the lives of others through their jobs and community service fulfill the university's mission not only to provide education to strengthen the local economy, but also to graduate people who demonstrate the ideals of an educated society.

GRIT GAINER™

GRIT BEGETS GRATITUDE Being happy is great. But you can do better. Happiness is a mood. It's fleeting. Beyond happiness is fulfillment, that deep sense of gratification that only comes from one thing. It comes from having set bold, tough ambitions for yourself, then achieved them, despite facing some powerful struggles along the way. Assuming you fulfill your quest, the greater the strife, the more gratifying the life.

GET PAID
from college to career

4 things future professionals need to know about preparing for a career

an effective job search takes time

Reading industry publications to stay current, preparing for and attending career fairs and recruiter information fairs, participating in several rounds of interviews, and building and maintaining a network are time-intensive activities. As you develop your degree plan, try to set it up so that you can take a lighter class load during your senior year, and even during the last term of your junior year, if possible. Taking courses in the summer is a great way to help reduce your course load during the regular academic year.

the best careers for college graduates are often overlooked

There are some companies in certain industries who have outstanding management development programs and who have a great reputation for training recent college grads to become effective in the workplace. And yet, some of these companies are relatively unknown by students, or are in industries that aren't popular among students. When you review the list of companies that are attending your university's career fair, take time to carefully consider every one.

the skills you're practicing to get your first job will be used throughout your career

According to a 2012 study by the Bureau of Labor Statistics, people born in the years 1957 to 1964 held an average of 11.3 jobs from ages 18 to 46. Most experts speculate that this number is probably even higher for younger generations. Even if we round the number to 10 jobs in someone's adult life, it's clear that your ability to identify the career that fits you best and secure employment in that career is a skill that you'll need to use many times in your lifetime. Learn it well!

every college experience is a potential source of evidence of your workplace skills

When you overcome conflict with a roommate or team member in a group project, that will provide evidence to an employer that you'll be effective at navigating the workplace. When you juggled four classes, a part-time job, and a club leadership role in the same semester, that's evidence of your work ethic and time management skills. Reflect on these experiences and how they are preparing you to be successful in your career. Be ready to talk about them in an interview!

THE GRIT ADVANTAGE

You can enhance your GRIT game now by asking yourself these questions:

1. What challenge can you take on now that would demonstrate your GRIT, and enhance your career prospects?

2. What is your best adversity story? What is the greatest challenge or obstacle you have had to successfully navigate to achieve positive results in your life?

3. List five people you most admire and from whom you would most want advice on how to have not just good, but *great* career options.

4. What community or group can you join that would be the most likely to challenge and improve you as a human being?

HOW GRITTY ARE YOU?

Now that you've completed this chapter, how committed are you to:

1. Doing things that use and prove your GRIT so you are more attractive and valuable to future employers?

Zero Commitment 0 ———————————————————————————————— 10 Fully Committed

2. Owning and relentlessly building your own career prospects by tapping the available resources and asking the right people for their advice?

Zero Commitment 0 ———————————————————————————————— 10 Fully Committed

3. Striving to clarify your values, goals, and mission and then pursuing a career where you can bring them to life?

Zero Commitment 0 ———————————————————————————————— 10 Fully Committed

Glossary

Academic calendar—A list of important dates. Included are vacation breaks, registration periods, and deadlines for certain forms.

Academic probation—A student whose GPA falls below a designated number can be placed on academic probation. If the GPA does not improve, then the student may be prohibited from registering for classes for a designated number of semesters.

Adjunct instructor—An instructor who is not employed full-time with the college. An adjunct instructor usually teaches one or two courses at the college.

Articulation agreement—A signed document stating that one college will accept the courses from another college.

Asynchronous communication—When two or more people do not have to be communicating at the same time. Email and discussion boards are asynchronous communication methods.

Audience—In essay writing, the audience is the person or persons whom you are addressing.

Bursar—The person at your college who handles payments for tuition and fees.

Chat room—An electronic method of communicating with other people in real time.

Corequisite—A course that you can take at the same time as another course. For example, if intermediate algebra is a corequisite for physical science, then you will take both courses during the same semester.

Cornell System—A note-taking system in which a student draws an upside-down "T" on a sheet of paper and uses the space to the right for taking notes, the space to the left for adding questions and highlighting important points, and the space at the bottom for summarizing the material.

Course catalog—A book that provides students with information about the college's academic calendar, tuition and fees, and degree/certificate programs.

Course objective—A goal that the instructor has identified for the student to meet once the course is completed. For example, a course objective could be to use MLA documentation properly.

Cover letter—A letter accompanying a resume that describes how a person's qualifications match the advertised requirements for the job.

Critical thinking—The ability to use specific criteria to evaluate reasoning and make a decision.

Curriculum—A term used to refer to the courses that a student must take in a particular field, or it can refer to all the classes that the college offers.

Dean—An administrator who is in charge of faculty or a division in the college.

Developmental classes—Sometimes referred to as *remedial classes,* developmental classes focus on basic college-level skills such as reading, writing, and math. Students who earn a certain score on standardized tests such as the ACT and COMPASS exams may be required to take developmental classes before enrolling in college-level courses.

Discussion board—An electronic method of interacting with other people by posting messages and reading postings from other people.

Family Educational Rights and Privacy Act (FERPA)—A federal law that ensures that a student's educational records, including test grades and transcripts, are not accessed or viewed by anyone who is not authorized to do so.

Full-time student—A student who is taking at least 12 credit hours of courses per semester.

Full-time worker—A person who is working at least 40 hours per week.

Grade point average (GPA)—The number that is used to determine a student's progress in college. It refers to the number of quality points divided by the number of hours a student has taken.

GRIT—Your capacity to dig deep and do whatever it takes—even sacrifice, struggle, and suffer—in the pursuit of your most important goals.

Growth—Your tendency to seek fresh angles on situations and to view success as a matter of effort, more than talent or smarts.

Information literacy—A set of abilities requiring an individual to determine when information is needed, locate appropriate information for the need, assess the information as to accuracy and relevancy, and use the information in an ethical manner.

Instinct—Your gut-level capacity to pursue the right goals in the most efficient and effective ways.

Knowledge—This comes from taking in information, thinking about it critically, and synthesizing one's own ideas about what one has read or seen.

Long-term goal—A goal that takes a long time to complete (within a year or more).

Major—The area that a student is focusing on for his or her degree. If a student wants to teach third grade, his or her major can be elementary education. (*See also* Minor.)

Matching question—A test question that provides one column of descriptors and another column of words that must be matched with the appropriate descriptor.

Minor—A second area that a student can emphasize in his or her degree. A minor usually requires fewer classes and is not as intensive as a major. For example, if a student majors in marketing but also wants to learn more about running his or her own business, the student may want to minor in business or accounting.

Mission statement—A declaration of what a person or an institution believes in and what that person or institution hopes to accomplish.

Multiple-choice question—A type of test question in which an incomplete sentence or a question is given and the correct response must be chosen from a list of possibilities.

Objective question—A question that presents a limited number of possible answers.

OK5R—A reading strategy developed by Dr. Walter Pauk that stands for Overview, Key Ideas, Read, Record, Recite, Review, and Reflect.

Part-time student—A student who is taking less than 12 credit hours per semester.

Prerequisite—A required course or score that must be completed or achieved before enrolling in a course.

Priority—Something that is important at that moment.

Provost—A high-ranking college administrator.

Purpose—What a student hopes to accomplish with his or her writing assignment.

Quality points—The number that is assigned to each grade. For example, an A is worth four quality points and a B is worth three quality points.

Registrar—The official record keeper at the college.

Remedial classes—*See* Developmental classes.

Resilience—Your capacity to respond constructively to, and make good use of, tough moments, including all kinds of difficulty, adversity, and challenges.

Resume—A page or two that provides a person's educational and work experience, career objective, and contact information.

Short-term goal—A goal that can be accomplished in a short period of time (within a week or a few months).

Stress—A physical and psychological response to outside stimuli.

Student handbook—A publication of the college that outlines what the college expects of the student.

Subjective question—A test question that requires a student to provide a personal answer. Usually, there are no "wrong" answers to subjective questions.

Syllabus—A document that contains an overview of the course, including objectives, assignments, and required materials as well as the instructor's policies for attendance, exams, and grading. It may also contain the college's policies on disability accommodations and academic dishonesty.

Synchronous communication—When two or more people have to be communicating at the same time. Internet-based synchronous communication includes chat rooms.

Tenacity—Your sheer persistence; the degree to which you commit to, stick with, and relentlessly work at whatever you choose.

Time management—Strategies for using time effectively.

Topic—The subject of a piece of writing.

Transcript—A record of the courses a student has taken and the grades the student has earned. Transcripts also note the student's grade point average.

Transfer—Refers to moving from one school to another. Students who transfer must apply for admissions to the second school and must request that their transcript(s) be sent to the new school.

T-System—*See* Cornell System.

Values—Part of a person's belief system that provides the foundation of what the person does and what the person wants to become. If a person values financial stability, then the person will look for opportunities to earn money and provide a secure future.

Work-study—A federal program that allows students to work at their college while taking classes. Students must qualify for work-study money and must meet college department requirements for work.

References and Recommended Readings

Chapter 1

Banner, J. M., & Cannon, H. C. (1999). *The elements of learning*. New Haven, CT: Yale University Press.

The College Board. (2008). *Succeeding in college: What it means and how to make it happen*. Plano, TX: College Board.

Dabbah, M. (2009). *Latinos in college: Your guide to success*. Scarborough, NY: Consultare.

Newport, C. (2005). *How to win at college: Surprising secrets for success from the country's top students*. New York, NY: Broadway.

Nist-Olejnik, S., & Patrick Holschuh, J. (2007). *College rules! How to study, survive, and succeed in college*. Berkeley, CA: Ten Speed Press.

Stoltz, P. G. (1999). *The adversity quotient: Turning obstacles into opportunities*. New York, NY: Wiley.

Watkins, B. D. (2004). *Everything you ever wanted to know about college: A guide for minority students*. Camillus, NY: Blue Boy Publishing.

Chapter 2

Beals, M. P. (1994). *Warriors don't cry*. New York, NY: Pocket Books.

Dickerson, D. J. (2000). *An American story*. New York, NY: Anchor Books.

Lazear, D. (1991). *Seven ways of teaching: The artistry of teaching with multiple intelligences*. Palatine, IL: Skylight Publishing.

Myers-Briggs Type Indicator. (2009). Retrieved September 22, 2014, from www.myersbriggstypeindicator.co.uk

Rodriguez, R. (1982). *Hunger of memory: The education of Richard Rodriguez*. New York, NY: The Dial Press.

Smiley, T. (2006). *What I know for sure: My story of growing up in America*. New York, NY: Anchor Books.

Chapter 3

Gurin, P. (1999). New research on the benefits of diversity in college and beyond: An empirical analysis. Retrieved July 11, 2011, from www.diversityweb.org/digest/sp99/benefits.html

Katz, N. (2005). Sexual harassment statistics in the workplace and in education. Retrieved July 5, 2005, from http://womenissues.about.com/cs/sexdiscrimination/a/sexharassstats.htm

Zemke, R., Raines, C., & Filipczak, B. (2000). *Generations at work: Managing the clash of veterans, boomers, xers, and nexters in your workplace*. New York, NY: Amacom.

Chapter 4

Allen, D., Schwartz, T., & McGinn, D. (2011). Being more productive. *Harvard Business Review, 89*(5), 82–88.

Dodd, P., & Sundheim, D. (2005). *The 25 best time management tools and techniques: How to get more done without driving yourself crazy*. Chelsea, MI: Peak Performance Press.

Hindle, T. (1998). *Manage your time*. New York, NY: DK Publishing.

Leland, K., & Bailey, K. (2008). *Time management in an instant: 60 ways to make the most of your day*. Franklin Lakes, NJ: The Career Press.

Nelson, D. B., & Low, G. R. (2003). *Emotional intelligence: Achieving academic and career excellence*. Upper Saddle River, NJ: Pearson.

Schwartz, T. (2007). Manage your energy, not your time. *Harvard Business Review, 85*(10), 63–70.

Sibler, L. (1998). *Time management for the creative person: Right-brain strategies for stopping procrastination, getting control of the clock and calendar, and freeing up your time and your life*. New York, NY: Three Rivers Press.

Tyson, D. (2009). *Personal finance for dummies* (6th ed.). New York, NY: Wiley.

Chapter 5

American Heart Association. (2009). Cigarette smoking statistics. Retrieved September 6, 2009, from www.americanheart.org/presenter.jhtml?identifier=4559

Gately, G. (2003, August 23). College students ignoring risks of unprotected sex. *Health Day News*. Retrieved August 29, 2005, from www.hon.ch/News/HSN/514968.html

Mayo Clinic. Interval training: Can it boost your calorie-burning power? Retrieved July 19, 2011, from www.mayoclinic.com/health/interval-training/SM00110

RAINN. (2014). Reducing your risk of sexual assault. Retrieved September 22, 2014, from https://rainn.org/get-information/sexual-assault-prevention

U.S. Food and Drug Administration. (2014). How to understand and use the nutrition facts label. Retrieved September 22, 2014, from www.fda.gov/Food/IngredientsPackagingLabeling/LabelingNutrition/ucm274593.htm

Chapter 6

Diestler, S. (1998). *Becoming a critical thinker: A user friendly manual* (2nd ed.). Upper Saddle River, NJ: Prentice Hall.

Dweck, C. (2006). *Mindset: The new psychology of success.* New York, NY: Random House.

Foer, J. (2007). Remember this. *National Geographic, 212*(5), 32–55.

Gunn, A. M., Richburg, R. W., & Smilkstein, R. (2007). *Igniting student potential: Teaching with the brain's natural learning process.* Thousand Oaks, CA: Corwin Press.

Harris, R. (2002). *Creative problem solving: A step-by-step approach.* Los Angeles, CA: Pyrczak.

Miller, G. (1956). The magical number seven, plus or minus two: Some limits on our capacity for processing information. Retrieved July 5, 2011, from www.musanim.com/miller1956/

Chapter 7

International Dyslexia Association. (2007). IDA fact sheets on dyslexia and related language-based learning disabilities. Retrieved September 22, 2014, from www.interdys.org

Orfalea, P., & Marsh, A. (2007). *Copy this! Lessons from a hyperactive dyslexic who turned a bright idea into one of America's best companies.* New York, NY: Workman.

Robinson, F. P. (1970). *Effective study* (4th ed.). New York, NY: Harper & Row.

Chapter 8

Beglar, D., & Murray, N. (2009). *Contemporary topics 3: Academic and note-taking skills* (3rd ed.). Boston, MA: Pearson.

Kline, J. A. (1996). *Effective listening.* Maxwell Air Force Base, AL: Air University Press.

Rowson, P. (2007). *Communicating with more confidence: The easy step-by-step guide* (Rev. ed.). Hayling, England: Summersdale Publishers.

Spears, D. (2008). *Developing critical reading skills.* New York, NY: McGraw-Hill.

Chapter 9

Bradbury, A. (2006). *Successful presentation skills* (3rd ed.). London, UK: Kogan Page.

Tracy, B. (2008). *Speak to win: How to present with power in any situation.* New York, NY: AMACOM Books.

Strunk, W., & White, E. B. (2008). *The elements of style* (50th anniv. ed.). New York, NY: Longman.

Wilder, L. (1999). *Seven steps to fearless speaking.* New York, NY: Wiley.

Zinsser, W. (2006). *On writing well* (30th anniv. ed.). New York, NY: Harper Paperbacks.

Chapter 10

Paul, M. A., & Paul, K. (2009). *Study smarter, not harder.* Bellingham, WA: Self Counsel Press.

Roubidoux, S. (2008). *101 ways to make studying easier and faster for college students: What every student needs to know explained simply.* Ocala, FL: Atlantic Publishing Group.

Chapter 11

The College Board. (2009). *Getting financial aid 2010.* New York, NY: The College Board.

Cress, C. M., Collier, P. J., & Reitenauer, V. L. (2005). *Learning through serving: A student guidebook for service-learning across the disciplines.* Sterling, VA: Stylus.

Lipphardt, D. (2008). *The scholarship and financial aid solution: How to go to college for next to nothing with short cuts, tricks, and tips from start to finish.* Ocala, FL: Atlantic Publishing Group.

Schlacther, G., & Weber, R. D. (2009). *Kaplan Scholarships 2010: Billions of dollars in free money for college.* Fort Lauderdale, FL: Kaplan Publishing.

Perkins Loans. (2011). *Student aid on the web.* Retrieved July 11, 2011, from http://studentaid.ed.gov/PORTALS-WebApp/students/english/campusaid.jsp

U.S. Department of Education. (2011). Types of federal student aid. Retrieved July 11, 2011, from http://studentaid.ed.gov/students/publications/student_guide/2006-2007/english/typesofFSA_grants.htm

U.S. Department of Veterans Affairs. (2011). What is the Post-9/11 G.I. Bill? Retrieved July 11, 2011, from www.gibill.va.gov/benefits/post_911_gibill/index.html

Chapter 12

The College Board. (2013). *Education pays 2013: The benefits of higher education for individuals and society.* New York, NY: The College Board.

Farr, M. J. (2004). *Same-day résumé: Write an effective résumé in an hour.* Indianapolis, IN: Jist Publishing.

Leider, R. J. (2005). *The power of purpose: Creating meaning in your life and work.* San Francisco: Berrett-Koehler Publishers.

Leonhardt. (2014). "Is college worth it? Clearly, new data say." *New York Times,* www.nytimes.com/2014/05/27/upshot/is-college-worth-it-clearly-new-data-say.html?smid=tw-share&_r=0

Marcus, J. J. (2003). *The résumé makeover: 50 common résumé and cover letter problems—and how to fix them.* New York, NY: McGraw-Hill.

Pew Research Center. (2014). "The rising cost of not going to college." www.pewsocialtrends.org/files/2014/02/SDT-higher-ed-FINAL-02-11-2014.pdf

Safko, L., & Brake, D. (2009). *The social media bible: Tactics, tools, and strategies for business success.* Hoboken, NJ: Wiley & Sons.

Shellenbarger, S. (2009, Dec. 16). "Weighing the value of that college diploma." *Wall Street Journal,* p. D1.

Index